SHAKESPEARE

A Study and Research Guide
Second Edition, Revised

DAVID M. BERGERON
& GERALDO U. DE SOUSA

UNIVERSITY PRESS OF KANSAS

Published by the University Press of Kansas (Lawrence, Kansas 66045), which was organized by the Kansas Board of Regents and is operated and funded by Emporia State University, Fort Hays State University, Kansas State University, Pittsburg State University, the University of Kansas, and Wichita State University.

Library of Congress Cataloging-in-Publication Data

Bergeron, David Moore.
   Shakespeare: a study and research guide.—2nd ed., rev. / David M. Bergeron & Geraldo U. de Sousa.
    p. cm.
   Includes index.
   ISBN 0-7006-0339-5   ISBN 0-7006-0340-9 (pbk.)
   1. Shakespeare, William, 1564–1616—Bibliography. 2. Shakespeare, William, 1564–1616—Study and teaching. I. De Sousa, Geraldo U., 1952– . II. Title.
Z8811.B44 1987
[PR2894]
016.8223'3—dc19   87-24967
                                                    CIP

British Library Cataloguing in Publication Data is available.

Printed in the United States of America
10 9 8 7 6 5 4 3 2 1

Contents

Preface

Confronted with the mass of materials on Shakespeare, where does the beginning student or even a seasoned one turn for guidance? Answering that question has been the central aim of this revised edition. Here one can find an overview of critical approaches to Shakespeare, summaries and evaluations of scores of books, and a guide to documentation (including a model paper). The organization of the book reflects the desirable pattern of moving from a general understanding of Shakespeare criticism to an investigation of resources to the actual writing of a critical paper. Each chapter, however, stands alone; and students may dip into the respective chapters as their need dictates.

This revised edition differs in several ways from the previous edition, published in 1975. Obviously, by trying to respond to the criticism of the past few years, it includes analyses of dozens of new books. It develops the section on the Romances, and it creates new sections on feminism and gender studies and on poststructuralism and the new historicism. These changes respond to profound new developments in Shakespearean criticism since 1975. Because the Modern Language Association has adopted a new system of documentation, this guide outlines this new system and also provides a new model paper, based on the MLA style. Last, but certainly not least, every sentence of the original edition has been carefully scrutinized, then kept, revised, or discarded. In a word, the original version has undergone thorough revision in every way possible.

We should add nonetheless that this new edition bears a strong resemblance to the original. That is intentional. We hope that we have preserved the virtues of the original, an edition that proved helpful to many students and teachers alike. We collaborated by dividing up the critical terrain of the post-1975 era and by together critically poring over the content and style of the original. Such collaboration has strengthened the book and made the seemingly insuperable task of revision more manageable.

We have received assistance from many people, beginning with colleagues who over the years have commented on the strengths and shortcomings of the original edition. Encouragement from various quarters indeed led to the idea of a revision. We are particularly grateful to William Carroll of Boston University for his careful, efficient, and helpful assessment of the revised text. His many good suggestions have been incorporated. David Paul Fidler assisted by rounding up some materials, doing some initial typing, and especially by offering his paper. Denisa Brown initially and then Pam LeRow worked the wonders of word processing; their kind and skillful help reduced anxiety and added pleasure to the task. The following university libraries (especially the first two) were crucial in providing materials for the revision: Kansas, Iowa State, Exeter, Warwick, and Cambridge.

Two final caveats: first, only book-length studies have been evaluated and typically only studies of groups of plays (thus no evaluations of, say, *Hamlet;* rather, studies on the tragedies). Second, our subjective judgment is at work, determining which books to include and what to say about them. On this score opinions will surely vary.

For the general encouragement of our universities and for the specific support of the General Research Fund of the University of Kansas, we are truly grateful. As with the 1975 edition, so here: this book rightfully belongs to our students, who have challenged our knowledge and often shared our enthusiasm for Shakespeare.

May 1987

David M. Bergeron
Geraldo U. de Sousa

CHAPTER ONE
The Subject in Context

In confronting the criticism and scholarship currently available on Shakespeare, one may be surprised to learn that such productivity is largely a twentieth-century phenomenon. Books, editions, and essays now proliferate at an astronomical rate—some 3,500 new items published in 1964 alone. Gone are the days when the professional scholar could reasonably expect to have some sort of mastery of the material being produced on his subject; he or she now stands in danger of being engulfed in a sea of criticism, often unable to distinguish the sharp rocks from the sheltering boulders. We seem not to have world enough and time to separate the important from the unimportant, and we look in vain for a guide. But a moratorium on publication is both unrealistic and undesirable; thus, students of Shakespeare simply must come to terms with the material in some way.

CRITICISM IN SHAKESPEARE'S TIME

What accounts for the lack of criticism during the dramatist's own lifetime? Of course, people did have opinions about Shakespeare and his work. Robert Greene, in fact, rather testily refers to him in 1592 as "an upstart Crow"; and in 1598, Francis Meres, in *Palladis Tamia,* praises Shakespeare's "sugred Sonnets" and judges him to be the most excellent of the English writers of comedy and tragedy. Ben Jonson, a fellow dramatist and a classicist, complains occasionally of Shakespeare's violation of

1

the traditional unities of time, place, and action; but in verses prepared for the publication of the first collected edition of Shakespeare's plays, the Folio of 1623, Jonson praises Shakespeare effusively, claiming, "He was not of an age, but for all time!"

At least two reasons can explain the lack of extensive early critical writing about Shakespeare. For one thing, no well-established tradition of literary criticism existed in the sixteenth century. Grammarians and rhetoricians defined different literary forms, but that is not criticism. Philip Sidney's *An Apology for Poetry* in the early 1580s remains the major statement of the century; but unfortunately, he wrote before the full flowering of English Renaissance drama, and thus he praises *Gorboduc* as the finest English tragedy. One must wait for John Dryden in the 1660s for pieces of sustained criticism. The period between Sidney and Dryden, though not a critical wasteland, experienced little traffic. Thomas Heywood's *An Apology for Actors* (1612), though it offers a justification for drama, breaks no new critical ground. Curiously, this most brilliant period of English literary history provoked so little criticism, practical or theoretical—perhaps because there were no English professors wandering loose in the country.

Furthermore, drama was not generally recognized as literature—hence no particular need to discuss it seriously as a literary form. One finds it difficult to intellectualize about mere "plays," which one saw at "playhouses." The location of the theaters side by side with the bear-baiting and bull-baiting arenas offers a striking commentary on the relationship between sport and play. The spectator might one afternoon watch *Hamlet* at the Globe and the next day watch a bear being torn apart by dogs in a nearby arena. Readers esteemed poetry as worthy literature. At least one dramatist, Ben Jonson, took his plays (and himself) seriously and published in 1616 a folio collection of his drama, which he had the audacity to entitle *The Works of Benjamin Jonson*— the term "works" was typically used to designate serious poetry or prose, not plays. Even the editors of the folio collection in 1623 of Shakespeare's drama entitled it *Mr. William Shakespeare's Comedies, Histories, & Tragedies*. Drama suffered a fate as a highly ephemeral art, a notion supported by the evidence that but a fraction of the plays ever saw light of day in printed form—only half (eighteen) of Shakespeare's plays appeared during his lifetime. With this general disregard for drama as literature—not, of course, a disregard for drama itself, which was extremely popular—one understands the absence of elaborate research and criticism about Shakespeare.

THE EIGHTEENTH AND NINETEENTH CENTURIES

The eighteenth century gave rise to the first serious and extensive research in Shakespeare, most of which focused on editing. Obviously, establishing a sound text has to precede criticism. Nicholas Rowe's edition of 1709 is the first "edition" of Shakespeare; it also includes a brief biography of Shakespeare, usually regarded as the first formal biography. Another significant editor was Lewis Theobald, unfortunately remembered most for being the target of Alexander Pope's *The Dunciad* (1728)—he had made the mistake of pointing out the shortcomings of Pope's own edition of Shakespeare (1725). In the latter part of the century, Edward Capell, George Steevens, and Edmond Malone contributed important editions; and Malone also worked on the problem of the chronology of Shakespeare's plays, a still unresolved, vexing problem, though we have a generally accepted order. Fortunately these serious editors ultimately carried the day, establishing the groundwork for continuing investigation; Pope and Samuel Johnson, whose editorial practices were often whimsical, highly subjective, involving free alteration of the text, have fallen into disrepute as editors, though Johnson's notes contain value.

Not surprisingly, the nineteenth century spawned even more editions, many of them offering nothing especially new. But the Cambridge edition—issued in 1864 as the one-volume Globe text, edited by Clark, Glover, and Wright—has achieved high status as an edition of importance. In fact, it became the standard text on which many twentieth-century editions have been based; and its line-numbering system is only now being altered in favor of continuous through-line numbering (one suspects that it may take another generation or two before we altogether surrender the Globe's system). That century also experienced the founding of societies in Germany and in England devoted to research and criticism of Shakespeare: in Weimar the Deutsche Shakespeare-Gesellschaft, founded in 1865 and publisher of the *Shakespeare Jahrbuch,* and in England the Shakespeare Society, founded in

1840, and the "New Shakespere Society," founded in 1873 by F. J. Furnivall. The bickering and contentiousness of the English members aside, these societies opened up new territories by understanding the importance of Elizabethan documents and by seeking information on Shakespeare's fellow dramatists. Furnivall's group, caught up in the wave of late nineteenth-century belief in science, sought scientific tests to measure and account for Shakespeare's verse in the hope of establishing chronology and settling questions of authorship. Led by the industrious Frederick Fleay, the society placed its faith in metrical tests that may seem to us either naïve and touching or simply misplaced. Other scholars in England and elsewhere pursued various kinds of linguistic studies that led to the publication of important glossaries and lexicons.

THE TWENTIETH CENTURY

The twentieth century is more fully accounted for below in the discussion of "schools" of criticism. (By "school" is meant simply a group whose participants share common critical ground, not an organized effort as such.) Suffice it to say for the moment that the present century has been exceptionally productive in many areas of scholarship. The publications exclusively concerned with Shakespeare—*Shakespeare Survey, Shakespeare Quarterly, Shakespeare Newsletter,* and *Shakespeare Studies*—have all first appeared in the past forty years. The Shakespeare Association of America became a national organization in the early 1970s; it sponsors annual meetings and encourages research. Important documents pertaining to Shakespeare's life were unearthed in the early decades of the century, largely because of the indefatigable researches of Charles Wallace and Leslie Hotson. Perhaps partly because of this kind of research, the twentieth century has been the period of Shakespearean biography, and we get the first full-fledged treatments of his life. In 1985, one scholar argued for Shakespeare's residence in Lancashire among Catholics during the presumed "lost years," and another discovered a poem allegedly written by Shakespeare. The twentieth century also has given rise to important studies in psychology, language, rhetoric, imagery, and feminism and gender. This has also been the time of textual and bibliographical studies, opening avenues of research and speculation undreamed of in previous centuries. Indeed, when the history of twentieth-century Shakespearean *scholarship* is written, textual research and theory may be deemed the most significant contribution for its overall impact—for both the questions it has raised and some of the answers it has provided.

SHAKESPEARE IN THE CLASSROOM

For the students who have made a forced march through probably *Julius Caesar* and *Macbeth* in high school, it may be cause for chagrin, reassurance, exasperation, or whatever to learn that such has not always been the lot of high school students. The teaching of Shakespeare is a relatively new activity, though it seems natural now for secondary schools and colleges to offer some kind of instruction in Shakespeare. (Of course, the study of American literature in American colleges is even more recent.) Seventeenth- and eighteenth-century schools did not teach Shakespeare primarily because education had principally a classical orientation, though clearly Shakespeare was being read—witness the spate of editions. His works did not become a regular subject of instruction in England until after 1858, which marked the beginning of the Oxford and Cambridge Local Examinations. Similarly, in the United States the mid-nineteenth century saw Shakespeare become part of the curriculum, but even then in very limited fashion. Both in England and in the United States the early teaching focused on such things as plot, historical background, characters, grammar and rhetoric, and the plays as vehicles for instruction in elocution. In a word, one seldom studied them as dramatic art, but rather as a means of illustrating something else. As early as 1825, the study of Shakespeare appeared in courses in moral philosophy at the University of Virginia, but not until 1857 was there a separate course on Shakespeare in the school of History and General Literature. Cornell University had a course in Shakespeare by 1868; Princeton, 1869; Johns Hopkins, 1877; and Columbia University, 1882. The first PhD degree for a dissertation on Shakespeare went to Robert Grant in 1876 for his work on the Sonnets, written at Harvard University; and the second such degree for work on Shakespeare went to S. B. Weeks, who graduated in 1888 from the University of North Carolina. Interestingly, a number of Americans and a few

Englishmen during this same period received PhD degrees from German universities for their studies of Shakespeare.

By the end of the nineteenth century the teaching of Shakespeare became widespread in the United States, with most schools offering at least one play as part of the curriculum. One teacher who helped move the teaching of Shakespeare away from its early, somewhat narrow concerns was George Lyman Kittredge, a popular teacher at Harvard for nearly fifty years (1888-1936). Though probably no one has ever known more about Shakespeare's language than Kittredge, his approach in the classroom was not strictly philological; rather, it emphasized understanding and appreciating Shakespeare's dramatic artistry. Not surprisingly, the growth of research in Shakespeare has gone hand in hand with the expansion of the teaching of Shakespeare. The productive critics and scholars of the past few decades have been, for the most part, teachers of Shakespeare; this contrasts with the general situation in the eighteenth and nineteenth centuries, when many of the critics were themselves poets, men of letters, or simply amateur lovers of literature.

SOME CRITICAL APPROACHES

In defining some of the various critical approaches to Shakespeare, one must necessarily be aware that most critics fit into more than one school of criticism. Of late we seem to be increasingly aware of the need for eclectic criticism—that is, criticism that uses several different methods in interpreting Shakespeare. Perhaps one might start negatively by reviewing the excesses of several different critical approaches, and the place to start would be with John Crow's witty, amusing, and incisive essay "Deadly Sins of Criticism, or, Seven Ways to Get Shakespeare Wrong," *Shakespeare Quarterly* 9 (1958): 301-6. Of course, Crow exaggerates and is a bit too despairing, but he hits on some of the weaknesses and flaws of Shakespearean criticism. His essay ought to be required reading for all who venture into criticism. An equally sobering account and analysis of current criticism can be found in Richard Levin's *New Readings vs. Old Plays: Recent Trends in the Reinterpretation of English Renaissance Drama* (University of Chicago Press, 1979), much of which focuses on Shakespeare. Even if one does not entirely agree with Levin's sometimes bleak assessment, one has to admit that he makes some telling points about excesses in criticism. Much of the problem boils down to the mistaken and regrettable view that some *one* method exists that will yield the best results or even reveal the truth.

Students will discover in chapter 2 the diversity of Shakespearean scholarship and criticism, but it might be helpful here to outline and group rather broadly some of the types of modern criticism.

HISTORICAL CRITICISM

We can call one large category *historical,* with its several subcategories. The emphasis on history comes partly as a reaction to the excesses of a highly romanticized, somewhat sentimental Shakespeare who emerged from some nineteenth-century criticism, which often took no note whatever of the context in which Shakespeare wrote. Historical criticism ideally steers a course between a Shakespeare exclusively Elizabethan, whom we can apprehend only if we become Elizabethans, and a Shakespeare our contemporary. This approach has validity only insofar as it leads us into the plays and poems. The sin to which this critical approach may be susceptible is what Crow might call "woods-for-treeism," not being able to see the forest for the trees—a variety of pedantry.

One manifestation of historical scholarship is biography: What are the facts of Shakespeare's life? Who were his family and friends? What was life like in Stratford, in London? Documents discovered in this century have filled in some of the gaps, and a rather large number of biographies have been written. The pursuit of the life of the world's best-known writer seems valid in and of itself, though some biographies have contributed little to our store of knowledge. With hard facts about Shakespeare frustratingly few, many critics have searched the works themselves to try to gather information about the man. But such a critical approach abandons historical criticism in favor of a more speculative and conjectural procedure.

Much effort has gone into getting a reliable picture of the social, economic, political, intellectual, and cultural life of the Shakespearean era. Clearly we have a much better-informed view than was available to previous centuries. As a man who came under royal patronage in 1603, Shakespeare had to be keenly aware of the political world; whether he set out especially in his histories to offer political propaganda or teachings remains open to debate. The strong nationalism of the Elizabethan reign, which can be easily documented, must have had some impact on Shakespeare. Whether he understood economic theory, he surely understood practical finance, for we can now document his economic success, his property holdings. And, of course, the social and economic rise of actors and dramatists adds another variable in the historical equation, providing new status to a group previously deemed vagabonds. Knowledge of the sports and customs of the people helps in understanding parts of particular plays and the whole impulse toward dramatic entertainment. Shakespeare's philosophical assumptions and predilections do make a difference in his drama; but the problem remains: What were those assumptions? Reading his contemporaries, both literary and philosophical, a number of scholars have drawn a composite, a paradigm, of what the "world view" might have been. That Shakespeare himself adhered to any system is problematical, and the "evidence" from the plays kicks up about as much dust as it settles. But certainly assumptions about the scientific, moral, political, and psychological world differ from twentieth-century assumptions. Historical knowledge of such areas at least provides a hedge against egregious error, though it does not provide any sure-fire interpretation. Again, we must somehow understand the dramatist's context without believing that that is the only context in which he can be understood and enjoyed.

Influenced by anthropology, Marxism, or political ideology, a number of critics have been moved to consider what is history: Is it a construct of facts, paradigms, or is it much more problematical? These critics, labeled neohistoricists, insist that no opposition exists between literature and history; indeed, literature helps create society. This idea differs radically from older historical assumptions that Shakespeare's work reflected society—as one finds in E. M. W. Tillyard's perspective. Critics engaged in the new historicism hope to escape the trap of reductionism that afflicts some earlier historical studies. Instead of searching for a paradigm, the newer critics focus on the complexity and sometimes indeterminate nature of Renaissance culture. They explore the interaction between state and culture, often finding the theater to be a prime location for the representation and legitimation of power. The new historicism witnesses a convergence of concern for politics, cultural anthropology, historical fact, literary theory, and an expanding awareness of the function of literature in society.

THEATRICAL CRITICISM

Knowing the historical details of the era also involves learning about the theater. The major research on the theaters, acting companies, and actors has come in the twentieth century; previous criticism had largely ignored the Elizabethan theater. And yet Shakespeare as a complete man of the theater had to face practical, day-to-day problems that in many ways shaped his art. The presence of the actor Richard Burbage in Shakespeare's group helped make possible such great tragic roles as Hamlet, Lear, Othello, and Macbeth—one obviously does not create dramatic roles that suit no one in the company.

What were the theater buildings like? What advantages, what limitations, did they offer? Clearly the jutting platform stage makes the soliloquy and the aside plausible dramatic devices because it places the actor in close proximity to the audience with whom he may communicate confidentially. What, if anything, happens to Shakespeare's drama when the King's Men also begin to perform regularly at the private, indoor Blackfriars Theater, in addition to the Globe Theater? Critics occasionally observe that Shakespeare wrote for the box office, and he certainly appealed to the audiences. But who made up the audiences—what social and economic groups? What were their tastes and expectations? Further, who were Shakespeare's fellow dramatists, how well did he know them and their work, what influence did they have on him, and with whom did he collaborate? To learn more about the drama of the time means understanding that many of Shakespeare's dramatic conventions and techniques were widely accepted practices at the time.

Another approach of theatrical criticism explores the stage history of plays since the seventeenth century and thus documents changing stage traditions and interpretations. How the great actors of the past have come to terms with Shakespearean characters obviously reveals dimensions and subtleties perhaps not before appreciated. The staging of the plays can involve historical study as one tries to reconstruct the performance likely in the Elizabethan theater, or it can be immediately practical, as in the mounting of a contemporary production. Either way, one has to grapple with and resolve certain issues that a reader may simply pass over. How does one, for example, stage the supposed plunging of Gloucester from the cliff at Dover in *King Lear?* And what about the Ghost in *Hamlet*—does one make him a character on stage or an offstage voice? Theater criticism in particular attempts to answer an almost endless list of such questions.

GENRE CRITICISM

As the evidence in chapter 2 suggests, a vast amount of critical energy has been expended in a study of the *genres*: comedy, history, tragedy, and sonnet. Critics have often created subcategories within the genres, as, for example, problem comedies, satirical tragedies, Roman plays, Romances, pastoral comedies, tragicomedies. We have yet to reach the full extent of Polonius's famous list of such forms in *Hamlet*. What were the definitions and practical understanding of these forms in the Elizabethan period? Were the practitioners of the art influenced by Aristotle's critical theory of tragedy or by the Italian critics of the sixteenth century? How does Shakespearean tragedy differ from Aristotle's description or our knowledge of Greek tragedy? We may observe that *Romeo and Juliet* differs from the later tragedy *Hamlet;* does this reveal some sort of development in Shakespeare's practice of writing tragedies? Similar questions can be raised about the other genres. Comedy may be defined by its themes, structure, and form; or one might emphasize comic characters as the most distinguishing feature of these plays. How do Shakespeare's comedies differ from, say, Jonson's in spirit and in form? What is a history play, and what are its precursors? Who else wrote plays about English history? Conceivably Shakespeare had little systematic theory of form, being more concerned with getting another play finished than with whether it fit some conception of genre. Some critics have suggested that we should not refer to Shakespearean tragedy or comedy but, instead, to Shakespearean tragedies or comedies, that each has an independent existence not tied to those that went before or came after. Whatever conclusions we reach about Shakespeare's critical knowledge of literary theory, we can safely assume that he did not first immerse himself in critical treatises and then proceed to write—such is not the usual path of creative genius.

The relationship among genres is the subject of an increasing number of studies, which challenge the notion that genre differentiation depends on fixed, stable boundaries. We have been aware for quite a long time that violations of genre boundary often occur in Shakespeare—comic elements in tragedy, tragic elements in comedy, for example—but only in the last few years have critics turned their attention to mixed forms to understand the double problem of boundary definition and genre differentiation. This problem can be tackled from a variety of critical approaches and methods. Historical criticism helps us understand genre theory in the Renaissance. Other critics have focused on the archaic or archeological strata embedded in the works themselves, thus helping us understand the ways in which Shakespeare at once represents and departs from inherited patterns. Many interesting questions have been posed: To what extent does one form or genre develop in opposition to another? How do comedy and tragedy overlap in terms of structure? Where does romance fit with the other genres? The influence of poststructuralist and deconstructionist critics is beginning to be felt, particularly in the notion that the text simultaneously erects and erases boundaries in a process often referred to as "closure." The text paradoxically includes what it is supposed to exclude: namely, its opposite. The full implications of genre boundary and differentiation studies are still to be determined.

ANALYSES OF LANGUAGE AND IMAGERY

Partly in reaction to excesses of pedantic biographical and historical criticism, a wave designated "new criticism" hit the critical shores in the early decades of the twentieth century. It places priority on the intensive exploration of poetic *language* (and, of course, encompasses much more than just Shakespearean criticism). Readers ought not be so concerned with biography or the historical milieu in which the writer wrote; instead, the sensitive reader should respond to the drama (or whatever) as poetry. To oversimplify, the reader ideally sits down with no other paraphernalia than the text itself (probably shorn of footnotes) and comes to terms with the work of art. The potential rewards and risks seem quite great. Such an approach has reminded us that Shakespeare was the master poet; the approach risks forgetting that he was also the master dramatist. At its most extreme, this critical method would make each play an expanded metaphysical poem. But probably no other school of criticism has had so profound an impact on the practical matter of teaching Shakespeare. It has led to specialized studies of Shakespeare's verse—meter, rhythm—and how these elements contribute to our apprehending the poetic meaning. A number of books and essays have explored the intricacies of Shakespeare's language—his use of word play, ambiguity, paradox, verbal irony. The design of the Elizabethan theater itself encouraged emphasis on language, as it provided a platform stage with consequent full focus on what the actors were saying; the drama was thus in the best sense "wordy." With limited printing and limited literacy, this was a time of oral communication, and the theater was only another manifestation. Sensitivity to the word was crucial for those who sat or stood in the Globe.

Of major importance in the work on language has been the study and analysis of *imagery*. This critical approach got its greatest impetus in the 1930s, when several seminal studies appeared. Today, commenting on the plays' images has become a widespread practice, and many books pursue this particular critical method. Some studies have examined or isolated individual images or grouped them, documenting, for example, the extensive sun imagery in *Richard II*, disease imagery in *Hamlet*, and garden imagery in the history plays. Patterns of repeated imagery, often referred to as iterative images, reveal a meaningful order. Or particular images may be found grouped together several times in the play. Some critics have seized on a single image as shaping the whole structure; the image of evil in *Richard III* may be so pervasive as to imply an ordering of the play around it. The dramatist obviously uses images to comment on theme and character. One cannot recall the image of Richard II as "glistering Phaeton" without understanding something about his dramatic character or the constant images of storm that accompany Lear without perceiving that they reflect the tempest in his mind. In other words, seldom does Shakespeare use images merely as decoration;

they have some dramatic function. Recent studies have under-scored the significance of visual images produced in the staging of the plays—gestures, poses, costume. As Richard and Boling-broke hold the crown momentarily together in Act IV of *Richard II,* they offer a striking emblem of the struggle for kingship and testify also to the compelling power invested in the symbol of the crown. The larger view of Shakespeare's imagery has at-tempted to trace his development as a dramatist through his use of imagery, from earlier fitful moments when the images seem mainly decorative to the full integration of images with dramatic action, character, and theme.

Reacting to these traditional views of language, a new critical movement, often referred to as Poststructuralism or Deconstruc-tion, focuses on differences, oppositions, and antitheses as it asks ever more challenging questions about the ways in which the text differs from itself. Questioning, probing, and reading against the grain of the text's language, poststructuralists examine the means by which the text achieves stability. Focusing on such oppositions as writing/speech, signifier/signified, literature/criti-cism, reader/writer, deconstruction challenges the desire for unity, a center, and metaphysical truths. Although unable to escape this desire for unity and center, we must recognize that the cen-tering equilibrium is momentary. Final meaning eludes; instead, we can only reach provisional meaning, provisional states of inter-pretation. Poststructuralism is helping revise and challenge many traditional assumptions about language, imagery, text, and litera-ture itself. Although its impact on Shakespearean criticism is still minimal, an increasing number of studies using some post-structuralist strategies are beginning to appear.

THE STUDY OF CHARACTER

In addition to matters of generic form and language, many critics have been preoccupied with the study of *character;* indeed, this may be one of the oldest critical approaches. Analysis of character inextricably links with the nature of drama itself. Though Aristotle insists that the soul of drama is plot, the exper-iences of readers and theatergoers may suggest that the most memorable element is some striking character—perhaps most apparent in Shakespearean tragedy. The characters seem so real that some critics choose to discuss them as if they are indeed real, not fictional, persons or as if they have an existence beyond the play. An extreme case occurs in the mid-nineteenth-century study of the childhood of Shakespeare's female characters. Obviously a potential problem with this critical approach appears as another variation of "woods-for-treeism," that is, gaining a dominant character but losing the whole play. What motivates Iago? What causes the sudden onslaught of irrational jealousy in Leontes? The questions could be multiplied considerably, but obviously we have keen interest in character motivation. How much ink has been spilled trying to explain what Hamlet does (or doesn't) and why he does it (or doesn't). If one judges by what has been written, Hamlet is perhaps the most fascinating character in all of Western literature—an extraordinary testimony to the creation of character.

PSYCHOLOGICAL CRITICISM

All this leads to *psychological* criticism. The complex psychology of character of most of Renaissance drama, Shakespeare in particular, remains one of the striking features that sets it apart from medieval drama. Thanks to Freud, we can rather casually hold the opinion, whether valid or not, that Hamlet suffers from the Oedipus complex (Freud draws generously from Shakespeare in his writings). Psychoanalytical criticism has thrown off sparks of illumination, but whether they catch fire or merely fizzle often depends on how well the critic remembers that these are fictional characters. Complications occur because of the inability of the characters to respond to psychoanalytical questioning except in the voice and words that the dramatist has given them. Some studies have sought to define Renaissance psychology and then to view the plays in that light. In order to understand many of the references in the plays, one does have to know some of the rudiments of Elizabethan psychology—the theory of the humors, for example; but reading all the Renaissance treatises on melancholy cannot finally explain our reaction to Hamlet or the construction of his character. Recent psychological studies have focused on such questions as identity, doubling, sexuality, and personality development. Inevitably, some critics have examined family structure and its psychological implications: problems of parent-child relationships, paternal narcissism, fratricidal rivalry, and especially father-daughter bonds—of great relevance in Shakespeare. Some less well-founded studies have attempted to move from the plays to say something about the psychological development of Shakespeare himself. Obviously, psychological understanding of the characters has had much to do with threatrical productions of the plays.

THEMATIC AND MYTHIC CRITICISM

Pursuing *thematic* criticism, a somewhat small but controversial group of critics has taken what can be termed the "Christian" approach to Shakespeare. For generations, Shakespeare has been searched out for what instruction he has to offer about righteous living; indeed, in the early days of teaching his plays, this became one of the purposes. For some time preachers, with varying degrees of actual knowledge, have borrowed freely from Shakespeare, usually a quotation to drive home a point. Much of the early response links to the notion that to be a good writer one must first be a good man. Shakespeare grew up in the midst of a solidly Christian culture; but about his personal religious practice or belief we know nothing, except that he was baptized, married, and buried in the Church of England. Studies have indicated his apparently extensive knowledge of the Bible as reflected in his plays and poems—that is not controversial. But when critics begin to interpret a work in specific Christian theological terms, difficulty ensues. Are the endings of certain plays or the overall themes specifically Christian? Does the Duke in *Measure for Measure* represent God's providence? Does Othello find salvation? One could go on raising questions that have been debated. The whole nature of "Christian tragedy" has been critically vexing, the idea seeming contradictory to some. The final Romances have been read as religious allegories; Christ symbols have been found here and there. The pitfalls of this particular critical approach should be obvious without denying that in its more sensible moments it has opened new perspectives on the plays. Other critics have examined dramatic themes not necessarily colored by religion, such as jealousy, justice, love, education, patience, duty, moral obligation, suffering, revenge, transformation, reconciliation, politics, substitution, inheritance, and greed. Thematic criticism argues for the importance of ideas in the plays.

Mythic criticism asserts that Shakespeare participates in and reflects myths common to different civilizations. Drama itself seems a form of ritual, or at least contains ritualistic qualities as it establishes a participatory relationship between actors and audience. Shakespeare's use of classical myths and ancient mythology appears obvious in the plays; on occasion he seems to have had in mind a specific myth that orders and structures the play, as in his dependence on the Pyramus and Thisbe and the Venus and Adonis stories. The legends of King Lear and Cymbeline come from a shadowy pseudohistory that Shakespeare fashions into drama. Critics have found especially in the comedies or in such a figure as Falstaff reflections and embodiments of a Saturnalian myth—the whole process of social and holiday indulgence, reminiscent of customs and practices current in Shakespeare's own time. The necessary aesthetic distinctions that should be made between a holiday occasion and formal drama have led to fascinating criticism. The myth of the seasons has been seen to underlie the nature of comedy and tragedy, with the winter's tale of tragedy in opposition to the summer, life-renewing spirit of comedy. Such criticism explores issues of anthropology and collective psychology. This mode of analysis runs the risk, as do other methods, of forgetting the theater. But surely if these critical approaches even approximate the truth, they should give the lie, once and for all, to the idea that Shakespeare was an untutored genius.

FEMINIST AND GENDER CRITICISM

The decade of the 1980s has witnessed an explosion in book-length studies that analyze Shakespeare from a feminist perspective or that at least have a gender approach to his works. Feminist criticism seems to struggle with two primary questions: What does it mean to be a female character in Shakespeare's fictional world, and what does it mean to be a female reader of Shakespeare in the late twentieth century? Only the first question had been broached earlier, but not in a satisfactory or sophisticated manner. Feminist criticism, as a result of these fundamental questions, has heavily relied on historical and psychological approaches. Thus, a number of the critics have tried to ascertain the position and plight of women in Shakespeare's time: What were the social conditions? What was the role of women in marriage, in commerce, in politics? What effect did the system of patriarchy have on women?

If one is able to answer these questions successfully—and they are not as simple or straightforward as they may seem—then how does one square this understanding with the way Shakespeare portrays women in his works? Do the plays reflect the actual world, contradict it, criticize it, or what? Is Shakespeare sympathetic towards women in ways that his society and his contemporaries were not? Was he a feminist? What does it mean if some of Shakespeare's female characters are strong and powerful when the historical record seems to say that women at the time were expected to be meek and docile?

Feminist critics have also explored on a psychological basis what it meant or means to be a woman. Is there some feminine principle that can be recognized and defined and that operates in the plays? Do the males feel threatened, endangered psychologically, by the presence of this opposing force? What does it mean to the male characters that the women have the power of birth, given them by nature? Are the women psychologically envious of the men, desiring their aggressiveness and prowess? What is the role of the female characters in sexual relationships? What is the nature of the father-daughter bond?

Additionally, feminist critics have tried to assess the relationship between gender and genre. Some have argued that there are comic women and tragic men, that one generic form is particularly compatible with the feminine principle and that the other suits the masculine perspective. But what is the connection between gender and genre in mixed forms, such as the history plays and the final Romances? Is there something in the understanding of gender that helps us understand and interpret the structure of the plays? Do some particularly strong women cross generic boundaries?

The studies listed and discussed in chapter 2 reveal the diversity of questions raised and approaches tried by feminist critics. Also, one should note that part of the contribution of such critics has been simply to counteract decades of male bias and insensitivity in the practice of criticism.

TEXTUAL CRITICISM

Another school of criticism deserves attention for its exceptional impact on Shakespearan studies—*textual* criticism. As suggested above, the practitioners of this form of scholarship have made a major contribution in the twentieth century. Students and other readers often feel little concern about the nature of the edition that they use; certainly, the standard editions mentioned in chapter 2 will not seriously mislead anyone. But such has not always been the case, as with many earlier texts, impressionistically edited and emended according to the editor's whim, whether on poetic or moral grounds. Textual criticism remains an art, though it has developed some objective, scientific methods. Fundamentally this approach seeks to determine what Shakespeare wrote—not questions of disputed authorship, but literally what he wrote—believing quite rightly that correct understanding and analysis can only come from a sound, reliable text. In the history of Shakespearean criticism, a number of examples exist in which the critic relied on a poor and incorrect text, thus damaging interpretation.

Textual criticism, according to Fredson Bowers, tries to deal with at least three major problems: (1) To determine the nature of the printer's copy; that is, on what did he base his printing—author's manuscript, scribal copy, promptbook from the theater, and so on. (2) To establish the relationship between all known copies of the text. For example, how do the three different versions of *Hamlet* relate to one another, and which provides the authoritative text on which to construct a sound edition? Or, what about a single edition that survives in several copies with variant readings? (3) To understand the nature of the printing process itself in order to know what effect this might have had on the transmission of the text. What was the typical method of setting a page of type? What were the common work habits in a given print shop? Did that shop have one or two presses? To pose such questions, and there are dozens more, involves one in descriptive or analytical bibliography—that is, the "science," the physical make-up of a book. Investigations into the printing process have led in some cases to the discovery and identification of the compositors who set the type; their spelling habits and preferences appear in the text, meaning that frequently we read their spelling, not Shakespeare's. Study of the First Folio has isolated with some certainty five, probably six, different compositors and the portions of the Folio that they set. All of these matters have a profound effect on how the textual editor goes about his business. Computers now assist in sorting evidence, thus providing a reliable base from which to work. In the early days of this whole critical movement, sometimes referred to as the "new bibliography," some felt that we should soon have all problems resolved if only we followed the methodological "rules." Less sanguine today, we watch almost every solution give rise to additional problems; but textual criticism remains an area of challenge and intellectual rigor, stimulating lively debate among its theorists and practitioners.

MAJOR SCHOLARS AND CRITICS

What follows attempts to single out some of the leading scholars and critics. The selection, of necessity subjective but not whimsical, encounters the vast quantity of available material on Shakespeare, which makes any kind of selection perilous and certainly difficult. The choices here should not in any way be construed as indicating the "top ten" among Shakespearean critics; at best it deals with those who have been especially influential. In a simpler day it may have been possible to name *the* outstanding Shakespearean; to do that now risks rushing in where angels fear to tread. A number of the persons mentioned here receive more extensive treatment in chapter 2.

Samuel Johnson (1709-84) epitomized and at the same time reacted against eighteenth-century neoclassical criticism. His *Preface to Shakespeare* (1765), an important critical statement, views Shakespeare as the poet of nature, holding up the mirror to manners and to life. The characters become genuine progeny of common humanity; we easily recognize them. Curiously, Johnson believes that Shakespeare's true genius lay in comedy, not tragedy. Rebutting critical tradition, Johnson exonerates Shakespeare on the issue of observing the unities; he also accepts the mingling of tragic and comic scenes. Though praise outweighs fault-finding, Johnson outlines a series of problems that he further documents in the notes of his edition. He complains that the plots are loose and that Shakespeare does not fulfill the function of moral instruction. The dramatist too readily indulges in a quibble—"the fatal Cleopatra," in Johnson's famous phrase. Johnson's concern for style and dramatic construction, his recognition of the significance of the characters, and his laying to rest the argument over the unities—all indicate a keen critical mind at work.

The next critic to dominate the scene was Samuel Taylor Coleridge (1772-1834), one of the ablest critics of any era. Coleridge never wrote a book on Shakespeare; we find his ideas scattered in notes, parts of essays, and lectures. The final view may be somewhat fragmentary, but several basic ideas emerge. Coleridge reacts as the supreme romantic critic against earlier criticism that had honored some concept of neoclassical rules. For Coleridge, Shakespeare's organic form, not mechanical in any way, shapes and develops itself from within. Coleridge also emphasizes Shakespeare the great poet as well as dramatist. Strangely, few before Coleridge had paid much attention to this obvious fact. The logical critical extension of such an assumption may be seen in the close reading of the poetry by the "new critics" and others. In one of his excessive moments, Coleridge likened himself to Hamlet, but more seriously he pointed the way to an emphasis on the characters as he observed the psychological and moral sensitivity of Shakespeare's creations. The willing suspension of disbelief constitutes poetic faith, and this doctrine has clear ramifications for our perception of drama. Scattered comments on some of the plays offer insight, but the ideas sketched above form the more permanent part of Coleridge's legacy to Shakespearean criticism.

A. C. Bradley (1851-1935) stands as a giant at the beginning of the twentieth century; his work on the tragedies has become one of the major works of this century, though in truth, Bradley may be seen as the culmination of Victorian criticism. In any event, his detailed analyses of characters and the primacy assigned to them provide a critical approach still quite appealing. E. E. Stoll (1874-1959), whose best-known book is *Art and Artifice in Shakespeare* (Cambridge University Press, 1933), worked in a critical direction opposed to Bradley. His ideas have also had long-range impact. He modifies biographical or character criticism, insisting instead that a play must be judged in light of its milieu. He places emphasis on the dramatic conventions that Shakespeare reflects and by so doing opens the door to the whole development of historical criticism. On the artistic level, Stoll comments: 'The greatest of dramatists is careful, not so much for the single character, as for the drama; indeed, he observes not so much the probabilities of the action, or the psychology of the character, as the psychology of the audience, for whom both action and character are framed" (168). Shakespeare's art focuses on being true to art, rather than being true to life. Stoll, much more than Bradley, emphasizes Shakespeare as a man of the theater. (Stoll's book was the first major critical work by an American to be published by an English press.)

Several others who began in the earlier part of the century have made special contributions in historical research and criticism. E. K. Chambers's (1866-1954) monumental four-volume study and collection of materials on the Elizabethan stage has had a major influence on the development of scholarship. Similarly, his collection of materials relevant to Shakespeare's life remains unsurpassed. Hardin Craig (1875-1968), noted as an editor and great teacher, did much to define the philosophical and historical context in which Shakespeare wrote. That critical concern E. M. W. Tillyard (1889-1962) shared; his brief book on the Eliza-bethan world has become a classic statement of the orthodox, hierarchical world view that the Elizabethans inherited. Though Tillyard wrote on the early comedies and on the late Romances, his influential book on the history plays has been his best-known book. His vision and interpretation of the histories became the accepted view for quite some time, though it has since been chal-lenged. It remains, nevertheless, a landmark in Shakespearean criticism.

The new directions in bibliographical and textual studies gained impetus from a number of scholars, among them R. B. McKer-row (1872-1940), A. W. Pollard (1859-1944), W. W. Greg (1875-1959), and John Dover Wilson (1881-1969). Singling out individual works remains difficult because these scholars pro-duced many and various books. McKerrow's introductory guide to bibliography and Pollard's (in collaboration with Redgrave) *Short-Title Catalogue,* of all the books printed in England, Scot-land, and Ireland between 1475 and 1640, have both been of enormous help and made possible additional research. Greg's influential essay on the rationale of the copy text, his bibliography of English printed drama to the Restoration, and his book on the First Folio have been major contributions to textual studies. Wilson, who produced books on *Hamlet* and on the comedies, explored many new avenues of textual theory as editor of the New Cambridge edition of Shakespeare.

The early analyses of Shakespeare's imagery by Caroline Spurgeon (1869-1942) and Wolfgang Clemen (b. 1909) (both discussed in chapter 2) influenced many later critical studies. Spurgeon's arguments have been much modified, but most studies of imagery start with her book. Unfortunately she reached conclusions about Shakespeare the man on the basis of the imagery and was not content with analyzing what the images reveal about the drama. Clemen's book, published in German in 1936 and translated in 1951, explores the development of the dramatist's use of imagery. G. Wilson Knight (1897-1985), whose productive critical career also began the 1930s, became an influential practitioner of the imagery approach. To see Knight as a critic who investigates the dramatist's imagery unduly restricts a view of him. His highly metaphysical, religious, symbolic, spatial vision of the drama does not fit neatly into any single category, though in a number of his essays he emphasizes imagery. He never fails to offer insight into the drama or poetry, even if one finally disagrees with him.

More recent years have witnessed enormous productivity, and only a few persons can be singled out for their contributions. G. E. Bentley and Alfred Harbage deserve special recognition. Bentley, in his seven-volume compilation of material on the Jacobean and Caroline stage, provides an impressive base from which additional research has sprung. Other books by him on the Shakespearean stage and on the profession of the dramatist during this period utilize some of his research materials and present an analysis of significant theatrical problems. Harbage has not only edited certain plays and served as general editor of the Pelican Shakespeare; he has also contributed important historical studies, principally, *Shakespeare's Audience* (1941), *As They Liked It* (1947), and *Shakespeare and the Rival Traditions* (1952). Harbage's view of the make-up of the theater and audience and his thesis of a profound cleavage between public and private theaters have provoked challenge, but his contribution remains considerable.

Geoffrey Bullough and S. Schoenbaum have been working also in a historical tradition. Bullough's multivolume collection on the narrative and dramatic sources of Shakespeare constitutes a major piece of scholarship, providing a sound text of and extensive guide to the sources—a work not likely to be supplanted. Schoenbaum has revised Harbage's *Annals of English Drama*, but his major work exclusively on Shakespeare has been his work on Shakespeare biography. In one book he sifts through the mass of materials concerned with constructing a life of Shakespeare. Given the increasing number of biographies, certainly the time had come for such a survey and assessment of them. Schoenbaum handles the subject with skill and wit. He has become *the* biographer of Shakespeare.

The present era has yielded many important textual studies; among the principal contributors have been Fredson Bowers and Charlton Hinman. This period of bibliographical research, often called the "age of Bowers," testifies to the impact of his work. His principles of bibliography and techniques of editing have been much imitated. His editorship of *Studies in Bibliography* provided an outlet for research and set high standards for it. The culmination of Hinman's work was his two-volume study of the printing and proofreading of the Shakespeare First Folio. The monumental examination of several dozen copies of the Folio yielded conclusions about how the book was put together and many other details associated with its publication. Additional compositor studies now supplement Hinman's study of the compositors who set the type for the book.

The post-World War II explosion of Shakespearean criticism renders suspect any attempt to single out the most outstanding critics of this era. Critical fortunes have a way of waxing and waning, while the contribution of research and scholarship may be easier to assess. The materials presented and evaluated in chapter 2 provide a partial basis for grasping contributions in Shakespearean criticism in the latter half of the twentieth century. Depending on one's perspective, the productivity of Shakespearean critics may either be a curse or a blessing, a burden or an embarrassment of riches. Time may be the final arbiter of what critical studies survive and have influence.

Only a willingness to suffer the fate of fools who rush in where angels fear to tread would lead one to speculate about where we will be in Shakespearean criticism (or anything else) at the beginning of the twenty-first century. We will doubtless have more editions of Shakespeare, and we will have critical studies that pour old wine into new bottles. Probably we will witness more interdisciplinary studies that link Shakespeare's works with other art forms—music, pictorial art and iconography, even other dramatic forms—that explore the full range of cultural implications (past and present) of Shakespeare's art, that examine the psychological and practical consequences of gender awareness. If we are lucky, we will have criticism that asks questions as yet undreamed of. Who a hundred years ago foresaw the diversity and richness of current criticism?

Part of the beauty and mystery of Shakespeare's art derives from its never-ceasing appeal and its ability to stimulate the intellect and emotions of people far removed from one another in time and place. Each passing decade and each passing century verify Jonson's seemingly extravagant claim that Shakespeare was "not of an age, but for all time."

CHAPTER TWO
A Guide to the Resources

This is the heart of the matter. This chapter presents a selection of some of the most valuable and useful books, arranged under the following categories: bibliographies and reference guides, editions, studies in the genres (comedies, histories, tragedies, sonnets), studies of groups and movements, interdisciplinary studies, periodicals, and biographical studies. With a few exceptions no essays are dealt with, only books. Students should consult the appropriate bibliographies in order to gain access to potentially helpful essays in periodicals; if they are trying to track down a particular critic here, they should simply consult the Index of Authors.

Obviously, summarizing and analyzing these several dozen books involve paraphrasing the authors' ideas and frequently include direct or indirect quotations. Names of publishers and dates of publication immediately follow each reference. Below is a list of abbreviations for the titles of Shakespeare's works:

Ado	*Much Ado about Nothing*	*2H4*	*Henry IV, Part 2*
Ant.	*Antony and Cleopatra*	*H5*	*Henry V*
AWW	*All's Well That Ends Well*	*1H6*	*Henry VI, Part 1*
AYL	*As You Like It*	*2H6*	*Henry VI, Part 2*
Cor.	*Coriolanus*	*3H6*	*Henry VI, Part 3*
Cym.	*Cymbeline*	*H8*	*Henry VIII*
Err.	*Comedy of Errors*	*JC*	*Julius Ceasar*
Ham.	*Hamlet*	*Jn.*	*King John*
1H4	*Henry IV, Part 1*	*LLL*	*Love's Labor's Lost*

Lr.	King Lear	Shr.	The Taming of the Shrew
Luc.	The Rape of Lucrece	TGV	Two Gentlemen of Verona
Mac.	Macbeth	Tim.	Timon of Athens
MM	Measure for Measure	Tit.	Titus Andronicus
MND	A Midsummer Night's Dream	TN	Twelfth Night
MV	The Merchant of Venice	TNK	Two Noble Kinsmen
Oth.	Othello	Tmp.	The Tempest
Per.	Pericles	Tro.	Troilus and Cressida
R2	Richard II	Ven.	Venus and Adonis
R3	Richard III	Wiv.	The Merry Wives of Windsor
Rom.	Romeo and Juliet	WT	The Winter's Tale

BIBLIOGRAPHY AND REFERENCE GUIDES

Part of the Goldentree Bibliography series, David Bevington's *Shakespeare* (AHM Publishing, 1978) offers nearly 4,700 entries, arranged by topics (such as bibliographies; social, political, and intellectual background; biography; editions and textual criticism; and studies in genre) and then entries on the plays and poems. The dates of coverage in this bibliography are approximately 1930 to the beginning of 1977. Bevington uses asterisks to mark those items that seem indispensable; otherwise there is usually little system of annotation. For a number of the plays Bevington creates subtopics of the criticism, thereby assisting the sorting out of the criticism. Clear and easy to use, this bibliography makes a good starting point for a survey of Shakespearean items between 1930 and 1977. One may find additional items in Andrew M. McLean's *Shakespeare: Annotated Bibliographies and Media Guide for Teachers* (National Council of Teachers of English, 1980), which is a three-part bibliography: (1) an extensive bibliography on teaching Shakespeare in the schools (high school and college); (2) Shakespeare in films and on television; and, (3) a guide to media for teaching Shakespeare (audio-visual materials).

A *Selective Bibliography of Shakespeare,* prepared by James G. McManaway and Jeanne Addison Roberts (UP of Virginia, 1975), contains some 4,500 items covering the period 1930-70, with a few exceptions. The table of contents reveals the organization of the book, which surveys material on individual plays and poems and specific topics. Some of the entries are annotated.

Larry S. Champion's *The Essential Shakespeare: An Annotated*

Bibliography of Major Modern Studies (G. K. Hall, 1986) includes 1,500 entries, spread over 435 pages. Champion covers the period 1900-84 and annotates what he considers to be the significant works in scholarship and criticism. He begins with a section General Studies, then moves to the individual works arranged by genre. His annotations are primarily descriptive rather than evaluative; they are thorough and helpful.

Much more extensive, but now a bit outdated, is Gordon Ross Smith's *A Classified Shakespeare Bibliography, 1936-1958* (Pennsylvania State UP, 1963). Over 20,000 items are cited in this book. On pp. xlix-li Smith discusses the use of this bibliography and its methods of compilation; on pp. vii-xli the two broad categories, "General" and "Works," are broken down, which should speed finding references on specific topics. For example, under the heading "General," one finds entries on bibliography, surveys of scholarship, life, sources, stage, literary taste, influence, criticism, and the Bacon controversy. This bibliography examines works individually and also includes a category on the chronology of the drama.

Smith's bibliography is a continuation of the earlier one by Walter Ebisch and Levin Schücking, *A Shakespeare Bibliography* (Clarendon, 1931) which had a cutoff date of 1929. A Supplement to this bibliography was issued in 1937, covering the years 1930-35, also published by Clarendon Press. Eight pages outline the contents of the volume; also included is an index of authors. The classification categories resemble those adopted by Smith; thus students should be able to thread their way through both bibliographies if they know the format of one of them (even so, they can be a bit perplexing).

The first full-fledged bibliography on Shakespeare was compiled by William Jaggard: *Shakespeare Bibliography* (Shakespeare Press, 1911; later reprints). Jaggard boasts of over 36,000 entries and references and claims that the book is "so simply arranged that a child can use it"—a most dubious claim. The entries appear alphabetically, according to author, title, and subject. Under the heading "Shakespeare," separate works are listed first, arranged alphabetically with each item in chronological order. Jaggard is especially strong on early editions of the plays but not very useful on matters of criticism or interpretation.

The student may find it beneficial to have two bibliographies that are available in paperback editions. Ronald Berman has produced what he calls a "discursive bibliography," *A Readers's Guide to Shakespeare's Plays,* revised edition (Scott Foresman, 1973; originally published, 1965). Each play is treated in terms of text, editions, sources, criticism, and staging, with criticism getting the main attention. Berman covers articles as well as books, and he does not hide his critical opinion of the material he reviews. Not an enumerative bibliography as such, this one offers a narrative guide to the scholarship and criticism of the plays and is on the whole both reliable and extremely helpful.

Stanley Wells has edited *Shakespeare: Select Bibliographical Guides* (Oxford UP, 1973). This book was planned as a selective guide to the best in Shakespeare scholarship and criticism; it offers seventeen essays by different critics who review criticism on specific topics, a specific play, group of plays or poems. The essayists sketch out the main critical views and provide reading lists. The essays cover such topics as Shakespeare's text, theater, sonnets, early comedies, middle comedies, problem comedies, late comedies, and English history plays; seven essays are on the tragedies. Though the book carries a 1973 imprint, not much after 1969 is included in these surveys; in any event, the student will find it of great assistance.

The Garland Shakespeare Bibliographies, general editor William L. Godshalk (Garland, 1980-), offer extensive, annotated bibliographies that survey Shakespeare criticism since 1940 for their respective plays. A general introduction assesses critical trends and offers an overview. Thorough indexes enable the user to retrieve information easily. Twelve volumes have appeared thus far in this series.

An ongoing project is *The Biblioteca Shakespeariana* (Microforms International), which is a series of 3,000 works on Shakespeare reproduced on microfiche. Some thirty units, including one on Shakespeare bibliography, make up the series. Other topics include Shakespeare's life and society, Shakespeare's texts, Shakespeare's reading, Shakespeare in performance, and Shakespearean scholarship and criticism. Various editors have chosen the material to be reproduced. One will find in the section on bibliographies, for example, six major bibliographies, reproduced in their entirety on microfiche.

Though not specifically prepared as a bibliography, the effect is the same for the *Folger Shakespeare Library: Catalog of the Shakespeare Collections*, 2 vols. (G. K. Hall, 1972). Not only is this a guide to one of the world's greatest Shakespeare collections, but it also serves rather handily the need for a bibliography, though, of course, it does not list essays in journals. Volume 1 covers the hundreds of editions of Shakespeare, both collections and individual plays, all arranged chronologically. Volume 2 treats Shakespeare as subject, with some fifteen categories, and Shakespeare as the first word of a title.

The *Cambridge Bibliography of English Literature*, vol. 1, edited by F. W. Bateson (Cambridge UP, 1940, with a supplement in 1957), offers a generous section on Shakespeare (pp. 540-608; Supplement, pp. 257-93). Bateson surveys such topics as bibliography, life, works, and criticism, with the entries arranged alphabetically and chronologically; also there are cross references to the appropriate parts of the Ebisch and Schücking bibliography. The most recent version of this bibliography is *The New Cambridge Bibliography of English Literature*, edited by George Watson (Cambridge UP, 1974). In volume 1 the extensive Shakespeare bibliography may be found in columns 1473-1636.

A specialized bibliography is John W. Velz, *Shakespeare and the Classical Tradition: A Critical Guide to Commentary, 1660-1960* (U of Minnesota P, 1968). This guide attempts to gather, classify, summarize, and appraise the commentary that has been written since 1660. The entries are arranged alphabetically by author under nine different categories, all geared to the topic of Shakespeare's participation in the classical tradition. Velz includes a valuable index. His book greatly expands the earlier one by Selma Guttman, *The Foreign Sources of Shakespeare's Works: An Annotated Bibliography of the Commentary Written on this Subject between 1904 and 1940* (Columbia UP, 1947; reprint, 1968). Guttman lists the foreign authors with the pertinent editions and translations that could have been known by Shakespeare. This bibliography includes foreign sources other than classical.

In addition to these sources that cover expanded periods of time, there are publications that annually list or comment on Shakespearean items: students will want to consult these publications in order to bring research up to date. The *Shakespeare Quarterly*, published since 1950, now under the auspices of the Folger Library, contains an extensive "Annotated World Bibliography" on Shakespeare. The subject index aids the researcher in tracking down potentially useful essays or books. There is a *Cumulative Index* to volumes 1-15 (1950-64) of the *Quarterly* itself, prepared by Martin Seymour-Smith (AMS Press, 1969), which offers easy access to the articles, reviews, and notes of the journal. The Modern Language Association produces annually the *MLA International Bibliography*, sometimes filed separately from the journal *PMLA*. The annual bibliography began in volume 37 (1922). The section on Shakespeare has entries on general topics and on the individual works. The *Shakespeare Association Bulletin*, published between 1924 and 1949 by the Shakespeare Association of America, also contains annual bibliographies. The *Annual Bibliography of English Language and Literature*, which began in 1920, is published by the Modern Humanities Research Association. Nearly 800 journals are surveyed by this bibliography, which contains a section on Shakespeare. The English Association publishes *Year's Work in English Studies*, begun in 1919/20, which presents in narrative form a summary and evaluation of materials published on Shakespeare, arranged under such categories as editions, textual matters, sources, bibliography, criticism, theater, reprints. This book includes helpful indexes as well. Beginning in volume 19 (1922) and continuing through volume 66 (1969), *Studies in Philology* published an annual Renaissance bibliography, which, of course, had a section on Shakespeare.

The student may want to consult more generalized bibliographies (often kept in special reference sections in college libraries). *The Reader's Guide to Periodical Literature* surveys the more popular magazines. Another H. Wilson publication, the *Essay and General Literature Index*, analyzes the content of books, which are listed at the back of this publication. Since it is often difficult to tell exactly the contents of a book by its title, this guide aids in efficient research. Published since 1960 is *An Index to Book Reviews in the Humanities*, arranged by author; the editions of Shakespeare are listed under his name. *The British Humanities Index*, published quarterly by the Library Association of London, contains a section on Shakespeare. The front of the issue lists all British publications that are surveyed, a number of which are not covered in the *MLA Bibliography*. The *Social Sciences and Humanities Index*, issued four times a year, has a section on Shakespeare and a convenient list of all the periodicals indexed in it. Begun in 1938,

Dissertation Abstracts International offers a guide to PhD theses. The simplest way to use it is to look in the index under "Shakespeare"; here are listed all the dissertations that deal with Shakespeare. *Dissertations in English and American Literature, 1865-1964,* prepared by Lawrence F. McNamee (Bowker, 1968), also provides access to graduate theses. A 1969 supplement covering the years 1964-68 includes a section on Shakespeare.

Much research involves some specialized knowledge of Shakespeare's language, and several books provide the means of understanding the patterns of usage and peculiarities of Elizabethan English. With the advent of computers, new studies and analyses of Shakespeare's language have become possible; one of the results is the publication of new concordances to his works. These concordances record each word that Shakespeare uses, where he uses it, and the frequency of usage. The first new one to be completed is Marvin Spevack, *A Complete and Systematic Concordance to the Works of Shakespeare,* 9 vols. (Olms, 1968-1980). Volume 1 provides drama and character concordances to the comedies; volume 2, the histories and nondramatic works; volume 3, tragedies, plus *Per., TNK,* and *Sir Thomas More;* volumes 4-6, alphabetical listing of all the words used by Shakespeare; volume 7, stage directions and speech prefixes; volume 8, the bad quartos; and volume 9, substantive variants. Spevack's work uses the Riverside Shakespeare edition for its references. *The Harvard Concordance to Shakespeare* (Harvard UP, 1973) is a one-volume abridgment of Spevack's concordance. Published in individual volumes are the *Oxford Shakespeare Concordances* (Clarendon, 1969-73), prepared by T. H. Howard-Hill. A separate volume appears for each play, with the copy-text being the one chosen for the Oxford Old Spelling Shakespeare edition.

Other books also deal with Shakespeare's language and offer reference sources. E. A. Abbott, *A Shakespearian Grammar* (1870; reprint Dover, 1966), remains the standard grammar. It surveys the various grammatical constructions and also includes a section on prosody. It contains illustrations from the plays and poems and often compares Shakespeare's usage with Early English and Middle English. In his book *Shakespeare's Vocabulary: Its Etymological Elements* (1903; reprint AMS Press, 1966), Eilert Ekwall explores the derivation of Shakespeare's language.

G. L. Brook's *The Language of Shakespeare* (Andre Deutsch,

1976) is a somewhat technical book that examines matters of syntax, accidence, word formation, rhetoric, dialects, pronunciation, spelling, and punctuation. This is essentially a reference book. On matters of syntax, Brook notes that Elizabethans preferred vigor to logic; and he discusses concord, word order, ellipsis, functional shift, nouns, pronouns, and other parts of speech. In the section on accidence he notes the presence of inflected forms in Shakespeare's language. With regard to punctuation, we are reminded that the Elizabethan system was rhetorical. The influence of regional dialects is to be found in Shakespeare's plays in vocabulary and pronunciation and to a much lesser extent in syntax and semantics.

A valuable reference book is Helge Kökeritz, *Shakespeare's Pronunciation* (Yale UP, 1953), the main purpose of which is to provide a comprehensive account of Shakespeare's pronunciation and to present the relevant phonological evidence for the reconstructions. Kökeritz believes that an adequate knowledge of pronunciation is essential for the understanding of the text and prosody as is, for example, a knowledge of grammar and syntax.

Disputing some of Kökeritz's conclusions, Fausto Cercignani, in *Shakespeare's Works and Elizabethan Pronunciation* (Clarendon, 1981), sets out to examine the question of pronunciation in light of contemporary external evidence and in the wider framework of historical English phonology. In contrast to Kökeritz, who argues that Shakespeare's pronunciation closely resembled modern English, Cercignani argues that the types of speech reflected in Shakespeare's works and in those of contemporary writers on orthography and pronunciation reveal considerable discrepancies between Elizabethan and present-day standard usage. The bulk of the book is a detailed examination and description of Shakespeare's phonology, the use of vowels and consonants.

A handy guide is C. T. Onions, *A Shakespeare Glossary* (Clarendon, 1911), based on usages from the *Oxford English Dictionary*. Definitions of words are given with their location in Shakespeare's text; these references are sometimes supplemented with evidence from other contemporary writers. Comparable but much more extensive is Alexander Schmidt, *Shakespeare Lexicon*, 3d ed., revised by Gregor Sarrazin (1901; reprint Blom, 1968). All words are listed with definitions and citations to Shakespeare's text (Schmidt cites the Globe edition).

Another book that deals with definitions, but of a very special kind, is Eric Partridge, *Shakespeare's Bawdy,* 2d ed. (Routledge & Kegan Paul, 1968; 1st ed., 1947). Partridge includes an essay on the sexual and bawdy in Shakespeare, but the major portion of the book is a 180-page glossary, listing every word suspected of bawdy possibilities. Definitions are given with references to location in the plays and poems. Partridge certainly sheds a quite different light on Shakespeare.

E. A. M. Colman, in *The Dramatic Use of Bawdy in Shakespeare* (Longman, 1974), explores Shakespeare's development in the use of bawdy language in his plays and poems. Eventually, Colman argues, the dramatist made such language one of the most potent weapons in his dramatic armory. In order to trace development, Colman treats the plays more or less chronologically and includes a separate discussion of the sonnets and poems.

Building on the work of Morris Tilley's *A Dictionary of the Proverbs in England in the Sixteenth and Seventeenth Centuries* and subsequent studies, R. W. Dent, in his *Shakespeare's Proverbial Language: An Index* (U of California P, 1981), lists all the known proverbs, play by play, in Shakespeare's canon. Appendixes give the actual proverbs, cite possible origins, and cross-reference them to the plays. Dent's Introduction indicates the principles by which he has compiled this valuable index.

In *How to Find Out about Shakespeare* (Pergamon Press, 1968), John Bate surveys some of the criticism and scholarship on Shakespeare. Bate, a librarian, describes and evaluates materials a researcher might need, centering on such topics as Shakespeare's England, his life, theater and production, text, sources, literary criticism, commentaries on the individual plays.

Of enormous value is *The Reader's Encyclopedia of Shakespeare,* edited by O. J. Campbell and Edward H. Quinn (Crowell, 1966; published in London by Methuen with the title *A Shakespeare Encyclopaedia*). This compendium of information covers a vast range of subjects and people, arranged alphabetically from *Aaron* to *Zuccarelli,* including excellent sections that review criticism and scholarship, arranged by century, as well as topics that comment on the various schools of criticism. The appendixes provide a chronology of events, transcripts of relevant documents, and a 30-page selected bibliography. Much less ambitious but nevertheless valuable is F. E. Halliday, *A Shakespeare Companion, 1564-1964,* 2d ed. (Duckworth, 1964), available in paperback. Arranged alphabetically, it offers all kinds of information about Shakespeare's works, characters in the plays, contemporary dramatists, history, actors, editors, scholars. Covering some of the same territory is *The New Century Shakespeare Handbook,* edited by Sandra Clark and T. H. Long (Prentice-Hall, 1974). Brief essays on Shakespeare's life, theater and play production, and his major poetry precede the alphabetical listing, but this volume adds little of importance. *The Concise Encyclopedic Guide to Shakespeare,* by Michael R. Martin and Richard C. Harrier (Horizon, 1971), offers a glossary and listing of critics, scholars, and people of the theater noted for their contributions. It includes lists of modern productions of the plays, composers of music based on Shakespeare, and recordings.

Two collections of essays offer a good view of the critical and scholarly terrain for students. The earlier one is *A Companion to Shakespeare Studies,* edited by Harley Granville-Barker and G. B. Harrison (Cambridge UP, 1934). This book gives a fair sampling of where scholarship was in the early 1930s and offers valuable introductions to several topics—biography, theater, Shakespeare's dramatic art, Elizabethan English, music, historical background, sources, text, drama of his time, Shakespearean criticism and scholarship. Among the outstanding contributors of essays are Pollard, Harrison, Granville-Barker, T. S. Eliot, Sisson. A follow-up volume *A New Companion to Shakespeare Studies,* edited by Kenneth Muir and S. Schoenbaum (Cambridge UP, 1971), contains a series of eighteen essays on comparable topics. Essayists include Schoenbaum, Hosley, G. K. Hunter, Bevington, Bradbrook, Ure, Sprague, Sternfeld. Like its predecessors, the more recent version, *The Cambridge Companion to Shakespeare Studies* (Cambridge UP, 1986), edited by Stanley Wells, pursues some of the same topics. But this new collection contains a fuller treatment of Shakespearean criticism, including an essay on new critical approaches. These volumes include reading lists, and they help researchers trying to get an assessment of fact and critical opinion on various subjects. They make a good starting point for background reading.

In a three-volume set *William Shakespeare: His World, His Work, His Influence,* edited by John F. Andrews (Scribner's, 1985), sixty writers explore various topics in a series of essays. These range from Shakespeare's culture, education, music, theater companies, language, contemporaries, psychology, criticism, texts, and theater productions to contemporary issues in Shakespearean interpretation. Each article concludes with a select bibliography. Volume 3 includes a comprehensive index.

As much for beginning students as for researchers is a series of books primarily concerned with providing necessary information and offering assistance with reading Shakespeare. The oldest one is Raymond M. Alden, *A Shakespeare Handbook,* revised by O. J. Campbell (Libraries Press, 1970; originally, 1932). This contains essays on pertinent topics; more than half of the book concerns Shakespeare's sources, including a reprinting of some of the basic ones.

Roland M. Frye, in *Shakespeare: The Art of the Dramatist* (Houghton Mifflin, 1970), seeks to aid readers by providing facts and approaches. The book offers an extensive discussion of key problems in reading and understanding Shakespeare. Frye outlines, for example, salient features of Shakespearean comedy; he discusses the tragic hero and the meter and rhythm of the verse. He focuses on such problems as structure, style, and characterization in Shakespeare.

A most notable Shakespearean scholar, Hardin Craig, presents in *An Interpretation of Shakespeare* (Dryden Press, 1948) chapters on all the plays and poems, with information about them and interpretation. Not technically a reference book, Mark Van Doren's *Shakespeare* (Holt, 1939) is a very stimulating little book of criticism. Van Doren writes on the poems and on each play; he is especially sensitive to the poetry of the drama.

In *William Shakespeare: A Reader's Guide,* Alfred Harbage (Farrar, Straus, 1963) explores the components of a Shakespearean play: its words, lines, and script, suggesting how the reader can learn to deal with these vital elements. Harbage comments extensively on fourteen plays, frequently scene by scene, demonstrating how one reads and understands the play.

In a much briefer book, *How to Read Shakespeare* (McGraw-Hill, 1971), Maurice Charney deals with such matters as the presented play: text and subtext, dramatic conventions, poetry of the theater, and Shakespeare's characters. This is a lively, sensible guide to the art of reading Shakespeare, generously illustrated with many examples from the plays as practical demonstrations of the points being discussed.

David M. Zesmer's *Guide to Shakespeare* (Barnes & Noble, 1976) serves as a fine introduction. Zesmer surveys the major subjects, such as Shakespeare's life, theater, philosophical ideas, problems of the text, chronology, and the likely sources. In subsequent chapters he moves through the entire canon, beginning with the narrative and lyric poems and closing with the Romances. Generous footnotes provide the key to many other sources that one might consult. Zesmer offers a commentary and interpretation of each work, varying from fewer than two pages on *Err.* to fourteen pages on *Ham.*

EDITIONS

The importance of reliable editions of Shakespeare to the researcher cannot be overestimated; for one thing, students may be assured of having a satisfactory text, and furthermore, they may find valuable introductory materials and notes in many of the editions.

Both the Oxford and Cambridge University presses are in the process of publishing individual texts of each play, edited by various scholars. Oxford Press has also issued a single-volume *William Shakespeare: The Complete Works* (Oxford UP, 1986), edited by Stanley Wells and Gary Taylor. Two additional 1987 volumes accompany: an original-spelling edition of the plays, and a volume of textual apparatus, entitled *William Shakespeare: A Textual Companion*. The volume of modern spelling represents several years' work and a complete rethinking and reediting of the works. Because it offers very brief introductions and no commentary notes, undergraduate students may not find this edition as helpful as some others. It will in all likelihood prove controversial, for the editors have made some radical departures from the standard procedure in Shakespeare editions. They include, for example, both the quarto (1608) and Folio (1623) texts of *Lr.;* and they use the Folio text of *Ham.*, believing it to be the more theatrical version of the play. The text of *Per.* has been "reconstructed" by including lines from George Wilkins's prose version of the story. *H8* has been renamed *All Is True*. The editors have not been timid in their decisions; the scholarly community will decide whether they have been right.

In *The Riverside Shakespeare*, general editor G. Blakemore Evans (Houghton Mifflin, 1974) has reexamined the original editions and collated all major editions since the Nicholas Rowe edition of 1709. In addition, Harry Levin contributes a general introduction that includes consideration of Shakespeare's heritage, biography, linguistic medium, style, theatrical setting, and artistic development. Evans writes an essay on Shakespeare's text and includes a quite useful glossary of bibliographical terms. Herschel Baker prepared the introduction and notes for the histories; Frank Kermode, the tragedies; Hallett Smith, Romances and poems; Anne Barton, introductions for the comedies. The volume includes extensive appendixes, such as the comprehensive essay by Charles Shattuck on stage history from 1660 to the present, and a selected bibliography.

David Bevington has completely revised Hardin Craig's edition of *The Complete Works of Shakespeare* (Scott, Foresman, 1980; Craig original ed., 1951). This new edition involves a complete reediting and resetting of the earlier edition and includes a new set of interpretive notes. Bevington writes on life in Shakespeare's England, drama before Shakespeare, London theaters and dramatic companies, the order of the plays, Shakespearean criticism, editors and editions, Shakespeare's English. He has placed in appendixes materials on the canon, dates, sources, and stage history. Students will find helpful the twenty-six-page bibliography, arranged topically. Bevington writes an interpretive essay before each play and more general ones for the various stages in Shakespeare's development. Both this and the *Riverside* edition are handsomely produced books.

In 1972 the previously issued single volumes of the Signet edition were brought together in a one-volume hardback edition, *The Complete Signet Classic Shakespeare*, general editor Sylvan Barnet (Harcourt Brace Jovanovich, 1972). There are multiple editors for the plays, which are arranged chronologically (including *TNK*, a play increasingly assigned to Shakespeare). Barnet contributes a long introductory essay covering such topics as Shakespeare's life, canon, theaters and actors, dramatic background, style and

structure, Shakespeare's English, intellectual background, comedies, history plays, tragedies, nondramatic works and texts. He
also discusses the development of the dramatist and assesses individual plays. Interpretative essays by the various editors precede
the texts and include information on the sources and a note on
the text, with some textual variants recorded. The edition includes a fourteen-page bibliography, "Suggested References," on
topics and on individual plays and poems.

Another edition that has been widely adopted for classroom
use is the Complete Pelican text, issued as a single-volume edition
in 1969: *William Shakespeare: The Complete Works,* general editor
Alfred Harbage (Penguin, 1969). This represents a revision of
the original paperback texts. The introductory matter has essays
by Ernest Strathmann on the intellectual and political background, Frank Wadsworth on Shakespeare's life, Bernard Beckerman on Shakespeare's theater, Harbage on Shakespeare's technique, and Cyrus Hoy on the original texts. The plays appear
according to genre categories, and each play has a brief critical
introduction by the individual editor.

One edition that has been much praised by textual scholars
is Peter Alexander, *The Complete Works* (Collins, 1951). Students
will not find here the kinds of apparatus that are available in
the editions mentioned above. Alexander follows the order of
the First Folio but also includes *Per.* and the poems. He writes
a brief introduction and includes a glossary at the end of the
book. Alexander was an excellent textual critic, and some scholars
view this edition as one of the most authoritative produced in
this century.

Another highly influential edition is George Lyman Kittredge,
The Complete Works of Shakespeare (Ginn, 1936). Kittredge reveals
his great knowledge of Elizabethan English in the glossary at
the back of this book. He arranges the plays in their Folio order
and includes *TNK,* which is one of the earliest editions to do
so. Several generations have grown up on the Kittredge text.
Recognizing its earned popularity, the publishers had it revised
in 1971 by Irving Ribner (Xerox, 1971), who radically altered
and simplified Kittredge's text and notes, thus producing a quite
different edition, which has been rather harshly reviewed by a
number of scholars. In this revision Ribner discusses Shakespeare
and the English Renaissance, Shakespeare's life, English drama

before Shakespeare, Elizabethan theaters and theater companies, publication of the plays, and Shakespearean criticism. He also includes a bibliography.

Noted both for its bold imagination and sometimes eccentricity, the *New Cambridge* edition of Shakespeare appeared in separate volumes, spanning a period of over forty years (Cambridge UP, 1921-66), edited by Arthur Quiller-Couch and John Dover Wilson, with Wilson doing most of the volumes. These texts have extensive introductions, involving interpretation, sources, stage history; the volumes also contain discussion of textual problems, commentary notes, and a glossary.

Two other series demand special attention. The *New Variorum* edition was begun in 1871 ("new" here as opposed to some of the earlier variorum editions) and is still incomplete. Some of the early volumes are being reedited. The whole project is now under the auspices of the Modern Language Association. These, too, are in single volumes and contain the most extensive discussion of the plays available. Their textual and commentary notes not only offer explanations but also trace historically the reaction to the particular problem—either text or meaning. The volumes conclude with an inclusive textual history, stage history, and history of criticism.

Somewhat less imposing but equally valuable are the editions that constitute the *Arden Shakespeare*. The original Arden editions were published between 1899 and 1924, with W. J. Craig as the first general editor. The "New" Arden editions, begun in 1951, are still in preparation. The general editors are now H. F. Brooks and Harold Jenkins. Because so many people have been involved in this project, the quality of individual volumes varies; but certainly taken altogether, they form a most impressive edition. Students will find in them a treasure house of information about textual matters, source studies, brief stage histories, interpretations, and usually valuable commentary notes.

Though not an edition in the sense of the others cited in this section, the latest facsimile edition of Shakespeare's First Folio, prepared by Charlton Hinman, certainly deserves attention: *The First Folio of Shakespeare: The Norton Facsimile* (Norton, 1968). This is the most reliable of the facsimile editions that have been published. Hinman drew from the vast collection of Folios housed at the Folger Shakespeare Library, in Washington, D.C.;

and by carefully picking the pages to be photographed, he has produced an "ideal" Folio—that is, examples of the best pages. Hinman's facsimile is thus unlike any one single copy of the Folio. In his introduction he writes about the Folio and its contents, the printing and proofreading of the book, and the facsimile itself. In every way this is an exceptional book. As the original Folio not only made literary but printing history as well, this facsimile earns its place in the history of facsimile printing. Hinman establishes in it a through-line numbering system for the texts, a system that may eventually replace the more traditional act/scene designations. The skill and care evident throughout this book bring great credit to the editor and to the publisher.

STUDIES IN THE GENRES

In the discussion that follows, books that cover more than one play are analyzed and summarized. For essays or books exclusively on individual works, students should consult the standard bibliographies, especially those prepared by Ronald Berman and Stanley Wells, which offer commentary on critical studies. Not to be overlooked are the editions of the plays, both the complete texts and particularly single editions of individual plays, such as the valuable Arden and New Cambridge editions mentioned earlier in this chapter.

The commentary here begins with the earliest most significant study on the comedies, Romances, histories, and tragedies, in order to demonstrate the initial foundation of the critical approaches. Other books are grouped as they complement or react against the first one, as they treat certain categories of the plays (such as early and late), and as they deal with topics or techniques common to that particular genre. What is revealed is a wide diversity of critical approaches, including historical, character, thematic, language-imagery, psychological, and mythic criticism. All of which illustrates not only the dramatist's but also the critics' infinite variety.

COMEDIES

Neither this section nor any of the others makes an attempt at a history of criticism of the comedies; nevertheless, as one reviews the books below, some ideas will emerge about how critics have treated Shakespeare's comedies. The past three decades have produced an increasing number of studies of the comedies, as will be seen. Some critics dwell on the theory of comedy and Shakespearean comedy in particular. Others are more concerned with the dramatic techniques involved in making comedy work. Shakespeare's development as a comic dramatist interests a number of critics. Of vital concern also are the basic comic themes, as well as comic structure. After examining the first major book on the comedies, the discussion proceeds to those studies that pursue other techniques in the comedies. Books that touch on all the periods of the comedies are considered next; then the focus narrows to a chronological pattern, moving from critical studies of early romantic comedies to the "problem," or middle, comedies. Finally, the section closes with books that focus on specific approaches, such as psychoanalytic, Marxist, and phenomenological.

A convenient review of criticism, though now in need of updating, is John Russell Brown, "The Interpretation of Shakespeare's Comedies," *Shakespeare Survey* 8 (1955): 1-13. Anthologies of criticism include the one edited by Laurence Lerner, *Shakespeare's Comedies: An Anthology of Modern Criticism* (Penguin, 1967), which contains essays on ten comedies through *TN* and five essays on the nature of comedy. An anthology prepared by Kenneth Muir, *Shakespeare: The Comedies* (Prentice-Hall, 1965), covers the whole range of Shakespearean comedy. A selected bibliography is included. Herbert Weil, in *Discussions of Shakespeare's Romantic Comedy* (Heath, 1966), focuses on the early comedies through *TN*, including excerpts from eighteenth- and nineteenth-century critics. One of the latest collections is David Palmer and Malcolm Bradbury, *Shakespearian Comedy*, Stratford-upon-Avon Studies 14 (Arnold, 1972), which has nine original essays on the comedies and bibliographical notes.

The first full-scale modern critical effort devoted to the comedies is H. B. Charlton, *Shakespearian Comedy* (Methuen, 1938), the purpose of which is to trace Shakespeare's growth as a comic dramatist. The essays that make up this book were originally eight lectures presented at the John Rylands Library over the course of eight years. Charlton sometimes seems victimized by his effort to trace a kind of evolutionary process, especially when he juggles chronology to place *TN, Ado,* and *AYL* after the "problem" comedies in order to find in this group the final "consummation" of Shakespeare's art.

Charlton sees the following qualities in the comedies: realistic temper, love, concern for the present; the objective is to attain mastery of circumstances. Chapter 1 emphasizes romanticism, specifically *TGV.* Elizabethan romantic comedy was an attempt to adapt the world of romance to the service of comedy. Charlton sees in *Err., Shr.,* and *LLL* a "recoil" from romanticism; and he later designates *Shr.* as a signpost along the road to the most mature achievements. *MND* is Shakespeare's first masterpiece, revealing his promise as the world's finest comic dramatist. Charlton finds *MV* somewhat troublesome, especially the ambiguity of Shylock, which makes the dramatist's intentions not very clear. He devotes one lecture to Falstaff but takes an unusually serious attitude toward him, finding Falstaff's denial of the value of honor, faith, love, and truth a kind of comic failure. On the other hand, he argues against the supposed cynicism, bitterness, and darkness of *Tro., AWW,* and *MM;* he views them as Shakespeare's effort to recover the spirit of comedy after the misleading comedy of Falstaff. All of which ultimately leads to Shakespeare's artistic consummation in *AYL, TN,* and *Ado*—his greatest triumphs in comedy.

An essay that has had a profound effect on the criticism of the comedies is Northrop Frye, "The Argument of Comedy," in *English Institute Essays 1948* (Columbia UP, 1949), pp. 58-73. This essay has been much anthologized and is enlarged and revised in Frye's *Anatomy of Criticism* (Princeton UP, 1957), pp. 163-86. A theoretical essay about the nature of comedy, it is a prime example of the mythic approach to criticism. According to Frye, the action of comedy begins in a world represented as a normal world, moves into the green world, goes into a metamorphosis there in which the comic resolution is achieved, and returns to the normal world. In ritualistic terms this process represents the victory of summer over winter. The essential comic resolution is an individual release that is also a social reconciliation. The ritual pattern behind the catharsis of comedy is the resurrection that follows death, the epiphany or manifestation of the risen hero. The fundamental pattern of our existence, according to Frye, is comic, while tragedy is really implicit or un-completed comedy.

Frye greatly expands this whole thesis in his book on the come-dies, *A Natural Perspective: The Development of Shakespearean Comedy and Romance* (Columbia UP, 1965). Believing that Shakespeare was primarily interested in dramatic structure, Frye also empha-sizes this approach, as opposed to moral ideas, images, vision, and theme. Anything that has the comic structure is a comedy, whether especially "happy" or not—this point leads Frye into several curious conclusions—for example, declaring *Tim.* a com-edy instead of a tragedy. As he had suggested in the essay, Frye argues that the mythical or primitive basis of comedy is a move-ment toward the rebirth and renewal of the powers of nature in which the predominating mood is festive. The movement of comedy is not only cyclical but also dialectical, as it lifts us to a higher world of the spirit. The emphasis is on reconciliation, the birth of a new society, frequently displayed in a marriage. In such a process the "anticomic" elements, like Shylock and Malvolio, have to be removed so that the resolution may occur.

A book that in some ways complements Frye's position is C. L. Barber, *Shakespeare's Festive Comedy* (Princeton UP, 1959). In this study of dramatic form and its relationship to social custom, Barber explores the ways that Elizabethan social and holiday cus-toms contributed to the form of festive comedy. The study fo-cuses on *LLL, MND, MV, H4, AYL,* and *TN.* These plays are distinguished by the use of forms of experience that can be termed saturnalian, hence "festive." The basic pattern of the com-edies is found in the formula, through release to clarification. The "clarification" achieved by the festive comedies is concomi-tant to the release they dramatize: a heightened awareness of the relation between man and "nature"—the nature celebrated on holiday.

In the first three chapters, Barber deals with Elizabethan tradi-tions of holiday, and two chapters give examples of holiday shows. The plays that Barber chooses are important, as they dem-onstrate the translation from social into artistic form. Shake-speare's comedies are not holiday shows but carefully structured drama. For example, *LLL* is not a show because Berowne can stand outside the sport and ruefully lament that it is only sport.

In *MND* the magical May game expresses the will in nature that is consummated in marriage; the play brings out the underlying magical meanings of ritual but keeps the comedy human. Barber notes how Shylock is outside the festive force; thus the play is more complicated, and the "threat" of Shylock is crucial in evaluating the play. But Shylock is comic insofar as he exhibits what should be human degraded into mechanism. Though in disguise, Rosalind in *AYL* is similar in function to Berowne. Barber emphasizes the liberty of Arden as the play itself articulates the feeling for the rhythms of life. Both misrule and liberty are explored in *TN*. For Barber, Shakespeare's comedy makes distinctions between false and true freedom and realizes anew the powers in human nature and society which make good the risks of courtesy and liberty.

In *Shakespeare and the Traditions of Comedy* (Cambridge UP, 1976), Leo Salingar explores the development of Shakespearean comedy, which brings into unison a diversity of traditions. From the medieval romance tradition, Shakespeare got the romantic elements; from the Roman playwrights, his sense of comic irony; and from the Renaissance, his feeling for comedy as festivity. Medieval romance provided Shakespeare with a point of departure, offering him two elements that would occupy center stage in his comedies—namely, prolonged trials by Fortune and the division and reintegration of a family. Classical comedy gave him a preoccupation with errors and mistaken identity. Finally, from the Renaissance writers, he got the double plot, which the Italians had elaborated upon, and from Italian *novelle* he borrowed stories about broken nuptials and crises involving the law.

Salingar divides Shakespearean comedy into three groups, depending on the types of source material that interested Shakespeare when he was writing the works: (1) The woodland plays, namely *TGV, AYL, MND,* and *LLL,* whose actions take place in a park or woodland, the leading idea for which came from Thomas Lodge's *Rosalynde* or from other works such as Montemayor's *Diana,* Sidney's *Arcadia,* or from earlier romances; (2) Plays of classical origin (*Err., Shr., Wiv.*), derived from classical or Italian learned comedies, which use the Renaissance double plot and the the classical notion of comedy as a matter of "errors" due to trickery, disguise, or Fortune; and (3) Problem plays, or *Novella* Plays (*MV, Ado, AWW, MM*), written between 1596 and 1604, which derive directly from Italian *novelle*. Though they rely on trickery and disguise, more serious elements appear: recourse to the law and prominent trial scenes, broken nuptials, interrupted completion of marriage, and plots revolving around the authority of a prince. Salingar traces Shakespeare's interest in what he calls the "complex of the judge and the nun" from *Err.* to *MM*—one of Shakespeare's central preoccupations—namely, the conflict in his mind over the claims of love and the claims of law in Elizabethan society.

Alexander Leggatt's *Shakespeare's Comedy of Love* (Methuen, 1973) considers each play as an experiment in the treatment of love and the dynamics of art, convention, and human nature. Each play has a dominant comic strategy, for example, dislocation in *Err.* and *TGV*. *Err.* interweaves the fantastic and the commonplace. *TGV* places love against a background, which ranges from hostile to indifferent; though mocked and displaced, love still remains the center of the play. Such dislocation creates comic tension. *Shr.* relies on traditional comic conventions; but at the same time some characters are able to manipulate convention and therefore transcend it, such as Katherina, who acquires a new identity as she crosses the border between one type of experience to another. *LLL*, though a formal play, constantly questions conventions. Its ultimate effect subsumes a delight in the changes and surprises of life. *MND*, a play that shows characters trapped in different kinds of perception and understanding, relies on dislocation, which becomes a double instrument of celebration and mockery. *MV* also explores the interplay of convention and human reality, combining complex characters and formalized action. Unlike *AYL*, which relies heavily on conventional comic intrigue, *TN* depends on plot complications and shows characters locked in their limited understanding. This play presents a fragmented world of confined spaces, self-enclosed perceptions, and barriers, which at least some of the characters must transcend. In his last chapter, Leggatt turns briefly to the dark comedies and the Romances, showing, for example, that the final plays return to the emphasis on convention and patterns of artifice.

Antic Fables: Patterns of Evasion in Shakespeare's Comedies (St. Martin's, 1980), by A. P. Riemer, discusses the uniqueness and individuality of Shakespeare's comedies from *Err.* to *Tmp.* Throughout his career, Shakespeare incorporates, changes, or challenges the usual conventions of the comic form; therefore, each play represents an attempt to write a particular type of play in an unexpected manner, and in such a way that its novelty would engender delight. Fascinated with "playfulness" and "playing," Shakespeare in *Err.*, for example, uses the conventions of farce, transforming the usual ingredients of the genre. In fact, all comedies employ a similar witty transformation of the conventions of comic drama. *LLL* is a comedy without a normal ending; *Shr.* plays with levels of theatrical illusion through its use of the play-within-a-play device; *MND* mingles an amazing variety of comic motifs and characters.

The comedies of the middle period seem to violate radically conventional comic modes: *MM,* which is a comedy because it has a happy ending, displaces comic conventions radically and can be considered an experiment in comic form. *AWW* may be considered Shakespeare's most abstract comedy, in which the usual conventions of love-comedy are turned upside down. The play contains a broad pattern of reversals. Such violations and reversals of conventions inevitably lead to excess. In *AYL,* we have the gratuitous arrival of the youngest of the de Boys brothers and the indecorous appearance of Hymen. According to Riemer, however, *WT* best exemplifies Shakespeare's skills. Finally, Riemer looks at the plays as emblems of art, how the plays turn to themselves. Shakespeare shows a preoccupation with the illusory power of art. This book, which is not thesis-bound, contains chapters that are more or less autonomous; and students will find chapters 2 and 3 to be most helpful.

In *Shakespeare's Comedies of Play* (Columbia UP, 1981), J. Dennis Huston argues that the defining quality of *Err., LLL, Shr., MND,* and *Ado* is their playfulness. Shakespeare's abiding concern is not only with the idea of the play but also with the idea of play itself. These works show Shakespeare playing with the contingencies of plot, staging an almost endless series of plays within plays, manipulating conventions and expectations in order to play with the audiences' responses, engaging his characters in games of elaborate wordplay, offering events and characters out of the play worlds of fairy tale and make-believe, playing with the difficulties and challenges of playwriting by drawing attention to them.

Err. plays almost exclusively with the dramatic possibilities of plot; *LLL* concentrates on language and the uses to which man puts it as he constructs schemes and pageants to suit reality to his desires; *Shr.* and *MND* show a celebration of the possibilities of the theatrical medium itself. *Ado* resembles the early plays, especially *Shr.*, hence its inclusion in this study, suggesting that Shakespeare may have had the outlines of *Shr.* in mind while writing *Ado.*

Huston traces a change in Shakespeare's career. The early plays celebrate an absolute self-assurance and joy in play making, but this exuberant optimism is qualified in *Ado;* for in this work the powers of the artist figure are noticeably diminished. These powers, Shakespeare suggests, may be turned as much to deception as to vision, as much to destruction as to creation. In *Ado* all reality does not submit to the playwright's almost magical energies and powers. This view of the possibilities of art and the intractability of reality shows a mature dramatist.

In *Comic Transformations in Shakespeare* (Methuen, 1980), Ruth Nevo examines ten early comedies in order to explore a theory of the dynamic of comic form and to demonstrate Shakespeare's development from early to mature. She sees the plays as experiments showing a gradual conquest of the medium. She argues that Shakespeare developed his own comic form out of the Donatan formula of comic plots and the battle of the sexes. But he modifies the Donatan formula in that the protagonists do not know what they want; they discover as they go along. As a result, formal development becomes a continual, unfolding process of disclosure for the protagonist and audience. The eventual recognition is retrospective as well as immediate for the protagonists and integrative for the audience.

The protagonists of Shakespeare's comedies become increasingly more self-perceptive, more aware of having gained in wisdom and insight. The early comedies culminate with *MND*. Nevo considers *Ado, AYL,* and *TN* masterpieces, as Shakespeare's praise of Folly. These plays exhibit an Erastian transvaluation in a battle of the sexes in which neither contender is defeated. The three plays epitomize Shakespeare's achievement in the invention of a New Comedy. She says that Shakespeare's plays represent an increasing experiment with a restorative, cathartic effect. Thus Shakespeare saves us from the trap of bipolarity, of mutually exclusive alternatives.

The Metamorphoses of Shakespearean Comedy (Princeton UP, 1985), by William C. Carroll, argues that virtually every comedy and two romances investigate a mode of metamorphosis or transformation. To Carroll, metamorphosis is more than mundane forms of change, such as natural mutability and normal human maturation; instead, metamorphosis entails fearful liberation and implausible possibilities, expressing itself in terms of a duality—both destroyer and creator. It figures as a kind of death or dissolution of identity and at the same time leads to the enchantments of love. In Shakespearean comedy, love cannot remain unfulfilled—an endless and unsatisfied longing—because it would be a one-way metamorphosis, a suspension in otherness or self-alienation. Instead, love is harnessed into marriage, a paradoxical state in which two must become one but also remain two, in which the self is given and therefore lost but miraculously received back. *Shr.* contains the central question of a psychological transformation, the "taming" of a shrew into a wife. In fact, all of the comedies suggest how marriage becomes a type of metamorphosis. In *Err.* and *TN*, Shakespeare focuses on doubling, disguise, and mistaken identity, not only as devices of intrigue plots but also as new and subtle versions of transformation. In chapter 4, "Forget to Be a Woman," Carroll explores the metamorphoses of Shakespeare's heroines. *MND* contains almost every type of metamorphosis. This play shows that the monstrous is a stage, temporal and dramatic, that the characters must pass through. Finally, Carroll looks at the changes of romance in *WT* and *Tmp.*

In *Shakespeare's Comic Sequence* (Liverpool UP, 1979), Kenneth Muir argues that it is difficult to define Shakespearean comedy because each play is unique: "There is no such thing as Shakespearian Comedy; there are only Shakespearian comedies" (1). He insists that the differences among the plays are more important than the resemblances. His main point, however, is Shakespeare's indebtedness to Plautine comedy, though Shakespeare's comedies are more didactic than those of Plautus and Terence. The traditions of Moralities and Interludes also influenced Shakespeare.

Thomas McFarland groups the comedies around a common motif in *Shakespeare's Pastoral Comedy* (U of North Carolina P, 1972). He devotes considerable space to a theoretical and historical discussion of both the pastoral and comedy. Shakespeare used the pastoral to strengthen and deepen comedy itself. The compatibility of comedy and pastoral resides first of all in a common tendency toward artificiality; also, they both function as social microcosms. The forms share an emphasis on the affections of the sexes. Brought together, pastoral comedy achieves for Shakespeare what neither form alone could accomplish. McFarland discusses five plays: *LLL, MND, AYL, WT,* and *Tmp.* In these plays the reciprocity of social and religious concern is seen as the common denominator of the plays' significance. The ideal setting in *LLL* counteracts the formlessness of the play and helps mold it. Theseus in *MND* declares from the beginning the existence of a state of comic and pastoral grace, and the play as a whole is less formed and more evanescent than *LLL*. *AYL* represents a darkening of action and tone; the play labors to keep its comic balance. Jaques's presence threatens as well as criticizes the pastoral environment. Acts IV and V bring about pastoral redemption in *WT*. In *Tmp.* the two great realities of Shakespeare's comic vision—movement toward social concord and the recognition of disharmony and disruption—come together in a final confrontation. The play reaffirms the happiness of *MND* as it reasserts the enchantment of brotherhood and social harmony.

In *The Heart's Forest: A Study of Shakespeare's Pastoral Plays* (Yale UP, 1972), David P. Young studies four plays (*AYL, Lr., WT,* and *Tmp.*) in relation to the pastoral tradition, arguing for close thematic, structural, and stylistic similarities between these plays and the pastoral. Like pastoral works, these plays show a concern with the exile of some of the central characters into a natural setting, their sojourn in that setting, and their eventual return. The plays also show a dual concern with innocence and happiness and a preoccupation with dualities, alternatives, and contrasts: urban versus rural, court versus country, and so forth. Differences in the treatment of the pastoral in the four plays can be accounted for by the influence of other genres and different stages of Shakespeare's career, as well as variations in the pastoral design introduced by Shakespeare's experimentation. According to Young, these plays are indeed versions of pastoral in a sense more literal than that used by William Empson.

In a topical approach Robert G. Hunter, in *Shakespeare and the Comedy of Forgiveness* (Columbia UP, 1965), deals essentially with six plays: *Ado, AWW, MM, WT, Cym.,* and *Tmp.* Hunter sees these comedies as constituting a special genre. They resemble their medieval prototypes, which help define the nature of Shakespeare's version. Hunter devotes one chapter to the medieval heritage and another to the pre-Shakespearean dramatic examples. He purports to show how the doctrine of forgiveness inspired the development of a literary form and to demonstrate the importance of a sympathetic understanding of that doctrine for the success of these works of art. *Ado* was the first comedy of forgiveness, and from *AWW* onward Shakespeare's work in comedy was entirely within the tradition. The fabric of society is threatened by strife in *Ado,* but love and order are finally restored after a revelation of truth and a consequent repentance and forgiveness. In *AWW* Shakespeare has deliberately changed his source into a comedy of forgiveness. The total effect of *Cym.* depends absolutely on a sympathetic understanding of Posthumus's contrition and an emotional involvement in his forgiveness (Hunter sees this play as the most overtly Christian of the romantic comedies of forgiveness). The resurrection of Hermione episode in *WT* is Shakespeare's most inspired moment of reconciliation and forgiveness. The charity that makes possible the happy ending of *MM* has as its source the knowledge and acceptance of our common humanity. *Tmp.* deals with the theme of forgiveness and the theme of romantic love in two separate actions. Hunter argues that Alonso is the principal one forgiven. Hunter rather successfully avoids some of the pitfalls that often beset critics who take an overtly "Christian" approach to Shakespeare; he is able to discuss the principal theme without altogether insisting that it be seen only in Christian terms.

In *Shakespeare's Comedies* (Clarendon, 1960) Bertrand Evans is concerned principally with dramatic technique. He deals with all the comedies, which he approaches through one of Shakespeare's dramaturgical characteristics: namely, his use of awareness and control. Evans's term for Shakespeare's technique is "discrepant awareness," which may involve disguise and, of course, irony. Disguise is only one of several means at the dramatist's disposal for creating a structure of discrepant awareness. Irony is one of the results and effects of this exploitation of different levels of awareness among the characters in the action. Shakespeare's regular practice after *Err.* is to expose to us at the outset the existence of the potential solvent. In *MND* for the first time, Shakespeare uses an outside force that interferes and controls the affairs of men. The climactic peak in the mature comedies regularly rises in the final scene of Act III or the opening scene of Act IV, or both. Also at this moment the exploitation of discrepant awareness is at its peak. *TN* represents the summit of Shakespeare's dramatic technique, for Viola's masquerade is sustained through the whole play. Evans notes that Helena in *AWW* is pivotal in Shakespeare's development, for after her, heroines do not control the world of their plays; instead, this role passes to men, benevolent, omniscient, omnipotent ones (like Prospero).

Several other books range over all the comedies, though taking a different approach from Evans's. One is Larry S. Champion's *The Evolution of Shakespeare's Comedy: A Study in Dramatic Perspective* (Harvard UP, 1970). The book includes forty-five pages of footnotes, which evaluate critics and usefully point the way to other books and essays. Champion groups the plays around four categories: comedies of action, comedies of identity, problem comedies, and comedies of transformation. In tracing the dramatist's evolution, he focuses on *Err., TGV, MND, Ado, TN, AWW, MM, WT,* and *Tmp.* The earliest comedies are essentially situation comedies in which the humor arises from action rather than from character. In the second group the plots emphasize problems of identity rather than physical action. The problem comedies present comically controlled delineation of character on the level of transformation; a central character falls to sin but is eventually pardoned after experiencing a comic catharsis on a moral level. The character development in the final comedies, which include sin and sacrificial forgiveness, involves a transformation of values. One of the concepts that Champion stresses is the idea of a character who serves as a "comic pointer," who provides the perspective for the audience.

S. C. Sen Gupta, in *Shakespearian Comedy* (Oxford UP, 1972; originally 1950), also surveys all the periods of Shakespeare's comic development. He devotes the first two chapters to discussing theories of comedy and the development of English comedy from its beginnings in medieval drama. Sen Gupta argues that for control of plot English comedy had to await the classical influence of Plautus and Terence. The principal characteristics of Elizabethan comedy are its richness and variety. And Shakespearean comedy excels in its multiplicity: its characterization, its unity and diversity, its logic and inconsistency. For Sen Gupta, Shakespearean comedy is the art of exploration, usually of a personal sort; and Falstaff is the dramatist's greatest comic character.

John Russell Brown, in *Shakespeare and His Comedies*, 2d ed. (Methuen, 1962; 1st ed., 1957), argues against the importance of characterization. In his survey of the whole range of comedy, Brown emphasizes the implicit judgments made in the plays; such judgments, Brown believes, reflect the dramatist's attitudes toward life. Brown draws on many of Shakespeare's other works in order to provide a basis for the judgments about the comedies. He suggests in a chapter on structure that the comedies often resemble the structure of the history plays. The ideal of love's wealth is the principal judgment of *MV,* while *MND* and *Ado* both explore the truth of love: the lovers establish their own truth, which seems to them most reasonable. *AYL* culminates in the fullest celebration of the ideal of love's order. These three judgments are repeated in *TN,* as it also repeats characters, situations, and devices from the earlier comedies. *AWW, MM,* and *Tro.* involve the ordeal of love and imperfect responses to love. The final romances share, albeit differently, most of the implicit judgments of the earlier comedies. But *Tmp.* seems an exception to the pattern, for the main action here turns on the conflict between Prospero's virtue and his desire for vengeance.

Examining the early comedies, critics try to determine the salient features of the plays from *Err.* through *TN* that often represent experimentation. In *Shakespeare's Early Comedies* (Chatto & Windus, 1965), E. M. W. Tillyard discusses *Err., Shr., TGV, LLL,* and *MV.* The first two chapters deal with the background and range of Shakespeare's comedy. Tillyard does not pursue a consistent theme or structure; instead, he deals with the plays as separate entities. He finds that what makes Shakespearean comedy different from other great comedy is the admixture of the status of mind proper to romance. In *Err.,* Shakespeare follows what was to prove his permanent instinct: Never forsake the norm of social life. *Shr.* is not quite consistent, not completely realized or worked out. In the approach to the theme of friendship in *TGV,* Shakespeare did not allow this theme to remain pure or uncorrected. The two main themes of adolescence and verbal excess in *LLL* are interrelated, and this comedy belongs to the central area of social comedy. Tillyard finds Shylock appropriate to the romantic comedy in which he appears.

A different approach to the early plays is Blaze O. Bonazza, *Shakespeare's Early Comedies: A Structural Analysis* (Mouton, 1966). The analysis centers on structure in *Err., LLL, TGV,* and *MND.* For Bonazza, structure means not simply plot mechanics but the whole fabric of the play, including incidents of plot and their design, characterization, and language. This book contains all sorts of information about dating, sources, textual matters, which seem at best tangential to the matter of dramatic structure. The whole analysis culminates in *MND* where Shakespeare solves the problems of comic structure. The earlier plays are in fact evaluated in light of the success of this drama, for in this play the earlier experimentation is successfully and dramatically realized. This book is not nearly as stimulating as some of the others.

Peter G. Phialas, in *Shakespeare's Romantic Comedies: The Development of Their Form and Meaning* (U of North Carolina P, 1966), sets out to define the distinctive qualities of the romantic comedies by analyzing the action. He includes numerous footnotes, many of them responding to other critics; in the text itself, Phialas takes special note of Charlton. Phialas believes that it is possible to trace a steady progress in Shakespeare's ability to develop comic character and adjust it to the expression of the central comic theme and in his ability to develop dramatic structure. The principal theme is to present the lovers' ideal against the fact of man's physical being; hence, the importance and centrality of love. Phialas includes *Err.* and *Shr.* because they prefigure some of the significant features of romantic comedy. *TGV* is the first "romantic comedy" because it explores the theme of forgiveness and reconciliation. *LLL* involves the committing of a comic error that in turn leads to reversal and recognition. Part of the superiority of *MND* is the device of the play within the play. In its achievement of a cohesive plot, *MV* surpasses the earlier plays. *Ado* carries further the attempt to elicit from its audience highly complex responses to its stage action. Important in *AYL* is the pastoral theme, which emphasizes and qualifies the theme of romance and romantic love; the play illustrates the successful form of romantic comedy. *TN* is distinguished by its reflectiveness, which at moments tends toward gravity; its chief theme is education in the ways of love of the disdainful, as well as of the romantic, lover.

R. Chris Hassel, Jr., in *Faith and Folly in Shakespeare's Romantic Comedies* (U of Georgia P, 1980), examines the Christian dimensions of Shakespearean romantic comedy and Shakespeare's indebtedness to Pauline and Erasmian teachings on faith and folly. According to him, the inevitably flawed characters progress through exposure and humiliation to a humble awareness and acknowledgment of their common folly. Hassel examines six comedies. *LLL* is the richest in doctrinal allusions, presenting the doctrinal controversy of love versus charity with the characters' eventual discovery of the wisdom of folly. *MND* explores the opposition between imagination and religious faith. *Ado, AYL,* and *TN* focus on the paradox of faith and folly. Finally, *MV* deals with the doctrinal controversy about the nature and efficacy of communion to which it alludes. In this play, Shakespeare deals with an ambiguity: namely, the characters' failure to achieve comic wisdom and to humbly acknowledge their imperfections. In the concluding chapter, Hassel explores the larger implications of Shakespeare's allusions to Christian doctrine.

Published in his eightieth year, John Dover Wilson's *Shakespeare's Happy Comedies* (Faber & Faber; Northwestern UP, 1962) attempts to define the nature of Shakespeare's comic genius; it also discusses the neglect of Shakespearean comedy. The "happy" ones include *Err., TGV, LLL, MV, AYL, TN, MND, Wiv.,* and *Ado.* Wilson defines Shakespeare's comedy as emotional, tender, fanciful, and human. The earliest comedies share the quality of serene happiness, liable to develop into merriment in the conclusion, yet threatening to become serious at times. The main ingredients of the happy comedies are a Continental or Mediterranean background (except *Wiv.*), clownage and foolery, quibbling by the gentry, merchants and mercantile life, and love and friendship among persons of high rank. Wilson views *LLL* as Shakespeare's most elaborate and sustained essay in satire and burlesque, with emphasis on the "feast of languages." He believes that *Wiv.* represents the nearest that Shakespeare came to writing a comedy after the fashion of Jonson. Shylock ought to be regarded as a tragic, not a comical, figure (but one wonders what happens to the "happiness" of the comedy). Wilson finds Malvolio the most interesting character in *TN* and Feste the subtlest of all fools. *Ado* is a grand game, and *AYL* has a vein of mockery present in the midst of its pastoral romance. From analyzing these particular comedies, Wilson concludes that Shakespeare delighted in experiment and would not be tied to a system—he sat loose to his own theories, if he had any.

John A. Hart's *Dramatic Structure in Shakespeare's Romantic Comedies* (Carnegie-Mellon UP, 1980) focuses on the dramatic structure of *MND, MV, AYL,* and *TN. TGV* and *LLL* are also briefly covered. Structure, to Hart, means a combination of locations (setting, limitations of characters, and exercise of authority or power). Shakespeare presents each world as self-contained and whole within its own terms; but he makes sure that we do not ever mistake it for all of experience, since he sets it against an alternative world, equally whole and equally limited. His technique enables him to present but not judge, not satirize, not moralize. Instead, he creates a variety of exactly described worlds, each partial and limited, each sharing some of the attitudes that the entire world of experience may exhibit.

In *Shakespeare's Comic Rites* (Cambridge UP, 1984), Edward Berry argues that Shakespeare's romantic comedies (*Err., Shr., TGV, LLL, MND, Ado, AYL,* and *TN*) incorporate rites of passage. These comedies focus on courtship and marriage, the separation of central characters from their familiar setting, the psychic turmoil as the main obstacle to their fulfillment in love, turmoil depicted through role playing and disguise, paradoxes of clowning, symbolic dislocations in place and time, and rites and customs of marriage. These elements, borrowed from rites of passage, provide endless variations and help explain the distinctive and peculiarly deep appeal of the romantic comedies. Chapter 1 focuses on the three phases of rites of passage: separation, transition, and incorporation; chapter 2, on "Separations"; chapters 3 and 4, on courtship as a transitional experience; chapters 5 and 6 also deal with transitional matters, discussing the role of clowns and fools and the temporal and spatial dimensions of the comic experience; chapter 7, on rites of incorporation that end the plays; and finally the Conclusion explores "social criticism" and the ways history can help us understand art.

Emphasizing form rather than character, Ralph Berry, in *Shakespeare's Comedies: Explorations in Form* (Princeton UP, 1972), covers ten plays from *Err.* to *TN*. He treats them as separate entities rather than evolving a common form or structure; instead, Berry emphasizes the organic form of each play. The object of each analysis is to detect the governing idea of the comedy and relate it to the action that expresses it. The central technique of the comedies concerns the relation of the overtly comic parts to the rest of the play, usually an extension of the social function of a jester: to criticize the behavior of social superiors. The grand theme of the comedies is illusion and its opposite, reality. Berry specifically argues against the "festive comedy" approach of C. L. Barber, believing it inadequate and incomplete. Berry pays special attention to the language of the plays—*LLL* and *MV*, for example. Though Berry is not concerned with tracing a particular development, he does see in *TN* a recapitulation and restatement of the themes that have been apparent since *Err.* He sees the comedies as a means of preparation for the tragedies—that is, the effect, if not the purpose, of them.

Several studies have dealt specifically with that group of comedies known, for better or worse, as "problem comedies"—usually *AWW, MM,* and *Tro.*. A survey of the criticism can be found in Michael Jamieson, "The Problem Plays, 1920-1970," *Shakespeare Survey* 25 (1972): 1-10. The first full-scale treatment of this group is William W. Lawrence, *Shakespeare's Problem Comedies* (Macmillan, 1931; revised, Penguin, 1969). Lawrence bases his designation on the suggestion first made by F. S. Boas in *Shakespeare and His Predecessors* (London, 1896).

The term "problem play" is useful for those plays that clearly do not fall into the category of tragedy and yet are too serious and analytic to fit the commonly accepted conception of comedy. The controlling spirit must be realism. The essential characteristic is a perplexing and distressing complication in human life presented in a spirit of high seriousness. The play probes the complicated interrelations of character and action in a situation admitting of different ethical interpretations. These plays represent a radical departure in Shakespeare's art.

Lawrence's treatment of the plays relies heavily on an analysis of the probable sources and traditions for these plays. In *AWW,* Helena is meant to be noble and heroic, and Bertram changes in a wholly conventional manner. This is basically the story of a noble woman passing through great afflictions into happiness.

The two movements of the play are the Healing of the King and the Fulfillment of the Tasks, which Lawrence finds traditional. The tone of *MM* is less depressing than tragic, and the play is best understood in light of earlier traditions and social usages. It is suffused with sympathy for the frailties of mankind. The basic issue in both plots of *Tro.* is failure. The last act is weak dramatically but strong psychologically. Lawrence also examines part of *Cym.* and briefly the other romances. He speculates on why Shakespeare wrote these plays at this particular time (a favorite critical activity). The most obvious explanation is increasing maturity, in part because of his larger vision and broader philosophic insight; perhaps also because of the loss of youthful illusions, and also the influence of prevailing literary and dramatic fashions. These are interesting speculations, some of which may be valid; but they cannot answer the artistic question of why Shakespeare did what he did when he did. Lawrence is strongest on his historical approach but weakest in actually analyzing the plays.

E. M. W. Tillyard includes *Ham.* in *Shakespeare's Problem Plays* (U of Toronto P, 1950). He suggests that *Ham.* and *Tro.* are problem plays because they deal with and display interesting problems; *AWW* and *MM* because they are problems. Tillyard admits that he uses the term "problem play" vaguely and equivocally. Some of the qualities that these plays share include concern with either religious dogma or abstract speculation or both; serious tone, revealing a strong awareness of evil; an acute interest in observing and recording the details of human nature. Tillyard finds *Ham.* not tragic in the fullest sense; it is partly deficient as a tragedy on the point of a regenerate Hamlet. The play is preoccupied with explication, with an abundance of things presented; this forces the play out of the realm of tragedy. Tillyard's discussion of *Tro.* has to do mainly with sources, though he does deny the classification of the play as a tragical satire. *AWW* has a defective poetical style, and *MM* has an inconsistent style. He observes in the book's Epilogue that the theme of mercy and forgiveness observable in *AWW* and *MM* points the way toward the final Romances. All considered, this book is not one of Tillyard's triumphs.

Ernest Schanzer's *The Problem Plays of Shakespeare* (Routledge & Kegan Paul, 1963) takes Tillyard and others to task. His problem plays include *JC, MM,* and *Ant.,* which should make the reader wary of any set group deemed to be problem plays. Schanzer finds Tillyard too vague; and while he agrees with Lawrence that the "problem" should be confined to the sphere of ethics, he believes that the plays Lawrence groups together do not fit this assumption. Schanzer contends that one should look for a satisfactory definition of the term and then see which, if any, plays fit. Ambiguity of responses from the audience is one of the characteristics that the author finds, an ambiguity produced by the presentation of a moral problem that leaves us uncertain of our moral bearings. Thus our responses to the protagonists and main actions are not so much mixed as uncertain and divided.

William B. Toole, in *Shakespeare's Problem Plays: Studies in Form and Meaning* (Mouton, 1966), is less concerned with uncertainty than with the certainty that these problem plays are religious plays, betraying a considerable indebtedness to medieval morality drama. He goes back to the Tillyard group of plays; and in his first two chapters, Toole sketches the background for his argument, namely, an investigation of *The Divine Comedy* and medieval drama, which form the basis for his "Christian" approach to these plays. *Ham.* he finds to be a Christian tragedy that explores the problem and consequences of original sin. In *AWW* and *MM,* Shakespeare makes explicit what is implicit in the morality play; they represent the medieval comic pattern in dramatic form. Their protagonists move from what is, in effect, metaphysical adversity to metaphysical prosperity. The world of *Tro.* is one of retribution, lacking the implication of redemption; thus it remains a tragedy, quite different from the other problem plays—one wonders, then, why he includes it. Toole reviews much of the criticism of these plays, which is very helpful even if one is not quite willing to travel the Christian road of criticism with him.

As the subtitle of Richard P. Wheeler's *Shakespeare's Development and the Problem Comedies: Turn and Counter-Turn* (U of California P, 1981) indicates, Wheeler focuses on mutually balancing movements in Shakespeare's plays: attraction and repulsion, union and separation, trust and autonomy, love and authority. He examines *AWW* and *MM* to demonstrate that their problematic resolution dramatizes larger patterns of Shakespeare's development as a dramatist. He argues that our reading of one play depends on an interpretive context constructed from the others.

In *AWW,* Bertram embodies in embryonic form the essential components of a romantic rebel who can only thrive by rejecting the society that has shaped him. Bertram must be reinstated, however, for he threatens precisely those social and domestic values celebrated in the festive comedies. Although Shakespeare sketches out the logic of romantic flight in Bertram, the young count is released, ultimately, in order to be retrieved. The psychological underpinnings of Bertram's rejection of Helena creates for Shakespeare an unprecedented conflict between Bertram's experience and the demands of comic form. Wheeler places *AWW* in the context of earlier comedies, the sonnets, and the Romances, to help us understand the implications of Shakespeare's dramatization of psychological conflict. In *MM,* conflict converges most sharply on a sexually naïve young man thrust into a new relation to authority. It dramatizes an unpurged tension between sexuality and the moral order. In the rest of the book, Wheeler explores trends in Shakespeare's development as a writer. The earlier writings, the second tetralogy of English history plays, the comedies from *LLL* and *MND* to *TN,* and the sonnets demonstrate Shakespeare's development through three distinct genres. Development within each group suggests separate movements converging toward the central position that tragedy comes to command in Shakespeare's drama.

Although Joseph Westlund's *Shakespeare's Reparative Comedies: A Psychoanalytic View of the Middle Plays* (U of Chicago P, 1984) purports to be a psychoanalytic reading of the plays, it can be better described as reader response, focusing as it does on the comedy's effect upon an audience. The role of reparation and the therapeutic effect of Shakespeare's plays interest Westlund. He defines reparation as the ability to recognize a destructive impulse, to feel guilt for real or imagined destructiveness, and to attempt to repair the damage. By seeing the characters through this reparative strategy, the audience can work out its own problems and bring about reparation. The success of these plays depends on the various strategies whereby potentially destructive feelings in us—the viewers—are anticipated, contained, and transcended.

MV explores the problems of excessive trust and mistrust; *Ado* doubly suggests that control is good but that it can be bad when it deprives characters of their autonomy. *Ado* suggests that one must isolate oneself so as to avoid being manipulated beyond endurance. *AYL* presents a world of wish fulfillment in which the reparative impulses integrate into a way of life, thus making us feel sane and wonderful. In *TN* the characters idealize, losing touch with reality and imagining perfection where it does not exist; but the play suggests that we must want to believe in the existence of a world where idealizations, however unrealistic, prove true. The reparative effect of *TN* comes from the fact that this play makes us see a distinction between an idealized and a good object. *AWW* and *MM* present a more skeptical view. The former fully reveals the dangers of inventing what one wants, of idealizing others beyond what seems a reasonable extension of actual traits. The latter deeply frustrates our desires for certainties and clearly ideal, or nonideal, figures. Shakespeare thus explores the eternal struggle between fusion, on the one hand, and isolation, on the other.

In *Shakespeare's Universe of Discourse: Language-Games in the Comedies* (Cambridge UP, 1984), Keir Elam explores the centrality of discourse—that is, "language in use," not only in Elizabethan culture but also in Shakespeare. His study rests on Ludwig Wittgenstein's conception of language not only as action but also in action. He adopts Wittgenstein's notion of language "game" to indicate any form of language use that is subject to its own rules and defined within a behavioral context. Elam explores several classes of linguistic activities in the plays, including theatrical, semantic, pragmatic, and figural games. These games occur within well-defined *frames*. Elam describes a game-frame dialectic, exploiting language as activity and as objects. Apparent in Shakespeare's use of language are various forms of reflexivity or meta-language—language commenting on itself. The plays studied are *Err., AYL, Shr., LLL, MM, MV, Wiv., MND, Ado, TN,* and *TGV.*

In *Shakespeare's Rhetoric of Comic Character: Dramatic Convention in Classical and Renaissance Comedy* (Methuen, 1985), Karen Newman examines rhetorical devices that Shakespeare uses in soliloquies and monologic fragments to create what she refers to as the "lifelikeness of Shakespearean character." Such soliloquies and monologic fragments contain a rhetoric of consciousness. This rhetoric shows the characters' divided minds through particular features which the audience perceives as signs of psychological complexity and realism. She examines the rhetorical features that represent an inner life to both reader and audience in *MM, AYL, TN,* and *Ado.*

Traditional readings of the comedies identify a primary world and a secondary or "green" world in which the conflicts of the primary world are resolved. In *A Marxist Study of Shakespeare's Comedies* (Macmillan, 1979), Elliot Krieger sees these two worlds as part of the same reality. The changes that take place in the secondary world seem to resolve the conflicts of the primary world, but in fact they do not. The protagonists develop "a second world strategy," which protects them from change and perpetuates their interests. The protagonists in *MV, MND, AYL, TN,* and *1H4* transform their environment into a manifestation of their subjective needs. This secondary world thus advances the interest of the ruling classes and is therefore antagonistic to the interest of other classes. The comedies examine the process through which a class creates and perpetuates its ideology.

W. Thomas MacCary, in *Friends and Lovers: The Phenomenology of Desire in Shakespearean Comedy* (Columbia UP, 1985), studies nine comedies and *WT* from a phenomenological standpoint. MacCary explores the complex relations between erotic orientation and identity, showing the dynamics of love relationships in the comedies as a series of assimilations and differentiations between self and other. In the plays examined, we see the action from the point of view of one character, a young man, who must learn to love. The characters start out by not knowing themselves or their appropriate objects of desire, and so they learn to love. Shakespeare takes his young heroes through four stages of object-desire: they love themselves (or seek themselves); then they love images of themselves in twins or friends; they love those same images in transvestized young women; and finally they learn to love young women in all their specific, unique, and complex virtues. In the early comedies (*Err., TGV, LLL, Shr.*), Shakespeare focuses on the danger to a young man of committing himself—his happiness, his whole identity—to a young woman in courtship and marriage. In the mature comedies (*MND, Ado, MV, AYL*), he shows how the lovers must fight against preconceived notions of female sexuality and yield, in some cases, the lead in love to the lady. Finally, *WT* brings all the concerns of the previous plays together.

Critics have grouped another series of comedies, the final Romances, *Per., Cym., WT,* and *Tmp.* Philip Edwards surveys the criticism of these plays in "Shakespeare's Romances: 1900-1957," *Shakespeare Survey* 11 (1958): 1-18. This was followed by a similiar survey by F. David Hoeniger in *Shakespeare Survey* 29 (1976): 1-10, covering the years since 1958. *Shakespeare's Romances Reconsidered* (U of Nebraska P, 1978), a collection of essays edited by Carol McGinnis Kay and Henry E. Jacobs, contains eleven essays on the plays, including one that surveys critical approaches that have been taken in the Romances, and a helpful bibliography of over 600 items on these plays.

Derek Traversi presents detailed analyses of the plays in *Shakespeare: The Last Phase* (Stanford UP, 1955). He suggests that at the heart of the plays lies the conception of an organic relationship between breakdown and reconciliation and that the plays, completely removed from realism, are properly definable in symbolic terms. *Per.* experiments in poetic symbolism, asserting nothing less than a concept of spiritual resurrection. *Cym.* presents the theme of loss and reconciliation, both in Cymbeline's sons and daughter. *WT* is a finished achievement that explores the divisions that time and passion create in love and friendship and the final healing of these divisions. For Traversi, *Tmp.* represents a further and logical development in the symbolic technique. In the final part the sublimation of the human state, foreshadowed in Miranda's romantic vision, is assumed as its crown into the full symbolic structure of the play.

In one of his first books, *Shakespeare's Last Plays* (Chatto & Windus, 1938), E. M. W. Tillyard also discusses these final plays, though he omits *Per.* because of uncertainty about the reliability of the text. He comments on the plays first under the heading "The Tragic Pattern." The old order collapses in the last plays as thoroughly as in the main group of tragedies, and this element of destruction sets them apart from the earlier comedies. But the total scheme is prosperity, destruction, and recreation; Tillyard illustrates how this works in each play. He admits in the

"Planes of Reality" chapter that to speak of different planes implies a state of mind akin to the religious and renders probable a certain amount of symbolism, but he does not suggest religious dogmatism. He finds the planes somewhat blurred in *Cym.*, but set in striking and successful contrast in *WT*, while in *Tmp.* they form a brilliant pattern of bold contrasts, subtle constrasts, and delicate transition.

G. Wilson Knight, in *The Crown of Life: Essays in Interpretation of Shakespeare's Final Plays* (Methuen, 1948; originally 1947), adds *H8* to the group, arguing that it is the culmination of the vision implicit in the Romances. This book includes Knight's much earlier essay "Myth and Miracle" (1929), which lays the groundwork for much of his criticism as it defines the belief that Shakespeare is moved by vision, not fancy, that he creates not merely entertainment, but myth in the Platonic sense. Thus, in the final plays the dramatist expresses a direct vision about the significance of life. Present in *Per* is the depth and realism of tragedy within the structure of romance; it might be called a Shakespearean morality play. Great nature, unpossessive, ever-new, creative, is the overruling deity in *WT;* against this Leontes has offended. Resurrection does not occur until Leontes completes his repentance and Perdita returns. Knight emphasizes in *Cym.* the Vision of Jupiter, which he finds in tune with the play's theological impressionism. But he lavishes greatest praise on *Tmp.*, which he calls the most perfect work of art and the most crystal act of mystic vision in our literature. He insists on the identification of Prospero with Shakespeare; through this play Shakespeare looks inward and traces the past progress of his own soul—on this point many critics would demur. The play itself, Knight suggests, is poor in metaphor because it *is* metaphor.

Less mystical but not less spiritual is Joan Hartwig's *Shakespeare's Tragicomic Vision* (Louisiana State UP, 1972). She attempts to see the final plays within the confines of the genre of tragicomedy, one of the most elusive forms to define. Part of her approach revolves around audience perception of the stage reality; somehow the audience is able to hold apparently opposite responses in equilibrium. The plays use illusion to illuminate the world of the actual, but the audience is aware of the difference. The final vision of the plays reunites the realm of human action and the realm of the divine. Hartwig emphasizes in *Per.* the dramatist's control of the audience and his techniques for doing this as he creates a conscious distance between staged illusion and the audience. Like the others, this play creates the achievement of "joy," shared with the audience. The discrepancy between man's true nature and his outward appearances dominates *Cym*. At the end of *WT*, Paulina fuses illusion and reality into joyful truth; she builds the imaginative excitement required of tragicomic recognition. The audience suspends its rational judgment so that for a special moment it may glimpse the wonder in the world of human actions. Prospero as magician and man incorporates the power and presence of divinity. All the major emphases of Shakespeare's tragicomic vision are announced and enacted in *Tmp.* with great self-consciousness. The play in effect begins at the denouement of the other Romances. Looking over the final plays, one may observe that the dramatist moves from direct supernatural manifestation to human embodiment (Prospero). Also, he changes the almost totally passive hero in Pericles to the thoroughly active Prospero, who participates in providential knowledge. Hartwig's approach is refreshing as she abandons the impulse to mythic vision in favor of how we the audience perceive and participate in these tragicomedies.

In his *Shakespeare: The Dark Comedies to the Last Plays: From Satire to Celebration* (UP of Virginia, 1971), R. A. Foakes argues that Shakespeare in his later plays learns how to liberate himself from a commitment to characters presented with psychological and linguistic consistency in order to achieve different kinds of effects, especially distancing the audience from the characters. Foakes focuses on the last plays as structures designed for performance. Thus the author moves from *AWW, MM,* and *Tro.* through satiric plays by other dramatists to arrive eventually at a discussion of Shakespeare's Romances. Documenting the satiric detachment in the problem comedies enables Foakes to sketch the achievement of the last plays. He also finds that the late tragedies, such as *Cor.,* form a natural link between dark comedies and the last plays. The masque in *Tmp.* may be taken to exemplify in the final plays Shakespeare's move away from character emphasis and a search for motives toward a visionary sense of wonder, as we also see clearly in the restoration of Hermione in *WT*.

In the opening chapter of *Shakespearean Romance* (Princeton UP, 1972), Howard Felperin seeks to answer this question: What are we to make of romance as a literary genre? He traces the three strands of romance that intersect Shakespeare: classical romance, medieval chivalric romance, and medieval religious drama. In subsequent chapters, Felperin establishes the pervasive presence of romance within Shakespeare's entire work, even within the major tragedies, arguing in part that the Romances would not have been possible without the preceding tragedies. *Cor.*, *Tim.*, and *Ant.* make a clear transition from tragedy to romance. With this well-established background, Felperin then turns to the final plays. He traces *Per.*'s indebtedness to early religious drama and shows how the focus of the play changes to Pericles as man, husband, and father. *Per.* also reveals Shakespeare reassessing the premises on which his art had always been based. *Cym.* and *H8* illustrate some of the problems that arise from the conflation of history and romance. Felperin finds the action of *Cym.* nevertheless highly unified on three levels: sexual or romance plot proper, the familial and dynastic level, and the level of international politics. In *Cym.* the values of romance ultimately determine the value of history; a similar observation can be made about *H8*. This latter play ends in the golden world of romance: the mythic realm of a Tudor golden age. In its combination of romantic design with mimetic fidelity to life as we know it, *WT* not only transcends *Per.* and *Cym.;* indeed, it represents a breakthrough in Shakespeare's romantic art. This play fulfills the conventions of romance while testing them rigorously against the touchstone of reality. *Tmp.* asks to be seen as glittering illusion or as essential reality, and its cast divides the possibilities of response among them. In some ways the play is also an ironic commentary on Renaissance travel literature. The art of power and the power of art become in Prospero's hands one and the same thing. Felperin argues that *Tmp.* finally resists all attempts to allegorize or idealize experience, thereby illustrating the limitations of the idealizing imagination. The world that emerges in the final scene is neither so brave nor so new as Prospero himself could have wished.

In a book strong on background material, *Shakespeare's Romances* (Huntington Library, 1972), Hallett Smith explores the romance tradition, the pastoral world, and the connections between comedy and romance and between tragedy and romance. Smith establishes that Shakespeare's Romances evolve in a natural way from the tragedies and also from the comedies. He develops fully the relationship between *WT* and Greene's *Pandosto*. Problems of reality and illusion inhere in both *MND* and *Tmp*. The final two chapters concern scenery and landscape, and language and style of the Romances. Smith uses landscape to signify that world which is described in visual terms but not shown on the stage, and he finds *Tmp.* to be the greatest achievement in landscape. In the Romances, Shakespeare's style achieves a new complexity and beauty, bringing about in the audience a heightened awareness of the improbable, the incredible, and the marvelous.

Douglas L. Peterson, in *Time, Tide, and Tempest: A Study of Shakespeare's Romances* (Huntington Library, 1973), explores the modes of dramatic illusion in the Romances, the problem of time, and the emblematic nature of these plays, which often involved the participation of the audience. Peterson suggests that generative and destructive love becomes the means by which the principal characters in the last plays influence the processes of growth and decay. Shakespeare depicts man's position within the natural order metaphorically in terms of time. Peterson sees *Per.* as a complex emblem, with Gower as a guide who controls audience perspective. Each of these plays discloses structures deriving from the dual aspects of time: duration and occasion. Shakespeare celebrates the power of a love grounded in trust. *Cym.* also shifts from representational to emblematic narrative. Peterson finds the turning point to be when Pisanio renews Imogen's faith and she decides to seek out Lucius; the action then moves steadily toward the restoration of trust and the reconstruction of the social order. *WT* emphasizes the dependence of seeing upon belief, the confirmation of nobility through action, and natural love and concord as the only basis of community. Generative powers of love begin the process of renewal in the play after Leontes has nearly destroyed himself and the kingdom. Peterson views *Tmp.* as the culmination of the issues that he has singled out in analyzing the other Romances. He argues that consideration of the past as memory and its influence upon the future leads to the deepest concerns of the play. In Prospero's use of time, he reveals his belief in a purpose and meaning in the flow of events; and his decision to forgive figures forth the dependency of the restoration pattern upon faith. Peterson also explores ways in which Prospero resembles Shakespeare.

Believing that the meanings of the Romances intricately connect with their form, Barbara A. Mowat, in *The Dramaturgy of Shakespeare's Romances* (U of Georgia P, 1976), examines *Cym.*, *WT*, and *Tmp.* for their dramatic tactics and strategy. Each chapter concentrates on a separate dramaturgical issue. Mowat first explores the way in which these plays exhibit a careful blending of tragic and comic effects, thereby offering a double perspective on life. Shakespeare's tactics include soliloquies and other presentational devices. In *Tmp.*, for example, the most important presentational devices are the spectacles. Through these various techniques, Shakespeare makes an audience's experience parallel that of the characters on stage. One primary strategy avoids the mid-play climax, common in most of Shakespeare's plays, and thereby upsets dramatic expectations. The persistent use of narrative devices in these plays in part accounts for their characteristic quality: witness Prospero's function as narrator in *Tmp.* Adding these tactics and strategies together, Mowat argues that the Romances are a kind of "open form" drama, a drama that goes against standard dramaturgical practices. Prospero, for instance, opens the closed form of his play. Like the characters, we also experience bewilderment and uncertainty in the face of the unstable, true/false world of Romance. Mowat convincingly argues that the meanings are contingent on the play's dramaturgy.

In an introductory chapter, Robert W. Uphaus, *Beyond Tragedy: Structure and Experience in Shakespeare's Romances* (UP of Kentucky, 1981) examines the qualities that define romance and the ways in which Shakespeare's Romances move beyond tragedy, projecting a sense of destiny in the guise of Providence. Analyzing *Mac.*, *Lr.*, and *Ant.*, Uphaus shows how these tragedies introduce elements that intimate the idea of romance. *Per.* remains a skeletal romance, one in which all the conventions of romance are displayed though rarely individualized. But *Cym.*, for Uphaus, with its prominent emphases on disjunction and mortality, becomes at once romance taken to its dramatic limits and a skeptical response to the optimism of *Per.* Indeed, *Cym.* parodies romance. *WT* takes romance conventions and invests them with extraordinary human significance, while being Shakespeare's most defiant romance. Paradoxically, Prospero's art in *Tmp.* performs the dissolution of art in such a way that the imaginative representation or fiction of romance becomes the actual experience or fact of romance. The characters and the audience participate in ways uncommon to the other Romances: *Tmp.* becomes its own hierophancy. *H8* constitutes a historical version of the literary experience of romance; thus for example, Act V presents a hierophantic spectacle of the triumph of a new Protestant order. All the plays, as Uphaus persuasively argues, take us beyond tragedy.

Frances A. Yates's approach to the last plays in her *Majesty and Magic in Shakespeare's Last Plays* (Shambhala, 1978; published in 1975 by Routledge & Kegan Paul under the title *Shakespeare's Last Plays: A New Approach*) can be characterized as historical-topical. She argues for an Elizabethan revival in the early years of King James's reign and that this harkening back pervades Shakespeare's final plays. Thus, the preoccupation with royal children in the Romances parallels what was occurring in the Jacobean court as James sought to arrange suitable marriages first for Prince Henry and then for Princess Elizabeth. Yates even identifies the royal children in *Cym.*, the two sons and a daughter, with the children of James. Thus these plays reflect actual events in the life of the Jacobean court, according to Yates, who also suggests that Shakespeare was a whole-hearted supporter of Henry and Elizabeth. She focuses on *Cym.*, *H8*, and *Tmp.*; in the last she finds a link between its practice of magic and German Rosicrucianism. This book should be read with caution and with a skeptical mind.

Gary Schmidgall's *Shakespeare and the Courtly Aesthetic* (U of California P, 1981) pulls together information and insights from several disciplines in order to sketch the Jacobean courtly aesthetic and to determine how Shakespeare's Romances fit. In a word, Schmidgall argues that the new Jacobean court established an artistic fashion to which Shakespeare responded, especially in *Tmp.*. In one chapter Schmidgall explores themes common to courtly art: praise and encouragement of a healthy *civitas* or *polis,* the golden age, the dynastic or imperial theme, and the ideal of the perfect ruler. He also examines the influence that the new Jacobean royalism in the arts had upon Shakespeare's late plays, noting, for example, the effect of the court masques on these plays. *Tmp.* exhibits the prominent themes and structures of courtly fiction, and it also manifests a strong political interest. Caliban has central political significance because he symbolizes the opposite of order. Two separate chapters treat Caliban and

Prospero extensively. If Caliban is the rebel capable of all ill, then Prospero is Shakespeare's vision of the ruler capable of all good. *Tmp.,* at once about the power and the vanity of art, itself contributes to the Jacobean courtly aesthetic. Schmidgall touches on all the late plays, but he emphasizes *Tmp.*.

In an investigation of the topicality and intertextuality of Shakespeare's last plays, David M. Bergeron, in *Shakespeare's Romances and the Royal Family* (UP of Kansas, 1985), argues that the family of King James I constituted a "text" that Shakespeare "read" and incorporated into his drama. The issue is not identification of members of the Stuart royal family with characters in the plays, such as Yates argued; rather, it is one of "re-presentation," how Shakespeare took the facts of the public and private lives of the royal family and represented them in the Romances. The royal family becomes part of the intertextual nature of these plays. Bergeron provides the historical and dramatic context for the last plays by examining in detail the Stuart royal family and the comic drama that immediately preceded Shakespeare's Romances. He notes the satiric nature of most of the comedy, a drama that demystifies the family and pays little attention to politics. By contrast, Shakespeare's final plays, including also *H8,* through their romance mode emphasize and celebrate royal families, which are themselves inevitably linked with politics. Indeed, these final plays intertwine politics and family as Shakespeare pursues questions of dynasty and succession. Bergeron analyzes the plays in terms of the twin issues of family and politics. From Pericles' quest in Antioch for a wife, so that he might propagate "an issue," to Henry VIII's presence at the baptism of his daughter Elizabeth, Shakespeare examines the politics of royal families, especially how the future will be secured by the royal children, such as Marina, Imogen, Florizel and Perdita, Miranda and Ferdinand, and Elizabeth. The royal children redeem their kingdoms by providing much-desired stability. Bergeron points out how the usually presumed sources for the final plays do not emphasize familial politics in the way that Shakespeare does, and he suggests that the text of the Stuart royal family may account for the difference. The plays then contain not merely exotic romances of remote places and times; rather, they become dramas that reflect the political world of their creation. *H8,* Bergeron argues, culminates the concern for politics and family in these plays, focusing, as it does, on an actual English royal family, one that links explicitly with the Stuart royal family.

HISTORIES

To this day, defining the history play as a genre remains rather imprecise. One area that has been explored extensively is the dramatist's use of possible sources: Which chronicle histories did he conceivably consult? How did he use them? How does the dramatic art correspond to the chronicle account, or whatever source might have been used? These plays, grounded in English history, have provoked much research into contemporary political theory and how the apparent assumptions of the plays do or do not reflect current political thought. Was Shakespeare in fact trying to teach his fellow Elizabethans some lessons about their own political world? How did the dramatist regard the function of Providence in the working out of history? Critics have certainly been divided on this issue. The plays seem to serve the cause of Tudor nationalism; but was this intentional or coincidental? Are the plays full of propaganda, or does a coherent political system emerge from them? Of interest to critics has also been Shakespeare's developing artistry as illustrated in the histories.

A review of criticism can be found in Harold Jenkins, "Shakespeare's History Plays, 1900-1951," *Shakespeare Survey* 6 (1953): 1-15. *Shakespeare: The Histories: A Collection of Critical Essays*, edited by Eugene M. Waith (Prentice-Hall, 1965), reprints eleven essays, Waith's introduction, and a brief selected bibliography. Irving Ribner's *The English History Play in the Age of Shakespeare*, 2d ed. (Barnes & Noble, 1965; 1st ed., 1957), outlines a dramatic context in which Shakespeare participated. In the opening chapter, Ribner discusses history and drama in Shakespeare's age; then he turns to the emergence of the genre, which Ribner sees as greatly indebted to medieval drama, specifically morality plays. There is a long consideration of the various history plays of the sixteenth century, including Shakespeare's. Appendix B provides a useful chronological list of extant English history plays, 1519-1653; appendix D has a select bibliography.

In Peter Saccio's reference book *Shakespeare's English Kings: History, Chronicle, and Drama* (Oxford UP, 1977), one finds excellent summaries of the history that forms the background of Shakespeare's ten plays on English history. Beginning with a sketch of fifteenth-century history, Saccio then moves through each play, recounting the history on which it rests. Such a summary helps us understand what Shakespeare did with the historical chronicle that he inherited.

All criticism of the histories emanates from E. M. W. Tillyard's pioneering work *Shakespeare's History Plays* (Chatto & Windus, 1944), whether one agrees or disagrees with it. Tillyard's has become the traditional interpretation of the history plays. He devotes a large part of the book to the background: cosmic, historical, literary nondramatic, and literary dramatic. Tillyard argues that Shakespeare was primarily influenced by the historical vision that he found in Hall's chronicle and that he expressed successfully a universally held scheme of history, one fundamentally religious, by which events evolve under a law of justice and under the ruling of God's Providence. The protagonist in the histories, especially the first tetralogy (*1H6, 2H6, 3H6,* and *R3*), is England, producing a structure that reflects the dramatist's indebtedness to medieval morality drama.

Tillyard emphasizes the idea of a "Tudor Myth" of history: namely, that the Tudors under Henry VII successfully ended the War of the Roses and brought a new unity and peace to the land. The theme of order is powerful, as is the continual insistence on cause and effect in the unfolding of history. The play *1H6* involves the testing of England, including the assumption of divine interference, whereas the problem of dissension at home develops in *2H6,* with the Duke of York as the emergent figure. In *3H6,* Shakespeare shows us chaos itself, as full-scale civil war breaks out. *R3* completes the national tetralogy and displays the working out of God's plan to restore England to prosperity, a view that does not take enough note of Richard's dramatic character. A political theme binds together these four plays: order and chaos, proper political degree and civil war, the belief that such had been God's way with England. *Jn.* offers the political problems of succession, the ethics of rebellion, and the kingly character. Tillyard finds *R2* the most formal and ceremonial of the histories; and he argues that Richard's crimes never amounted to tyranny, and hence the rebellion against him was treasonous. In *H4,* Hal, first tested in the military or chivalric virtues, becomes the mean between the extremes of Hotspur and Falstaff; in the second part he encounters the civil virtues and must choose between disorder or misrule and Order or Justice (the supreme kingly virtue). By *H5*, Shakespeare had finished the theme of England and thus could allow a concrete hero to dominate, though Tillyard finds many shortcomings in the play itself. Tillyard's criticism provides historical study in the political orthodoxy of the plays, demonstrating the dramatist's awareness and use of a providential view of history.

Lily B. Campbell's *Shakespeare's "Histories": Mirrors of Elizabethan Policy* (Huntington Library, 1947) complements Tillyard's study. It, too, sketches the orthodox political approach to the history plays but discusses only *Jn., R2, H4, H5,* and *R3*. Part 1 deals with historiography and politics—the different views on the meaning of history, the English historians. For Campbell the history play is a literary medium for history, concerned with politics as it mirrors patterns of behavior. In *Jn.,* Faulconbridge is not the hero; instead, he serves as a kind of vice from the moralities to prick others to action. *R2* reflects contemporary problems or concerns, namely, the deposition of a king: thus Shakespeare uses Richard to set forth the political ethics of the Tudors with regard to the rights and duties of a king. Henry IV, who was a rebel and usurper, in turn is punished for his sins by rebellion. Meanwhile Henry V is an ideal hero, and the play mirrors the English as triumphant in righteous cause, achieving victory through the blessing of God. *R3* combines the elements of both tragedy and history.

M. M. Reese, in *The Cease of Majesty: A Study of Shakespeare's History Plays* (Arnold, 1961), largely hews the Tillyard line. History demonstrates the logic and reason of God's control of human affairs; history also teaches through the examples of the past how to bear misfortune in the present. Reese discusses the Tudor historians—Polydore Vergil, More, Fabyan, Hall, and Holinshed—and literary works by Daniel and Drayton and *The Mirror for Magistrates*. According to Reese, the history play developed naturally from the folk dramas of the Middle Ages, the miracle and morality plays. Uniquely Shakespearean are the depth and range of his penetration and the undogmatic balance of his conclusions. Through the histories Shakespeare searches for the ideal public figure and finds in Henry V the man who most nearly fits. The parts of *H6* offer only an occasional glimpse of real people and human predicaments. While Richard gives *R3* boisterous energy, the play is not just about him. The dramatist argues in *R2* that rebellion is always wicked, but character and destiny cooperate in Bolingbroke's ruthless drive toward the crown. The real victim of Richard's tragedy is England (shades of Tillyard). *Jn.* is an unsatisfactory play because it lacks a focal point. The two parts of *H4* treat the education of the Prince, and the morality pattern inheres. In *H5*, Shakespeare celebrates England's recovered majesty in the mirror of the Christian king. Consistently the plays reflect on the plight and destiny of the country as well as occasionally presenting interesting dramatic characters.

S. C. Sen Gupta, in *Shakespeare's Historical Plays* (Oxford UP, 1964), reacts very much against the Tillyard school. Sen Gupta assumes that the greatness of Shakespeare consists chiefly in his ability to create men and women who have the vividness of living characters, a view of the histories that differs greatly from those who seek some pattern of morality throughout the plays. In his discussion of Tudor political philosophy, Sen Gupta doubts that the dramatist was primarily interested in propagating a particular political or moral idea. In fact, the notion that Shakespeare tried to express the Tudor view of history is somewhat naïve. The histories are neither moral homilies nor political treatises. They emphasize instead the personal, human aspect of events, the conflict and clash of Nature and Fortune in the lives of men and women. Sen Gupta sees in the first tetralogy an increasing tendency to simplify the network of history and to assign changes to the unpredictable element in human character. Though *3H6* remains largely a chronicle of events, rather than a historical play, *R3* is the first attempt to organize the various materials of history by placing the center of interest in a tragic character. Even so, the materials remain partly recalcitrant until the end. *R2* seems a human drama rather than a political document or a moral homily, indeed a personal tragedy. The theme of *H4* focuses, not on the education of Prince Hal, but on the fortunes of Falstaff; the plays are not morality plays centered on Hal's struggle between virtue and vice. In *H5*, Shakespeare presents a fusion of epic and drama, with the Chorus providing a perspective from which to view the events and personalities. Sen Gupta offers a healthy corrective by insisting that these histories are plays, not historical documents or pieces of propaganda.

Robert Ornstein, in *A Kingdom for a Stage: The Achievement of Shakespeare's History Plays* (Harvard UP, 1972), also emphasizes the aesthetic qualities of these plays. This work, in which the author discusses all of the histories, reacts somewhat to the earlier critical treatments, especially Tillyard and Campbell. Ornstein argues that for all practical purposes Shakespeare originated the historical dramatic genre, and that the histories must be judged by artistic standards and not by any effort to recreate the "Elizabethan world picture."

Ornstein doubts that Shakespeare wrote his tetralogies to set forth the Tudor myth of history, a myth that, if it existed, should more properly be called a Yorkist myth. Whatever source materials Shakespeare used, his interpretation of the past was his own. The tetralogies are themselves too separate and too different from one another to be regarded as the complementary halves of a single oddly constructed panorama of English history. Shakespeare journeys in the history plays toward artistic exploration and self-discovery, leading almost unerringly beyond politics and history to the universal themes and concerns of his most mature art. The dramatist demonstrates in the *H6* plays the possibilities of characterization and the range of dramatic and poetic techniques. In *3H6* as Henry approaches saintliness, he becomes less a dramatic character than a moral symbol, while Richard gains a new psychological complexity. For the first time in the histories, Shakespeare's plotting in *R3* has vertical as well as horizontal form because each step of Richard's rise and fall offers a fresh discovery of political and moral reality. As Ornstein suggests, Richard plays the moral teacher for quite a long time before he becomes the moral lesson of the play. More than simply a dramatic protagonist, Richard II is also the poetic voice of his era and the quintessential expression of its sensibility. The play presents a subtle revelation of the protagonist's nature. The author finds *1H4* remarkable for its unity of vision and of plot, which embraces and demands the interplay of comedy and history; but *2H4* is heavy with disillusion and debilitation of age. One wonders that Shakespeare succeeded as well as he did in celebrating English heroism in *H5* because he also makes damaging admissions about the methods and motives of the principal characters.

In *Shakespeare's History Plays: The Family and the State* (Ohio State UP, 1971), Robert B. Pierce also deals with all the histories except *H8*. The discussion proceeds chronologically in order to observe the developing skill of the histories in relating the family and the state. Pierce covers three basic areas: figures and analogies based on the family and relying on the habit of seeing correspondences; scenes of family life injected into the middle of historical events; and passages and whole plays in which the family is inextricably mixed with the political situation. The ideas of the plays and the craft come together, with some attempt at understanding the audience's likely response. In the *H6* plays the family functions almost entirely as a commentary on the causes and consequences of political disorder. The family in *R3* makes nemesis more than just a Senecan doom, gives it weight and ethical meaning as a force of Providence. *R2* embodies the most prominent family theme in the histories, focusing on the issue of inheritance. The play centers on fathers and sons, not only in its emphasis on orderly succession, but also in its study of moral inheritance. Shakespeare displays in the *H4* plays the quest for political order as fundamentally like the quest for personal order within the family—only the scale is different. The family theme has little consequence in *H5*, which does at least carry out the function of making the family an echo of political themes. Pierce sums up the argument of the book in an excellent conclusion.

Focusing on the second tetralogy, Derek Traversi, in *Shakespeare from "Richard II" to "Henry V"* (Stanford UP, 1957), sees the plays as centered on the life and career of Prince Hal; and the plays pose the question: What are the personal, as distinct from the political, qualities that go into the making of a king? As the personal implications of the royal vocation in Hal progressively unfold, they constantly relate to the state of an England that at once reflects and conditions the central presentation of royalty. *R2*, with its simple plot but elaborate style, has as its most original feature the effort to diversify artificial forms, to make the elaboration of contrasted styles respond to the tensions that constitute the true tragic theme. The drama emphasizes a conflict of personalities, with the tragic impotence of the king balanced by the purposeful advance of his rival. The play *1H4* represents a remarkable growth in significant complexity of structure. The development into full consciousness of the effective political Prince exists against the background of the English realm, threatened by anarchy. Falstaff's disintegrating, ultimately corrupting force cannot be overcome by his exuberance. The Lord Chief Justice balances Falstaff in *2H4*. The play includes the concepts of repentance and restitution, thus marking a changing spirit from the comic to the severely moral. The principal theme in *H5* is the establishment in England of an order based on consecrated authority and crowned successfully by action against France. Like most of Shakespeare's plays of this time, this play shares the concern with the mastery of passion and its relation to action. *H5* combines an acute analysis of motive in its hero with a conception of the royal office that has been carefully built up. Traversi argues that the play ends with a decided pessimism that somehow fails to attain the note of tragedy.

Michael Manheim follows a particular theme through some of the histories in *The Weak King Dilemma in the Shakespearean History Play* (Syracuse UP, 1973). He examines a group of plays that represent the ambivalence of subject toward monarch, be that monarch wanton or meek. For Manheim this reveals the universal contradiction about monarchy, which was beginning to run deep in the Elizabethans of the 1590s. This critical approach also involves consideration of the manipulation of audience sympathies toward the monarch. Manheim includes in the discussion an examination of several non-Shakespearean plays, such as *Edward II* and *Woodstock*. The central dilemma of the weak king is whether deposition is justified. Richard II first excites antagonism then sympathy, once he appears vulnerable. In the death scene the play approaches tragedy as Richard finally shows signs of new self-awareness. Bolingbroke, of course, embodies strength. The *H6* plays stretch to its limits the dilemma of whether an inadequate monarch ought to be deposed. Henry's weaknesses drag him down in the face of the inhumanity and strength of the nobles. In all these plays an imbedded Machiavellianism may be seen as an alternative to the weak king; the successful and strong king learns the practical lessons of a kind of Machiavellianism. *Jn.* is a transitional play, for it demonstrates a rapprochement with the new political methods as seen chiefly in the character of the Bastard. It thus stands between *H6* and *H5*, bridging the chasm between anti- and pro-Machiavellianism. The culmination comes in *H5*, which presents a strong king not plagued by the vacillation and weakness of other kings. Henry V makes desirable and attractive his brand of strength and Machiavellianism. One of the difficulties with Manheim's book is his sometimes careless attention to the texts of the plays as he fails to recall very precisely some of the details. He also neglects to correlate his thesis with Shakespeare's necessary dependence on some sort of source; in other words, the dramatist cannot make Henry VI strong because factual history dictates otherwise.

A more valuable book is James Winny, *The Player King: A Theme of Shakespeare's Histories* (Barnes & Noble, 1968; Chatto & Windus). Winny argues against Tillyard's view that the tetralogies form a coherent thematic unit embracing a moral argument. Instead, Winny believes the historical order of the six reigns irrelevant to Shakespeare's imaginative purpose, though the chronological order of the plays is important. Throughout the series (*R2* to *H5*) the king sits uneasily on the throne, under assault from rivals whose ambition he must contain if he is not to lose his crown; his task is one of personal domination. Winny focuses on the idea of the king, not as a political concept, but as an imaginative one, developed from play to play. In *R2* Richard's identity seems to exist in his name and title. The shock of political disaster forces him to acknowledge the emptiness of his grand identity and to fall back toward the basic, simple human character that he has ignored. The play centers on the confrontation of a majestic imposture (Richard) by the robust reality (Bolingbroke) it has attempted to avoid. Bolingbroke as Henry IV evades some realities himself, as he adopts a façade of moral responsibility. But while he maintains an outward majesty, Falstaff parodies this pose in his comic stateliness and aplomb. Hal debases the royal standard by submitting it to indignity and therefore continues the process initiated by the usurper, his father. But he ultimately restores dignity to both the king's office and person. Winny finds *H5* a seriously flawed play, and he dislikes the idea of Henry as the ideal Christian king. For some reason Shakespeare's historical matter seems intractable, the play being most alive at those moments of uncertainty and doubt in the king.

Though ranging through comedies and tragedies and ending with an analysis of *Tmp.*, Eileen Jorge Allman's *Player-King and Adversary: Two Faces of Play in Shakespeare* (Louisiana State UP, 1980) devotes one-third of its space to the history plays. She argues that in Shakespearean dramaturgy Henry V culminates the history plays' decade of search for a Player-King. Compared to the Player-King, who wills his being into the perpetual enactment of metaphor, Richard II is an Audience-King, enjoying the activity before him as if it were a spectacle he had no part in. Even Bolingbroke in *R2* recreates the paralyzing split between the word and the act. Allman sees the confrontation at Flint Castle as the turning point in the play, marking the end of hope and the opening awareness of futility. But this episode also points to the search for self and no longer for power. Allman explores the ways in which Henry IV and Falstaff resemble one another and how Prince Hal must ultimately be free of them both. Hotspur meanwhile cannot see that he stands alone. Hal, trained in play, becomes in *H5* a king who enacts metaphors and heals division, who creates his own realm in the way an artist creates an imaginary landscape. Henry V creates the garden and gives the players in it free will.

In *Shakespeare's Heroical Histories: "Henry VI" and Its Literary Tradition* (Harvard UP, 1971), David Riggs emphasizes the literary, dramatic, and rhetorical traditions available to Shakespeare, rather than the chroniclers, Hall and Holinshed. In the first chapter the author develops a set of assumptions about history and literature relevant to the actual business of making an Elizabethan history play; he considers issues of providence and historiography. Riggs questions the assumption that a humanistic approach to history came intuitively to the Elizabethan dramatists, while the providentialism of the chroniclers was more the exception than the rule. He further explores the rhetorical basis of popular history, giving special attention to Marlowe's *Tamburlaine*. Chapter 3 presents a survey of the "heroic example" from Marlowe to Richard III, distinguishing between parentage and deeds in the evolution of the Herculean hero. The trilogy of *H6* encompasses Shakespeare's presentation of "agents" who gave the reign its distinctive contours, as opposed to a consistent moral history or view of providence. Riggs pursues through all three plays Shakespeare's treatment of the gradual deterioration of heroic idealism; this trilogy is at once an embodiment and a criticism of the literary traditions described here. In a final chapter the author includes consideration of *R3* and *1H4*, reappraising the heroic tradition and its significance in English history; these two plays try to resolve the dilemmas. For example, *1H4* takes the erosion of traditional standards for granted and thereby redefines the intentions that lead a prince to elect the chivalric vocation. Riggs includes a helpful bibliography.

Examining the *H6-R3* tetralogy, Edward Berry, in *Patterns of Decay: Shakespeare's Early Histories* (UP of Virginia, 1975), argues for the dramatic integrity of the sequence. The conjunction of chivalric heroism and ceremonial mystique that unifies *1H6* represents an important tendency in Elizabethan thought. Stages of social disintegration appear in *2H6* in the concepts of justice and law, which erode until they collapse in the confusion of civil war. In *3H6*, Shakespeare depicts the gradual dissolution of a society at war with itself, a society in which the single bond of kinship becomes increasingly corrupted and is finally destroyed. Berry emphasizes the isolation of Richard III as his play explores the nature of this self alone as Richard moves from conquest to destruction. The aggressive egocentricity that gradually reduces the state to chaos ultimately destroys the self. In a final chapter Berry assesses the relationship between these early history plays and the later ones, which become much more concerned with the development of character.

Because almost every writer on the histories sooner or later says something about the role of Providence, it was both inevitable and desirable that someone should make a full study of this important issue in the plays. Henry A. Kelly's *Divine Providence in the England of Shakespeare's Histories* (Harvard UP, 1970) pursues the topic. Part 1 deals with the various "myths" of history as revealed in the contemporary accounts of fifteenth-century England. The sixteenth-century prose chroniclers Vergil, Hall, and Holinshed synthesized these views. Kelly argues for no absolute sense of the working out of divine punishment or judgment in the chroniclers, though Daniel's 1595 version of *The Civil Wars* has a strong sense of providential design. Though providential themes occur in *R2*, no final sense exists that God actively brings about any of the actions of the play. In *1H4* the themes are occasionally introduced for rhetorical effect, and in *2H4* Shakespeare does not make it clear that he believes either side in the conflict to have God's full approval or full condemnation. The actions of the *H6* plays do not come as some consequence of providence from the earlier reigns; the conflicts arise as a new situation with causes of their own. Nor does *R3* demonstrate that Henry VI and his family were being punished because of the "sins" of his grandfather, Henry IV. Kelly suggests that the providential aspect of the Tudor myth as described by Tillyard is an ex post facto Platonic form not substantiated by the drama or literature itself. Instead, Shakespeare dramatized the characters and thus eliminated all the purportedly objective providential judgments made by the histories on historical characters.

In his *The Lost Garden: A View of Shakespeare's English and Roman History Plays* (Macmillan, 1978), John Wilders sketches the philosophical background of Shakespeare's history plays, examining such topics as time and change; fortune and nature; prayer, prophecy, and providence; knowledge and judgment; dilemma and discovery. All of these concepts point to the image of the lost garden. The human condition that Wilders outlines while solving one problem never attains the ideal. Shakespeare portrays history as a series of attempts by individuals to satisfy their need for permanence, and the necessary failure to create it. Shakespeare sees in the histories the spectacle of human failure. At the heart of his conception of politics lies the paradox that a rule of law is necessary to protect men against their own inherent savagery; yet few men are willing to be governed. Wilders reinforces his thematic approach with generous evidence from the history plays.

Looking at the second tetralogy (*R2-H5*), James L. Calderwood, in *Metadrama in Shakespeare's Henriad* (U of California P, 1979), finds a self-contained metadrama in which the dramatist examines his art through his art. Calderwood sees Shakespeare as solving problems of language by means of politics, which become metaphors for art. Thus in the *Henriad* the main metadramatic plot centers on the "fall of speech." The sacramental language of a Richard II gives way eventually to a much more pragmatic language. The debasement of kingship also involves the secularizing of language in which the relation between words and things is arbitrary, unsure, and ephemeral. A wedge driven between words and their meanings leads in *R2* not merely to the fall of a king but also to the fall of kingly speech. Bolingbroke regards words as mere vocal conveniences. To raise such questions about the function of language forces the dramatist to look at his own artistry. Falstaff, Calderwood says, is a perfect embodiment, a final profane reincarnation of Shakespeare's impulse to create verbal worlds sufficient unto themselves. Hal, on the other hand, is an "interior" version of Shakespeare the controlling play-wright. In *2H4,* Shakespeare repeats the form but not the sub-stance of *1H4.* At Agincourt Henry V redeems English kingship in a self-conscious way. In *H5* the dramatist has moved to rhetor-ical speech in which words acquire pragmatic value as instruments of action. The Epilogue reminds us of what Henry V soon lost, as it may remind us that Shakespeare's own dramatic achieve-ments are fugitive: he must move on to other kinds of problems and attempted solutions.

Basing his analysis on J. L. Austin's work on speech acts, Joseph A. Porter in *The Drama of Speech Acts: Shakespeare's Lancastrian Tetralogy* (U of California P, 1979) explores several dimensions of language in the *R2-H5* tetralogy. Simply stated, Porter uses "speech act" to mean an act performed in speech. He argues that this tetralogy is, in part, about language and its function. Talk about name, naming, title, and the like constitutes the most prominent body of references to language in *R2;* therefore, to Richard, Gaunt, and Bolingbroke the idea of name is of great importance. For Richard, to lose the name of "king" is also to lose the name "Richard," so thoroughly are they intertwined in his mind. Richard also conceives of language poetically, as material from which to construct literary objects. The overall action of the play is, Porter suggests, the decline and fall of Rich-ard's conception of language. His universal, unilingual, absolutist world of nomenclature and ceremonial performatives contrasts with Bolingbroke's world of tongues and silence. In *1H4* we con-front practical questions of dealing with proliferated tongues. Porter likens Hotspur to Richard II in that Hotspur ties his ear to his own tongue and its world of figures. Prince Hal, mean-while, responds to the fact of the variety of languages, a fact made explicit in the appearance of Rumour in *2H4.* Reporting is one of the most frequently mentioned and frequently occurring speech acts in this play. Porter observes also the importance of the subject of deafness. In *H5* the variety of languages, excluded from Richard's absolutist conception of language, becomes a prominent example of the manageable order of the world. Ulti-mately, Porter argues that the tetralogy is about language with respect to the genre of drama and that the verbal form, drama, is itself a major unifying subject or theme of the tetralogy. Or to put the issue slightly differently, the tetralogy is about a shift of allegiance from nondramatic to dramatic literature. Porter takes time toward the end of his book to explain fully the methodology that he has used and to conclude with an overview of the entire tetralogy.

In a detailed analysis of the plays *R2-H5,* Herbert R. Coursen, *The Leasing out of England: Shakespeare's Second Henriad* (UP of America, 1982), seeks to define the world of these plays. He explores the question of the presence of God in the Henriad plays. For Coursen this second tetralogy represents a long denouement, beginning with Richard II's defection from duty and the evocation of a paradise lost—a lost sacramental vision of the world. Bolingbroke, instead, sets up a new feudal system in England; and the political world of Henry IV consists of broken contracts, duplicity, political calculation and miscalculation. In *2H4,* England sinks even below the baseness represented by a purely commercial ethic. Henry V, inheritor of an intrinsically meaningless crown, provides an artistic simulation of true kingship; and his play explores the limits of Henry's vision. In the plays of the Henriad, morality tends to be what power says it is.

Kristian Smidt's perspective in *Unconformities in Shakespeare's History Plays* (Macmillan, 1982) is stylistic, governed by a belief that Shakespeare often hesitated and sometimes ran into perplexities, revised his manuscripts, and was quite capable of making structural alterations while the plots were growing. Such a view determines Smidt's approach to all the histories. Expectation and fulfillment become the key concepts in Smidt's structural analysis. He argues, for example, that the second and third parts of *H6* were not at first envisaged as two separate plays but rather that Shakespeare expanded his original Henry VI/Duke of York play by stages. The succession of plays about Henry VI assumes an epic as well as dramatic character, and the traffic of relations runs both backwards and forwards. *R3* contains a web of stated intentions, curses, prophecies, and dreams, with most expectations fulfilled. But *Jn.* suffers from lack of focus, the king's centrality threatened by the Bastard. Smidt argues that *R2* underwent some major changes of design in the course of its shaping; the attitude of the play as a whole remains ambiguous. Prince Hal not only redeems his own lost opinion but also helps vindicate his father's legitimacy. Smidt finds the choruses in *H5* not in complete agreement with the main body of the play; they may not have been in the original version. King Henry seems at least two persons: the meek and pious Christian hero and the bragging conqueror. *H8* focuses on character rather than on plot and intrigue, and it has a shifting center. Smidt admirably confronts seeming lapses, discrepancies, or contradictions in Shakespeare's histories.

John W. Blanpied, in *Time and the Artist in Shakespeare's English Histories* (U of Delaware P, 1983), argues that the historical tetralogies have a coherence born of the dramatist's sustained attention to the evolving relationship of subject to medium, history to drama. Thus the book examines the ways in which the playwright *acts* in his historical material—how he manages to transform his own inevitable presence in the histories into the means of sounding out their huge and elusive energies. The central device is the king figure. In his challenging analysis, Blanpied explores all of the English histories except *H8*. Blanpied suggests that though *1H6* fails to enact the central issue between the dramatist and history, it nevertheless is the bedrock fabricated for the future. Enlarging his sense of history, Shakespeare in *2H6* adds silence, absence, impotence, and flux, qualities that demand active involvement of the audience. The mutual dependencies of Henry, Gloucester, and York reveal that history becomes the product of interwoven human action that drama is especially suited to convey. In the king-centered plays, such as *R3* and *R2*, Shakespeare begins the process of searching out the meaning of history in the very art and artistry of his own plays. *R3* culminates an old parodic mode of theatricality; *R2* initiates a new, more deeply sentient one. What happens to Richard II also happens to the play: an emergence from an unconscious to a conscious process of self-destruction. In *1H4* rebellion—more than the subject of the play, more even than its central metaphor—becomes its style. Falstaff brings to light the design of the play's rebellious energies. On the other hand, *2H4* is a play about thwarted effort, in a sense parodying *1H4*—a point that Blanpied develops persuasively. *H5* comes to us already full of its particular, scripted audience: the "audience" addressed by the Chorus is a part in the play that we are urged to fill. The play isolates the primary relationship of evidence and play as it has operated throughout the history sequence.

In his Introduction, Larry S. Champion, *Perspective in Shake-*

speare's English Histories (U of Georgia P, 1980), sketches the background of Shakespeare's history plays. Champion argues that from the earliest histories to *H8*, Shakespeare continually modifies his dramatic design, balancing the sweep of history with effective psychology of character. In separate chapters Champion analyzes all of the histories, noting, for example, that Henry is the central figure in the design of the *H6* plays, and his ambivalence modulates to provoke a complex response from audiences. In both *R3* and *R2*, Shakespeare narrows the focus in order to explore fully the principal characters; and in these plays he has also moved significantly toward his profound tragedies. In the *H4* plays and *H5*, Shakespeare essentially returns to the broad perspective and the skeletal characterization of the early histories; but he does achieve a level of genuine human complexity by manipulating and modifying the spectators' angle of vision. Champion examines the techniques of detachment in *H8*. Throughout his discussion he pays attention to dramatic techniques, such as soliloquies, and how these shape the play's perspective.

The opening chapter of C. G. Thayer's *Shakespearean Politics: Government and Misgovernment in the Great Histories* (Ohio UP, 1983) concentrates on the death of divine kingship in *R2*. The book examines the second tetralogy, *R2-H5*. This tetralogy undercuts the idea of passive obedience and reinforces the emerging strength of the sovereign, epitomized in Henry V. The whole movement goes from injustice to justice, according to Thayer. Richard II differs from his successors in that they are worthy of obedience whereas he is not: blind, passive obedience is wholly inconsistent with good government and human dignity. Richard, Thayer argues, suffers from the psychopathology of divine kingship; but Bolingbroke forces Richard out of games and into the objective facts of life. In *R2* the state is badly wounded by the follies of the king; in *H4* the wounds are mainly healed; in *H5* the state again becomes a healthy organism. Henry IV and later Henry V embody the concept of a man-centered kingship. Thayer suggests that Henry V is the antithesis of Richard II, and he pursues the topic of this final play's relevance for the political world of 1599.

Robert Rentoul Reed, Jr., in *Crime and God's Judgment in Shakespeare* (UP of Kentucky, 1984), examines matters of guilt, conscience, and divine retribution in several of the history plays and in *Ham.* and *Mac.* Reed assumes the divine function of conscience, and he analyzes the histories as an eight-part epic. The fundamental theme running through them is that of political homicide, prompted by self-interest, and God's ultimate judgment upon the perpetrator or his heirs. Reed emphasizes the theme in the histories of inherited guilt from generation to generation, and he suggests that Richard and Carlisle in *R2* possess a divinely granted clairvoyance in their prophecies. The theme of *nobilitas,* Reed observes, emerges also as a unifying motif in Shakespeare's double tetralogy: its qualities are valor and selflessness, betokening manhood. Reed basically argues that concepts of God's judgment control the principal destinies of each play world. Thus, Bolingbroke functions as an avenging agent of God, avenging Gloucester's murder. Reed also traces the responses to the death of Richard II through the histories. For example, Henry IV, in order to assuage his guilt, constructs an image of unqualified ineptitude of King Richard. In *H5* we find Shakespeare's most complete statement of the Lancastrian dread of God's vengeance for the death of Richard. The Wars of the Roses in the *H6* plays become an arena of vengeance and unwarranted bloodshed. The Ghosts that appear to Richard III, signs of God's judgment, paralyze his capacity to focus upon the objective at hand. Reed closes the book with a chapter on *Ham.* and *Mac.,* analyzing them also in light of divine retribution and judgment.

In an intricately and persuasively argued book, Graham Holderness, *Shakespeare's History* (St. Martin's, 1985), fulfills two tasks: to describe as precisely as possible the *production* of Shakespeare's historiography and to demonstrate the fate of those historiographical texts in history, particularly the story of their subsequent *reproduction.* He focuses primarily on the *R2-H5* tetralogy, and he argues that specific historical conditions attending the genesis of Shakespeare's drama inscribed into it patterns of meaning. In so doing, Holderness devotes considerable time to confronting the principal critics of the histories, especially Tillyard, exposing their own often nationalistic biases in their interpretations. Examining the Tudor historians, he concludes that these sources for Shakespeare were more complex than we often take them to be. Therefore, Shakespeare's history plays are not just reflections of a cultural debate: they are interventions in that

debate, contributions to the historiographical effort to reconstruct the past. Specifically these plays embody a conscious understanding of feudal society as a peculiar historical formulation,
and they analyze that society. *R2* reflects Shakespeare's sophisticated understanding of medieval history, and it dramatizes the
process of the destruction of the concept of divine monarchy.
The play epitomizes the struggle between royal authority and
feudal power. Richard, Holderness observes, is a historian, constructing and creating the myth of his own tragic history.

The *H4* plays show a continuation of the struggle between
sovereign and nobles, complicated by the change of dynasty. Bolingbroke's earlier victory only centralizes and deepens the unstable and contradictory forces of the society he hopes to rule.
Falstaff, in his function as carnival, constitutes a constant focus
of opposition to the official and serious tone of authority and
power, his attitude being always parodic and satiric. Holderness
sees the eventual collision of Hal and Falstaff as the inevitable
confrontation of patrician and plebeian dramatic discourses, or
ruling-class and popular cultures. He views Henry V as a feudal
overlord, not the ideal Renaissance prince; the play's historical
vision is an image of the declining feudal society of the fifteenth
century. The king's triumph is a barren military triumph, not
the prelude to a peaceful and harmonious commonwealth. The
remainder of the book examines how critics and theater produc-
ers have treated these history plays, the reproduction of history
that Holderness refers to. One recurrent thread is the barely dis-
guised, though perhaps unconscious, ideology of these interpretations, usually nationalistic.

Paul N. Siegel, in *Shakespeare's English and Roman History Plays:
A Marxist Approach* (Fairleigh Dickinson UP, 1986), distinguishes
himself from other critics who examine the historical and political
backgrounds of Shakespeare's plays. Siegel believes that class
struggle is the "motor force" of history and that the ruling ideas
of an age are the ideas of the ruling class. He thus analyzes the
interaction of the history plays with their culture and the economic base upon which the political structure was dependent.
Siegel argues that Shakespeare not only demonstrates the changing relationship between monarchy, aristocracy, and the bourgeoisie but that he also shows the changes in his own time and
foreshadows the time when the bourgeoisie will help overthrow a

Stuart king. From such a perspective Richard III becomes very much of the new capitalist world, obsessed with financial language and attitudes; but his energy is that of the bourgeoisie. In *Cor.* Shakespeare shows the class struggle that was present in the early Roman republic. The social systems depicted in these plays are only stages in the development of human society. This book needs a much more intellectually rigorous approach to its subject.

TRAGEDIES

Criticism of the tragedies has often focused on the study of characters; indeed, the leading protagonists of the tragedies are most memorable, and their motives, psychology, and spirit produce fascination both on the stage and in the printed text. The great actors of any generation aspire to the role of some Shakespearean tragic hero. Critics have examined both the spirit and the form of tragedy and have marked the movement of Shakespeare's development as a writer of tragedies. Questions of influence from his contemporary dramatists and from tragic theories have been discussed. Several critics have grouped common themes that bind together certain of the tragedies. Matters of style and imagery have likewise been considered.

An extremely helpful review of some criticism of the tragedies can be found in *The Major Shakespearean Tragedies: A Critical Bibliography* (Free Press, 1973), edited by Edward Quinn, James Ruoff, and Joseph Grennen. This book reviews and evaluates criticism and scholarship on *Ham., Lr., Oth.,* and *Mac.* The work on each play divides into five categories: criticism, editions, text, sources, staging—the emphasis is on criticism, treated chronologically, usually starting with the eighteenth century. An index to the critics accompanies the discussion of each play. An essay by Clifford Leech, "Studies in Shakespearian and Other Jacobean Tragedy, 1918-1972: A Retrospect," *Shakespeare Survey* 26 (1973): 1-9, also reviews criticism. Specialized studies can be found in Leech's essay "Studies in *Hamlet,* 1901-1955," *Shakespeare Survey* 9 (1956): 1-15; and in Helen Gardner, " 'Othello': A Retrospect, 1900-67," *Shakespeare Survey* 21 (1968): 1-11. Anthologies of tragedy criticism include Laurence Lerner, ed., *Shakespeare's Tragedies: An Anthology of Modern Criticism* (Penguin, 1963), which contains essays on nine tragedies and theoretical essays on tragedy and Shakespearean tragedy in particular; Clifford Leech, ed., *Shakespeare: The Tragedies: A Collection of Critical Essays* (U of Chicago P, 1965), reprints eighteen essays, ranging from Dryden to contemporary critics, with an Introduction by Leech, reviewing some of the criticism on Shakespeare's tragedies. *Shakespeare: The Tragedies: Twentieth Century Views, New Perspectives* (Prentice-Hall, 1984), edited by Robert B. Heilman, reprints sixteen essays and excerpts from books by a number of prominent critics.

What has been perhaps the most influential work on the tragedies and in fact one of the most influential pieces of Shakespearean criticism is A. C. Bradley's *Shakespearean Tragedy* (Macmillan, 1904). Its being reprinted over twenty times surely attests to its eminence. Bradley presents an intensive analysis of *Ham.*, *Oth.*, *Lr.*, and *Mac.*, emphasizing the characters and attempting to define their psychology. In the opening chapters Bradley discusses the "substance" and the "construction" of Shakespearean tragedy. For Bradley the center of tragedy lies in action issuing from character or in character issuing in action; calamities and catastrophes follow inevitably from the deeds of men, and the main source of these deeds is character. While discussing the nature of the tragic hero, the author observes that his tragic trait, also his greatness, becomes fatal to him.

The whole play of *Ham.* turns on the peculiar character of the hero, whose main difficulty is internal. Bradley denies Coleridge's notion that this is a tragedy of reflection; instead, the cause is a quite abnormal state of mind, a state of profound melancholy that grows out of Hamlet's moral shock. This emotional condition of melancholy explains most of his actions, which Bradley examines in detail. The sparing of Claudius in the prayer scene constitutes the turning point in the play, from which all the disasters follow. Bradley finds Claudius interesting, both psychologically and dramatically. *Oth.*, the most painfully exciting and most terrible of all the tragedies, concerns Othello, himself the most romantic figure among Shakespeare's heroes. His mind simple, he is by nature full of the most vehement passion; where he trusts, he trusts absolutely. Contrary to Coleridge, Bradley has no trouble finding sufficient motivation in Iago. Iago possesses remarkable powers of intellect and will, and his desire to satisfy the sense of power drives him on.

For Bradley, *Lr.* is Shakespeare's greatest achievement but not his best play. He finds, for example, the blinding of Gloucester to be a blot on the play as a stage play. But the chief fault comes from the play's double action, the Lear and Gloucester stories, though Bradley admits that this technique helps give the play its universal quality. Bradley's own dramatic sense calls for a "happy ending"–the suffering has been enough. He believes that Lear's final accents and gestures should express an "unbearable joy." In *Mac.*, the most vehement, the most concentrated of the tragedies, Bradley finds the witches an influence but nothing more. Ambition fires Macbeth and Lady Macbeth. After the murder of Duncan, Macbeth exhibits psychologically the most remarkable development of a character in Shakespeare. Curiously, Macbeth never loses our sympathy. Lady Macbeth's greatness lies in her courage and will.

The acceptance of Bradley's views has waxed and waned in the history of criticism during this century. This and other matters have been documented by Katherine Cooke, *A. C. Bradley and His Influence in Twentieth-Century Shakespeare Criticism* (Clarendon, 1972). This book deals with a biography of Bradley, his critical theories, the attacks by other critics on him, and an assessment of his contribution. On the whole, Cooke believes that Bradley is now held in very high regard and that he is being read for the right reasons, devoid of some envy of his success that afflicted earlier decades.

A self-confessed disciple of Bradley's, H. B. Charlton, in *Shakespearian Tragedy* (Cambridge UP, 1948), emphasizes the means by which Shakespearean tragedy achieves its effect of inevitability. In the greatest tragedies human nature shapes morality by some ultimate and mysterious impulse; Shakespearean tragedy is, then, the apotheosis of the spirit of man. Charlton deals with some of the early tragedies as apprentice pieces or experiments. Hamlet creates his ideal world and then mistakes it for a true intellectual projection of the real one, and he thus becomes largely incapable of action. Othello's downfall is the core of the tragedy, but he is a tragic figure in a tragic world, a world that is the disastrous meeting point of two cultural and spiritual traditions. Iago's malignity propels from within him. In spite of all his premonitions of agony, Macbeth's ambition overcomes all his moral scruples. He murders Duncan, and retribution begins. By its very process of primitive simplicity, *Lr.* universalizes the tragedy that it represents, involving all humanity in the tragic conflict of life.

In *Shakespeare's Tragic Sequence* (Hutchinson, 1972), Kenneth Muir observes that there is no such thing as Shakespearean tragedy, but only Shakespearean tragedies. He therefore examines each of the tragedies from *Tit.* to *Tim.* separately. Although the book does not have a controlling thesis, Muir treats the plays in chronological order, arguing for the evolution of Shakespeare's art. This book essentially rehashes several well-known critical arguments about the plays. Not an original or challenging book, *Shakespeare's Tragic Sequence*, like Muir's *Shakespeare's Comic Sequence*, may be valuable to beginning students who want to get acquainted with some of the general issues of the Shakespearean critical debate.

In *Shakespeare's Tragic Practice* (Clarendon, 1979), Bertrand Evans follows the approach of his 1960 book on Shakespeare's comedies. He studies Shakespeare's habit of creating and exploiting discrepant, or unequal, awareness as a means of producing various dramatic effects. He focuses on the dramatist's use of awareness/unawareness gaps in the tragedies, especially the dramatic effects created by the protagonist's unawareness of the tragic outcome. Whereas in the comedies the opposition of our awareness to the participants' awareness results typically in incidental, passing effects that have little to do with determining the outcome, in the later tragedies the unawareness of the protagonist becomes an integral part of the movement towards catastrophe.

In *William Shakespeare: The Tragedies* (Twayne, 1985), Paul A. Jorgensen studies ten tragedies from *Tit.* to *Cor.*, advancing the argument that what defines the tragic experience in Shakespeare is not death or fear of death but "felt sorrow," how the hero suffers. Titus changes from a man of rigorous honor to one who can feel. In *Rom.* separation and stoniness of heart function as major agents of evil. In *JC*, Brutus suffers feelingly, learns from his tragic ordeal, and ultimately improves as a human being. Hamlet must struggle to make of man more than a beast, and in so doing, he must constantly endeavor not to become a dehumanized creature. Othello experiences an ordeal in jealousy, a dehumanizing experience. His becomes a pilgrimage of known and feeling sorrow. *Lr.* epitomizes Jorgensen's main point because it constantly tests the human heart, striving to rescue "threatened humanity" through "known and feeling sorrow." *Macbeth* experiences a torture of the mind, which humanizes him; but *Tim.* shows a man turned to stone. *Ant.* must be seen as the disgrace and defeat of a Herculean hero. In *Cor.*, Shakespeare primarily focuses on nobility and nobleness of heart, a civilized or civilizing human tendency. Finally, Jorgensen suggests that Shakespeare's tragedies are "open-ended," something illustrated by the many questions that they pose—some of central concern to us.

Several critical studies deal with groupings of the tragedies according to when they were written. Nicholas Brooke, for example, in *Shakespeare's Early Tragedies* (Methuen, 1968), examines *Tit., R3, Rom., R2, JC,* and *Ham.* The book makes no particular attempt to trace development or to outline a common theme; instead, it focuses on the "style" of the individual plays. In *Tit.* the central theme is that passion causes men to deteriorate into beasts. Brooke emphasizes the poetic stylization as the unifying element of the play. Concentration on the moral history has tended to divert attention from the centrality of Richard III's disturbing vitality. In *R3*, Shakespeare admits a skepticism and in so doing discovers the tragic dilemma of his own orthodoxy. *Rom.* emphasizes a formal structure but also continually questions and penetrates it. The formal surface not only restrains but also reveals the inner experience. Shakespeare establishes the equation of love and death as part of the youth of Romeo and Juliet; this forms the center of the play's general insistence on paradox. In *R2* the king's tragedy is his humanity, his sufferings only marginally related to his faults. The structure of *JC* provides a dual vision, pointing to nobility but also to sham, the ludicrous. As with the others, this drama explores men as men. In *Ham.* the rhetorical high style of ghost, heaven, and hell, where events are significant in an established scale of values, opposes the vivid presence of a mortal world, where ideas of heaven and hell explain nothing. Shakespeare makes Hamlet's behavior and utterance oscillate between these polarities and yet lets him be convincingly one man.

Understandably much critical attention has been focused on the middle period of the tragedies, the mature plays of *Ham., Lr., Oth.,* and *Mac.* An early study is Lily B. Campbell, *Shake-*

speare's Tragic Heroes: Slaves of Passion (Cambridge UP, 1930). In this work of historical criticism, Campbell presents an extensive background of Renaissance philosophy and psychology; the four major tragedies reflect mirrors of passion. In *Ham.*, Shakespeare undertook to answer the fundamental problem of the way men accept sorrow when it comes to them; the play is thus a tragedy of grief. *Oth.* becomes a study in jealousy and how it affects those of different races. *Lr.* is a tragedy of wrath, planned as a tragedy of old age. In such a study of passion, *Mac.* becomes a study in fear, set against a background of its opposite. The passion of the characters is throughout more important than action. Campbell's book, thoroughly documented with Renaissance references, may finally disappoint because of the simplicity of its conclusions.

A radically different approach, but one also somewhat historical, is Carol Carlisle's *Shakespeare from the Greenroom: Actors' Criticisms of Four Major Tragedies* (U of North Carolina P, 1969). This book brings together widely diffuse information and illustrates the actors' major accomplishments as critics. Carlisle includes actors from the past to the present (an appendix gives brief biographical sketches). Each chapter consists of three major divisions of the criticism: the play, the characters, and from criticism to theater. A valuable introduction and conclusion evaluate the contributions of the actors and establish the context of their criticism. Altogether the book represents an impressive array of research and explores an area too often overlooked.

In *Shakespeare's Mature Tragedies* (Princeton UP, 1973), Bernard McElroy argues that the common foundation of all four tragic worlds is the complementary viewpoint (opposites); and he examines the relationship between the world of the play and the subjective, perceived world of the hero. The central focus of Shakespearean tragedy is the experience of the tragic hero. McElroy finds five principal qualities that the mature tragic heroes share in common: (1) a tendency to universalize; (2) an extraordinary sense of self-awareness; (3) a consciousness of themselves not only as individuals but also as part of a broad structure; (4) an ethical sense that sees hypocrisy and misrepresentation of truth as abominable crimes; and (5) a vulnerability to having their view of reality and of themselves undermined at the level of its basic assumptions. Qualities of the Hamlet world include perilousness, elusiveness, and widespread decay. Hamlet's most consistent and conspicuous reaction to his world is his rage. The tragic conflict derives from what he is told to do and what he wants to do. Two principal spheres in *Oth.*—Venice and Cyprus—reveal a play primarily about suffering, more especially about suffering in ever-deepening isolation. The action hinges on belief. Iago believes what his own psychic needs dispose him to believe. Othello stakes everything on a belief in love that can transcend all differences, but then discovers that he cannot sustain that faith once it is called into question. *Lr.*, a paradigm of the waning medieval hierarchy confronting the onset of pragmatic materialism, offers worlds of very basic primal energy, violently opposed extremes, constantly shifting identities—greatest in Lear himself. His death suggests the human capacity to hope when there is nothing left to hope for. Above all, *Mac.* is a tragedy about self-loathing, about self-horror that leads to spiritual paralysis, a world in which nature seems dead and wicked dreams abuse sleep.

A book concerned with the last tragedies is Willard Farnham, *Shakespeare's Tragic Frontier: The World of His Final Tragedies* (U of California P, 1950). Farnham groups together *Mac., Tim., Ant.,* and *Cor.* Deeply tainted rare spirits occupy the center of Shakespeare's last tragic world, a world so paradoxical that it is in danger of overwhelming the tragedy. The "heroes" of the final world are deeply flawed: Timon's seeming love is really a form of selfishness; Macbeth gives himself to evil in order to gain worldly position; Antony knows the threat that Cleopatra poses to his honor yet embraces her; Coriolanus, so blinded by regard for himself, commits treason. But each of the heroes does show a paradoxical nobility. Farnham relates all of this to the Jacobean world as exhibited in its poetry and drama. In summary, *Tim.* emphasizes the beast theme; *Mac.* is a morality play written in terms of Jacobean tragedy; Antony and Cleopatra provide finished studies in paradoxical nobility; Coriolanus becomes a tragic figure as the paradox of his pride brings his downfall.

Several critical studies have grouped the Roman plays in order to examine the common ground among them. J. C. Maxwell, in his essay "Shakespeare's Roman Plays: 1900-1956," *Shakespeare Survey* 10 (1957): 1-11, reviews some of the criticism. An anthology of criticism, *Discussions of Shakespeare's Roman Plays* (Heath,

1964), edited by Maurice Charney, includes fourteen essays from Coleridge onward.

The first full-length study of the Roman plays is M. W. Mac-Callum, *Shakespeare's Roman Plays and Their Background* (Macmillan, 1967; originally 1910). This imposing work, strong on the use of sources, has as its chief critical approach the characters, with detailed analyses (modeled somewhat on Bradley). But the book pays almost no attention to the plays as plays. A long introduction explores other Roman plays of the sixteenth century, Shakespeare's treatment of history, and the source ancestry of these Roman plays. MacCallum discusses in considerable detail the three plays, focusing both on Shakespeare's use of his sources and on an analysis of the principal characters.

More analytical, G. Wilson Knight, *The Imperial Theme* (Oxford UP, 1931), examines the Roman plays. The whole of *JC* is alight with erotic perception; the vision remains optimistic, vivid, startling. All the people are "lovers"—an emotional, fiery, but not exactly sexual love. The theme of *Cor.* illustrates the intrinsic fault in any ambition, indeed any value, that is not a multiple of love. The bare style of the play has little brilliance or color. In Knight's view, *Ant.* is probably the subtlest and greatest play in Shakespeare. The finite and infinite blend throughout. The play as a whole presents a visionary and idealistic optimism, though there is no absence of realistic matters or of tragic pathos. Knight explores what he calls the "transcendental humanism" of *Ant.* Ultimately Antony and Cleopatra find not death but life, the high metaphysic of love that melts life and death into a final oneness.

In *Shakespeare: The Roman Plays* (Stanford UP, 1963), Derek Traversi explores the dramatic development from *JC* to *Cor.*—from the most obvious and most familiar to *Cor.*, if not the greatest of Shakespeare's tragedies, the most balanced and complete of all his political conceptions. The dramatic growth revealed in the Roman plays corresponds to the growth of Shakespeare's tragic vision. This long, extremely detailed analysis, frequently scene by scene, finds in *Ant.* a world in which ripe universal intuitions of empire turn persistently toward decay. Here two themes interplay—political and "metaphysical"—making the play one of the culminating achievements of Shakespeare's genius. Death becomes, unlike in most of the other tragedies, an instrument of release. Irony is the key to the peculiar effect of *Cor.* A largely sardonic estimate of human possibilities, personal and political, leads to a desolate and disconcerting conclusion.

In *Shakespeare's Roman Plays: The Function of Imagery in the Drama* (Harvard UP, 1961), Maurice Charney examines style in the Roman plays. The book considers the Roman plays as poetry of the theater, principally through their imagery, both verbal and nonverbal. All of this leads to a close examination of the plays themselves. An introductory chapter discusses the function of imagery, and a second one analyzes generally style in the plays. Separate chapters interpret the imagery of *JC, Ant.,* and *Cor.* In *JC* the style is most notable in the sharply limited vocabulary of the play and the correspondingly limited imagery. The chief image themes are the storm and its portents—blood and fire. Contrastingly, *Ant.* contains rich imagery and stylistic effects. The imagery tends to be implicit, meanings suggested rather than stated; thus the style is elliptical, complex, and "hyperbolical." The imagery of dimension and scope powerfully expresses the world theme, essentially the movement toward decay and devaluation of the world. Within this the worlds of Egypt and Rome remain in symbolic contrast. The style of *Cor.* contrasts especially with *Ant.* by being curiously cold, aloof, and objective. The imagery centers on food, disease, and animals. These image themes help establish the peculiarly satirical quality of the play, and the images revolve around the conflict between plebeians and patricians.

J. L. Simmons takes quite a different approach in *Shakespeare's Pagan World: The Roman Tragedies* (UP of Virginia, 1973). Simmons argues that these three tragedies essentially differ from *Ham., Lr., Oth.,* and *Mac.* and that the most important element in their integral relationship is the historically pagan environment out of which each tragedy arises. The insight that Brutus, Caesar, Antony, and Coriolanus have into their own tragedies is severely limited, largely because of the ultimate darkness of Rome; they also do not have a moment or the possibility of recognition. Exiled from Rome, the Roman heroes must therefore, in the falling action of their tragedies, confront their city—there is no world elsewhere. Ironically, although Rome finally destroys, it gives what immortality it can to the tragic hero.

Simmons begins his study with *Cor.,* which he regards as the clearest and final statement of Shakespeare's idea of the Roman tragedy, with its focus on a protagonist whose moral vision is unblinkingly the moral vision of Rome. Coriolanus and Rome become finally incompatible because of the conflict that man must endure in his allegiance to two worlds, the real and the ideal. Simmons argues that both Brutus and Caesar in *JC* have ever but slenderly known themselves. Brutus's ambiguities in his tragedy mirror the reverse image of the enigmatic Caesar. Throughout, Brutus beholds himself only in the eyes of Rome. Paradox and irony lie at the heart of *Ant.*, for the play evokes ideals that are finally incapable of realization but that, nonetheless, ennoble man even as they lead to his destruction. In death Antony embraces both what he was, the noblest Roman, and what he has, the Egyptian, but with no reconciliation. Simmons believes that Cleopatra will put together the fragments of Antony's vision. Simmons argues persuasively throughout the book that the pagan setting limits the characters, preventing the possibility of reconciliation for them; no real means of grace or hope of glory exists.

To illustrate Shakespeare's sensitivity to the differences between the Roman Republic and the Roman Empire, Paul A. Cantor, in *Shakespeare's Rome: Republic and Empire* (Cornell UP, 1976), concentrates on *Cor.* and *Ant.* Cantor argues that these two plays were written as companion pieces. His initial chapter seeks to define "Romanness" in Shakespeare—what it meant to be Roman, as Shakespeare understood the matter. One finds, for example, the austerity of *Cor.* countered by the indulgence of *Ant.*, qualities defined by their reflection of the Roman world. Heroic virtue and the sense of serving a cause larger than oneself are qualities associated with the Roman Republic. Civic religion gets much attention in *Cor.*, in which the city is lavish with honors that it bestows upon public service. Paradoxically, the plebeians must accept the senate's right to rule and yet dispute bitterly the way it rules. Politics in Rome make Coriolanus face troubling issues about himself, such as his dependence on the city. This conflicts with his goal of having the self-sufficiency of a god. Paradoxically, Coriolanus's banishment prevents him from ever becoming free of Rome. In contrast to the Republic, the Empire sets Eros free with a new power, evident in *Ant.*, a play that intertwines love and politics. This play also shows the remoteness of the ruler from the ruled. The problem of fidelity, central in the politics of the Empire, is also the central problem: the love story of *Ant.* But the love of Antony and Cleopatra is a curious mixture of deep passion and profound insecurity; their deaths reinforce the paradoxical nature of their love. Indeed, love becomes a kind of tyranny. Either Rome—the Republic or the Empire—is potentially tragic in the disparity between human aspiration and the reality it encounters. The Republic seems to offer men nobility but only at the price of wisdom and self-knowledge; whereas the Empire offers freedom in private life but only at the price of a lasting and meaningful public context for nobility.

Opening his book with a review of Elizabethan classicism, Robert S. Miola, in *Shakespeare's Rome* (Cambridge UP, 1983), traces Shakespeare's preoccupation with things Roman from *Luc.* to *Cym.* Miola takes an organic approach to the problem of coherence in Shakespeare's Rome, identifying internal similarities in the poem and plays while recognizing differences. Miola argues that Shakespeare viewed ancient Rome as a place apart and that his vision of the city and people evolved dynamically. These Roman works are connected by an intricate network of images, ideas, gestures, and scenes. At the center of the vision stands the city of Rome, defined variously—sometimes metaphor, sometimes myth, but serving as a central protagonist. *Luc.,* Miola suggests, balances itself between tragedy and history as it progresses through disorder, loss, and sorrow to the costly expiation of evil and the chastened emergence of new order. The poem also provides a glimpse of many themes that will occupy Shakespeare's attention in the Roman plays. The clash between private interest and public duty reverberates in *Tit.,* destroying the life of the individual, the unity of the family, and the order in the city. The play features two important symbols: the Capitol and the walls. In *JC,* Rome shapes the lives of its inhabitants, who struggle to act according to Roman heroic traditions. Portia and Calphurnia represent forces and ideals crucial to the city but tragically unrecognized and unappreciated; they reflect Shakespeare's increasingly critical conception of Rome and Roman values.

Places in and outside Rome take on symbolic precision and importance for the first time in Shakespeare's Roman canon. *Ant.* examines the struggle of Romans with Rome, portrayed as a physical locality and an imagined ideal. This play world is one in which politic bargaining often prevails rather than military might. Rome in *Ant.* is also a kingdom divided against itself in bloody civil war, and the Empire is in spiritual conflict with itself. Least Roman of all Shakespearean women, Cleopatra is, paradoxically, most Roman as well. In *Cor.*, Shakespeare exposes the paradoxes inherent in the civilized community. Coriolanus's exit from Rome, like his entrance, is a complex symbol of his ambivalent relationship with the city; and his tragedy is to die, not on the battlefield, but in an alien marketplace. Unlike other critics, Miola includes discussion of *Cym.*, whose Roman elements, he suggests, color the entire play and appear unexpectedly at various places. The play reflects in part Shakespeare's increasingly critical scrutiny of Rome. Miola's helpful Conclusion sums up what he has been arguing. Also, his regular references to the influence of Vergil add another useful dimenson to this important study.

Other critical studies cover a varying range of tragedies and focus principally on matters of technique or definition of Shakespearean tragedy. For example, William Rosen's *Shakespeare and the Craft of Tragedy* (Harvard UP, 1960) focuses on dramatic technique, specifically studying *Lr.*, *Mac.*, *Ant.*, and *Cor.* Rosen examines how an audience's point of view toward the protagonist is established. Rapport between audience and protagonist, evident in *Lr.* and *Mac.*, largely disappears in *Ant.* and *Cor.* How we get to know the characters is important. We come to see the world through Lear's eyes and thus accept his point of view. In *Mac.*, Shakespeare molds the audience response by establishing a certain point of view toward Macbeth. The problem is vexing because of the villainous nature of the protagonist. We constantly change our point of view in *Ant.;* hence the often contradictory interpretations of the play. *Cor.* scrutinizes the problem of human integrity, its conception, worth, and how it may be destroyed; this is revealed in the manipulaton of our attitude toward Coriolanus—here the judgments by the other characters are quite explicit.

Brents Stirling, in *Unity in Shakespearian Tragedy* (Columbia UP, 1956), examines how the dramatist achieves unity within individual plays through his use of certain psychological themes. Stirling points to the haste theme in *Rom.*, and he pursues the antic theme in *Ham*. *JC* explores the integrity of conduct that leads the protagonist into evil and reassures him in his error. The reputation theme is important in *Oth*.; whereas the themes of darkness, sleep, raptness, and contradiction become crucial in *Mac*. Stirling sees *Ant*. as a satire that denies the idealism of the love that the title characters have for each other. Shakespeare saw tragic insight as a quality of the play and only secondarily, although often, as a quality of the protagonist.

In *"King Lear," "Macbeth," Indefinition, and Tragedy* (Yale UP, 1983), Stephen Booth argues that what characterizes the tragic experience is indefinition, incompleteness, and boundlessness. In tragedy, both the characters and the audience constantly seek definition; yet definition cannot be attained. Indefinition does, however, generate an illusory sense of pattern and therefore of wholeness and identity. But this sense of pattern only underscores further that all categorization, limitation, and definition are arbitrary and unreliable constructs. The greatness of *Lr*. derives precisely from the play's confrontation with inconclusiveness, hence a trial of our endurance. Booth also cites the example of *LLL*, a comedy that toys with tragedy and indefinition and also explores the conditioned reflexes by which we take contextual probabilities for certainties. In the play Shakespeare exercises these reflexes, frustrating them and stretching his audience's capacity to deal with the folly of relying on artificial, arbitrary limits. Finally, Booth turns to *Mac*. to argue that this play puts us through an actual experience of our finite minds' incapacity to apprehend the infinite universe. The tragedy of *Mac*., Booth affirms, occurs, not in the character Macbeth, but in the audience. The audience joins its mind to Macbeth both in his sensitive awareness of evil and his practice of it: "To be audience to *Mac*. is virtually to *be* Macbeth." Booth also notes that we confuse the form of a play that we call tragedy with the tragic experience, which cannot be defined or categorized. Tragedy thus becomes our attempt to cope with indefinition by giving it form.

John Lawlor explores the use of paradox in *The Tragic Sense in Shakespeare* (Chatto & Windus, 1960), where he examines primarily *Ham*., *Mac*., *Lr*., and *Oth*. Paradox, the foundation and center of the tragic experience, places overburdened human creatures between mighty opposites, trying to work out their salvation or damnation. Lawlor uses the *R2-H5* tetralogy to demonstrate the appearance/reality conflict. *Ham.* poses the question of whether man is the patient, never the agent of his destiny. The tragic conflict centers on the protagonist, who is averse to the deed required of him, seeking the cause of aversion and failing to know it for what it is. The conflict in *Oth.* occurs between accident and design, evil being the design played out in the accidents of domestic and military life. Perhaps the greatest "accident" is the one that brings together Iago and Othello. Against the background of the supernatural in *Mac.*, the perspectives of human action remain. The conflict in *Lr.* centers on the truth of imagination and the idea of justice. As Lawlor suggests, the illusion that Cordelia lives matches the illusion that reality is answerable to our contrivings and that repentance will undo the process of time.

For Irving Ribner, Shakespeare as a tragic dramatist grows in moral vision, a point he develops in *Patterns in Shakespearean Tragedy* (Barnes & Noble, 1960). Ribner touches on all the tragedies and includes also *R2, R3,* and *Jn.* He senses an evolution or development in Shakespeare's treatment of the tragic stories. The author perhaps presses too much the idea of development, as if each is some kind of improvement on what went before it. The basic theme of the tragedies is that the tragic hero through the process of his destruction may learn the nature of evil and thus attain a spiritual victory in spite of death. *Tit., R3,* and *Rom.* show the basic forms that Shakespeare will use: *Tit.*, the tragedy of the virtuous man's fall through deception; *R3,* the rise and fall of the deliberately evil man; *Rom.*, the ordinary man's growth to maturity. Better than before, Shakespeare in *JC* embodies intellectual statement in dramatic character; and in character conflict he exposes the implications of clashing ideologies.

In *Ham.* the hero has a universal symbolism; the total play provides the emotional equivalent of a Christian view of human life. Hamlet's life journey may be viewed as the affirmation of a purposive cosmic order. Shakespeare in *Oth.* gives dramatic form to a Christian view of mankind's enounter with evil, the destructive power of that evil, and man's ability to attain salvation in spite of it. All the elements of *Lr.* derive from the theme of regeneration that affirms justice in the world. Ribner greatly deemphasizes the characters as characters and sees them instead as performing symbolic functions. *Tim.* and *Mac.* concentrate on the operation of evil within the pattern of order. *Ant.* and *Cor.* illustrate the destructive power of evil and the magnificence of evil. But in *Ant.* there is a regeneration of the heroine in the final act; in *Cor.* the hero by his death demonstrates heroic altruism and self-sacrifice, and at least Rome is saved. In a sense this book represents a wide divergence from Bradley's approach because the total effect is to make the characters simple pawns in some larger structure of symbolism and order.

Ruth Nevo's approach in *Tragic Form in Shakespeare* (Princeton UP, 1972) counters Ribner's moralistic analysis. Nevo argues that within a given play the phases of the tragic progress can be distinguished; such a process helps not only in understanding the plays but also in apprehending the nature of the tragic idea. Shakespearean tragedy, according to Nevo, has an unfolding five-phased sequence: Act I or Phase 1 (not always the same) is the "predicament"; II, "psychomachia"; III, peripeteia; IV, perspectives of irony and pathos; V, catastrophe.

Nevo's discussion of the plays proceeds on this analysis of form, attempting to strip critical interpretation of its frequent moralistic, didactic bias. Brutus's career in *JC* follows the Shakespearean trajectory. The play stands on the threshold of the great tragedies, but the form remains largely empty of substance. Contrivance, conspiracy, concealment, and dissimulation in *Ham.* reach their crisis in the sequence that runs from the nunnery scene through the play scene to the killing of Polonius; this sequence articulates the peripeteia, or reversal. Iago's role in *Oth.* consistently expands to the culminating vision of the archdevil's taking possession of Othello's soul in Act III. The simultaneity of Othello's anagnorisis with the catastrophe of the play gives his final speech its power. *Mac.,* which is most rapid and compressed, presents a conflict between inner and outer. In Act III we watch a more profound disintegration of the tragic protagonist than in any of the other tragedies. The inadequacy of love to redeem is the burden of *Lr.* Act III (peripeteia) exhibits Lear's total reversal of his status and situation; Act IV offers the antiphonal dialectic of comfort and despair; Act V gives us Shakespeare's most unmitigated and quintessential tragic outcome. Cleopatra takes over the tragic role after Antony's death and carries the burden of the final phase of catastrophe. The psychomachia of Act II offers Coriolanus's first dilemma: he must choose integrity or mastery, since he cannot have them both. Reversal and anagnorisis come in the final turns of the catastrophe, giving rise to pure tragic poignance. While Nevo's approach may strike some as too schematic, it never fails to provide insight into the possible structure of the Shakespearean tragedies.

Matthew N. Proser, in *The Heroic Image in Five Shakespearean Tragedies* (Princeton UP, 1965), argues that tragedy ensues partly because of the discrepancy between the main character's self-conception and his full humanity as displayed in action, action often shaped by his heroic self-image. Proser examines *JC*, *Mac.*, *Oth.*, *Cor.*, and *Ant.* Brutus tends to visualize himself as a sacrificial priest, the savior or liberator of Rome. Brutus is the patriot. In *Mac.* the emphasis is on Macbeth's "manliness"—action is everything, verifies everything. In both *Oth.* and *Cor.*, Shakespeare takes a soldier-hero and places him in a situation with which his military training cannot cope. At the end Antony must rise to the image of lost nobility in order to recoup everything in one pure and self-defining gesture. The conclusion constitutes the heroic moment that each of the tragic heroes has faced. Throughout his book, Proser places much emphasis on the language of these plays.

In *The Music of the Close: The Final Scenes of Shakespeare's Tragedies* (UP of Kentucky, 1978) Walter C. Foreman, Jr., focuses on the final scenes of *Ham.*, *Lr.*, *Oth.*, and *Ant.* According to Foreman, each ending is an experiment, offering complex and fascinating variations on the tragic ending. The plays depict a process of moving from one order to another, usually going through a good deal of disorder. This disorder can be mental, sexual, familial, political or military, elemental or cosmic, and metaphysical. The disorder leads to disaster and a new order. The new order, however, is ironic because the world—dull and bounded—at the end of the plays seems diminished without the tragic figures. Shakespeare thus explores the separation of the tragic figures from the surviving community. *Ham.*, more than any of the other tragedies, is structured by a mutual, personal, increasingly recognized antagonism between Claudius and Hamlet—an antagonism that Hamlet sees as an inevitable duel. *Lr.* also depicts a tragedy of human insularity, rather than of human malice. *Oth.* has a fast and striking end, but *Ant.* closes inconsequently.

Audience response is the focus of E. A. J. Honigmann's *Shake-*

speare: Seven Tragedies: The Dramatist's Manipulation of Response (Macmillan, 1976). Honigmann argues that Shakespeare uses a variety of techniques to guide, control, and manipulate audience response to the plays. The intended effect in *JC* is a divided response to Brutus. *Ham.* invites the audience to judge Hamlet's judgment. *Oth.* gives audience response by focusing on secret motives, which are never quite fully revealed. In *Lr.* the audience has to adjust constantly to the vagaries of Lear's mind, an adjustment that affects our response to the entire play. In *Mac.*, Shakespeare carefully controls the flow of information, so as to encourage a sympathetic response to the victim/villain hero. *Ant.* invites an ambiguous and uncertain response to the hero; *Cor.*, contradictory ones.

John Holloway, in *The Story of the Night: Studies in Shakespeare's Major Tragedies* (Routledge & Kegan Paul, 1961), surveys *Ham.*, *Oth.*, *Lr.*, *Mac.*, *Ant.*, *Cor.*, and *Tim.* In his Introduction Holloway deals with different critical approaches and their implications and is generally dissatisfied with the kind of Shakespeare that they suggest. Holloway finds in the plays a developing pattern: the movement toward ritual sacrifice. He discusses the audience's response and participation in this activity as the plays ritualize reality. The protagonist moves from being the cynosure of his society to being estranged from it, a process of alienation. What happens to him may suggest the expulsion of a scapegoat, the sacrifice of the victim, or both. The issue in *Ham.* is not what kind of man he is, but what he does. While the play proceeds into decay, there remains an incessant play and thrust of frenzied intrigue, of plot and counterplot. Othello's whole nature transforms into a coherent sequence. Macbeth's act of revolt is an ultimate revolt. *Lr.* is in part a rehearsal of the terrible potentiality of Nature, the process of descent into chaos. *Ant.* exhibits the quintessence of vacillation in the world of politics and the world of love. The gradual isolation that the protagonist experiences in these plays becomes overt transformation into an outcast in *Cor.* and *Tim.* Holloway's anthropological method sheds new light on the fate of the tragic protagonists, though it may seem somewhat strained in places.

In *Passion Lends Them Power: A Study of Shakespeare's Love Tragedies* (Manchester UP, 1976), Derick R. C. Marsh studies the problems of love, primarily in three tragedies, *Rom.*, *Oth.*, and *Ant.*

In all three plays the lovers reject the world's ways of judging their situation and follow the demands of their love, even to death. Marsh starts, however, with the comedies, which show an awareness of the dangers and disasters inherent in any love situation. *LLL* focuses on the folly of attempting to shun love. *MND*, in its qualification of the love experience, has tragic undertones. *AWW* shows that individual love is not always enough. The problem comedies put the problems of love in further relief, exploring the relation between love and sexuality and one other element—justice in *MM*, forgiveness in *AWW*, and the collapse of a whole society in *Tro*. Marsh argues that *Rom*. is the tragedy of love's intensity, concerned with the nature of first love and intense sexual attraction. Othello's love becomes the central value in his life, replacing all other values and making him vulnerable. *Ant.*, a tragedy of love's triumph, depicts Antony and Cleopatra in their growing awareness of the irrelevance of all concerns except love. Their concentration on their love leaves them exposed to the worldly danger that their political importance has attracted. Finally, Marsh turns to love motifs as they echo in the Romances, especially *Cym.* and *WT*. These works look forward to a kind of future denied to the tragic heroes.

G. Wilson Knight, in *The Wheel of Fire*, rev. ed. (Methuen, 1949; originally 1930), writes mainly about the tragedies, though he includes some theoretical essays and one each on *MM* and *Tro*. Knight's introductory essay, "On the Principles of Shakespeare Interpretation," outlines his rationale and approach. As elsewhere, Knight is here metaphysical, "religious," and greatly concerned with the meaning of the plays' imagery. *Ham.* focuses on the central reality of pain. Hamlet's outstanding peculiarity in the action of the play may be regarded as a symptom of the sickness in his soul, which saps his will. From the first scene to the last, the shadow of death broods over this play, for Hamlet's disease is mental and spiritual death. Knight sees the style of *Oth.* as detached, clear and stately, solid and precise, generally barren of direct metaphysical content. This style necessitates an approach to the characters as separate persons, rather than the more generalized "atmosphere." Knight also works out a comparison between Brutus and Macbeth, with the symbolism in both plays centering on storm, blood, and animals. *Mac.* is Shakespeare's most profound and mature vision of evil, with fear as the dominant emotion. In an essay on *Lr.*, Knight explores the "comedy of the grotesque." The dualism in the play waits to be resolved either by tragedy or comedy; the Fool sees the potentiality for comedy in Lear's behavior. The Gloucester-Edgar scene at Dover reinforces the grotesque. In a second essay on the play Knight seeks to define the *Lr.* universe and explores the problem of human and universal justice. The author finds *Tim.* to be a parable or allegory about the search of perfected man to build his soul's paradise on this earth. Timon becomes the archetype and norm of all tragedy. The exaltation of Timon may strike many as unsupported by the text of the play; one suspects that Knight's argument has got the better of him here.

Roy W. Battenhouse follows a "Christian" perspective on the tragedies in *Shakespearean Tragedy: Its Art and Its Christian Premises* (Indiana UP, 1969). He discusses mainly *Rom.*, *Ant.*, *Ham.*, *Lr.*, and *Cor.*, with some attention to *Oth.* Battenhouse tries to steer between the thoroughgoing, sometimes excessive apologists and the denigrators. The discussion, firmly grounded in Biblical knowledge and knowledge of theologians, especially Augustine, argues that Shakespeare writes in a Christian context regardless of his personal beliefs (or lack thereof). The author suggests that knowledge of Shakespeare's background in medieval Christian lore can be of particular help in better understanding the tragedies. Like Judas's, Othello's tragedy involves not merely his mistakes but also the deeper sin of rejecting grace by neglecting the "mercy" of Desdemona. The recognition of Othello's overall likeness to Judas makes fully coherent his underlying psychology. The action of Romeo's visit to the tomb functions as a kind of upside-down analogy to the Easter story; he drinks the cup—a blind *figura* of the Christian Mass. Battenhouse finds the friar morally naïve and of questionable wisdom. Christian art reshapes the pagan story in *Ant.* The triumph in death turns out to be both glamorous and hollow. Hamlet's strategy for setting the world right perversely imitates the method of atonement in the Christian story. Lear's lack of charity and Gloucester's lack of faith suit them for their respective roles. Battenhouse sees Volumnia in *Cor.* as the woman of Revelation, the mistress of the beast. The fate of Coriolanus is tragic on two counts: by aspiring originally to a Grecian excellence and by accommodating to a Roman one. For Battenhouse, then, Christian tragedy reveals that beneath all other causes for tragedy man mislocates his chief end in the process of his passionate quest for bliss. Christian tragedy ends with a recognition of the divine Providence to which all sons of Adam are subject.

Other books on the tragedies also explore the Christian basis of Shakespeare's drama. Harold S. Wilson, in *On the Design of Shakespearian Tragedy* (U of Toronto P, 1957), separates ten tragedies according to those that exhibit Christian assumptions and those that do not. Those that exhibit the order of faith are *Rom.*, *Ham.*, *Oth.*, and *Mac.*; the order of nature, *JC, Cor., Tro., Tim., Ant.*, and *Lr.* Wilson further groups *Rom.* and *Ham.* as "thesis" and *Oth.* and *Mac.* as "antithesis"; the former are less somber, and the role of accident is more prominent in them; whereas in the latter the agents are willful and self-consciously deliberate. *JC* and *Cor.* become "thesis," and *Tro.* and *Tim.*, "antithesis"; the former are positive—studies of great and admirable men— whereas the latter are bitter and negative. But none of these four is comprehensive in its tragic scope; none is a very great tragedy. That honor belongs to *Ant.* and *Lr.*, which together represent the "synthesis" of Shakespeare's tragic vision and become his greatest achievements in tragedy. The value of human love, as comprehended in the love of Antony and Cleopatra and of Cordelia and Lear, ultimately emerges.

Two other books focus on Shakespeare and Christianity. Robert G. Hunter, in *Shakespeare and the Mystery of God's Judgments* (U of Georgia P, 1976), examines the impact that the Protestant Reformation had on Shakespearean tragedy (*R3, Ham., Oth., Mac.*, and *Lr.*). The second book, *Christian Ritual and the World of Shakespeare's Tragedies* (Bucknell UP, 1976), by Herbert R. Coursen, Jr., examines the Christian dimensions of *R2, Ham., Oth., Lr., Mac.*, and *Tmp.* Another closely related book is *Mankynde in Shakespeare* (U of Georgia P, 1976), by Edmund Creeth, which explores the connections between *Mac., Oth.*, and *Lr.* and the morality plays with "Mankynde" as their central character.

Virgil K. Whitaker focuses on the philosophical issues in the plays in *The Mirror up to Nature: The Technique of Shakespeare's Tragedies* (Huntington Library, 1965). Whitaker discusses Elizabethan tragedy to the end of Shakespeare's career and examines critical theory in England. While Shakespeare reflects these practices and theories, he surpasses others by using contemporary theology and metaphysics to develop the full implications of his tragedy. The author groups *R2, R3, Tit., Rom.,* and *JC* together as early experiments. But only *JC* achieves the tragic view of man characteristic of Shakespeare's great plays because a deliberate moral choice is central. In chapter 4, Whitaker isolates and describes the qualities of Shakespeare's tragic maturity. He sees *Ham.* as apprenticeship and *Lr.* as achievement. Lear's tragic stature comes from his moral strength, with which he fights to regeneration. *Ant.* and *Cor.* represent a falling off from the earlier creative power, lacking growth in the principal characters.

Identity in Shakespearean Drama (Bucknell UP, 1983), by James P. Driscoll, is a Jungian study, which explores a variety of archetypes and the Jungian view that the psyche is formed in multiple, interactive, hierarchical levels. Driscoll isolates four components of identity: real, social, conscious, and ideal. Shakespeare develops his conceptions of identity by defining his characters' conscious, real, and ideal identity. In the history plays, the characters create social identity from conscious identity. *Ham., Oth.,* and *TN* show a struggle between social and real identity to determine the conscious identity. Ideal identity becomes a significant motif from *MM* on; tension between the real and the ideal identities largely shapes conscious identity. In *Lr.,* Shakespeare explores archetypal wholeness in its full complexity and raises large psychological, philosophical, and theological questions. In *Tmp.,* Prospero transcends Lear's nervous striving to secure ego identity and attains serene faith in the greater self.

Michael Goldman's *Acting and Action in Shakespearean Tragedy* (Princeton UP, 1985) is an abstract, philosophical exploration of the relationship between "acting" and "action" in *Ham., Oth., Mac., Ant.,* and *Cor.* More specifically, Goldman distinguishes three types of action: the actions that the characters perform, the action of the audience's mind in responding to the events it watches, and finally, the actions by which the actors create and sustain their roles. This book examines the complex structure of these three types.

Directly concerned with the relationship between Shakespearean tragedy and his society, Paul N. Siegel, *Shakespearean Tragedy and the Elizabethan Compromise* (New York UP, 1957), suggests that the social compromise between the aristocracy and the bourgeoisie eventually broke down, bringing with it questionings and doubts of all kinds, reflected in Shakespeare's tragedies. Siegel relates the new social and philosophical world to the tragedies, examining in detail *Ham., Oth., Lr.,* and *Mac.* He argues that Shakespeare's method is, like that of the Christian humanists, ethical rather than theological. The tragedies thus explore the imperilment of the universal order by man's evil passions. Siegel does draw Biblical parallels and analogues for some of the plays— for example, Desdemona is the symbolic equivalent of Christ; Duncan and Malcolm are analogous to Christ; Macbeth, to Adam; and Lady Macbeth, to Eve. Lear achieves redemption since he cannot be saved on this earth. Certainly such views are a long way from those of Bradley.

A particularly challenging book on the tragedies is Howard Felperin's *Shakespearean Representation: Mimesis and Modernity in Elizabethan Tragedy* (Princeton UP, 1977). For Felperin, the modernity of Shakespeare is a part of the mimetic process. Mimesis arises in Shakespeare, not from direct imitation of nature, but from *re-presentation,* with a difference, of inherited models or constructs of nature or life. In a characteristic movement, Shakespeare's tragedies contain and at the same time depart from an archaic content—miracle play, revenge play, or historical morality. Shakespeare, Felperin demonstrates, at once invalidates older models even as he includes them, supersedes them in the very act of subsuming them. The result is a troubled awareness of the simultaneous resemblance and discrepancy between the play and its older models. *Ham.* at once repeats and surpasses the morality/revenge tradition, which constitutes its archaic core. Similarly, *Lr., Ant.,* and *Mac.* also subsume archaic structures. For *Mac.,* however, the inherited core is not the morality tradition, as it is for the other plays, but the tyrant plays of the Biblical cycles. For Felperin, the tragedies have "structures which can never quite reunite with their own dramatic models nor leave those models definitively behind" (87). Felperin argues that the critic's task is at once archeological, historical, and interpretive; therefore, interpretation cannot be isolated from literary history. The last chapter of the book focuses on the works of four of Shakespeare's contemporaries.

Susan Snyder's *Comic Matrix of Shakespeare's Tragedies: "Romeo and Juliet," "Hamlet," "Othello," and "King Lear"* (Princeton UP, 1979) argues that Shakespeare mastered the comic mode before he did the tragic one and that comedy became for him a point of reference and departure for writing the tragedies. The two modes, the tragic and the comic, interact in complex ways in the tragedies: at first the two are polar opposites, then two sides of the same coin, and finally, elements in a single compound. *Rom.* starts out as a comedy, but the well-developed comic movement diverts into tragedy by mischance. In this sense, Snyder argues, this play becomes, rather than is, tragic. *Oth.* is postcomic because it begins where the comedies usually end. The rather neat comic pattern, glossing over the vulnerabilities and ambiguities in Othello's and Desdemona's love and disposing too opportunely of the implacable forces represented by Iago, sets up a point of departure for what is to follow: the look beyond and beneath comedy. *Ham.*, on the other hand, transmutes the comic celebration of multiplicity into an existential nightmare of competing perceptions of reality. In *Lr.*, Shakespeare sets comic order side by side with comic chaos; and out of the resulting dislocation he develops his tragic effect. This perceptive study of the major tragedies demonstrates "how literary convention can operate to shape and enrich a work that is moving in a direction opposite to that convention" (16).

Another book that calls attention to the relationship between comedy and tragedy is Michael Long's *The Unnatural Scene* (Methuen, 1976), a work much indebted to Nietzsche and Schopenhauer. Long attempts to isolate the "thought-model" for the tragedies, arguing that Shakespeare was much concerned with the simultaneity of the personal and the social. Tragedy cannot be understood as an isolated event in the life of the protagonist; it is a social trauma. This dependency between the personal and the social appears in the isolation of Brutus in *JC,* in the crises of the hero's character and the crises of Rome and Romanness in *Cor.,* and in the psychological weakness of Vienna in *MM.* *Tro.* combines the tragic and the comic by exploring the underview of human societies and civilized consciousness; *Ham.* deals with the "philistine mind," presenting the traumatic experience of a man who has been thrust out of restricting civilization into the kinetic world. *Lr.* explores the tragic dynamics of a cultured and sophisticated man's relationship with the wild world of nature. Finally, in their lyric romanticism, *Mac.* and *Ant.* focus on a romantic apprehension of the Apollonian and of the Dionysian, respectively. These two opposites complement each other.

Also exploring generic relationships is David Scott Kastan's *Shakespeare and the Shapes of Time* (UP of New England, 1982), which focuses on the tragedies, histories, and Romances. For Kastan, dramatic structures are intimately connected with different conceptions of the experience in and of time. From the *H6* plays, Shakespeare reveals an interest in two temporal modes, linear and cyclical. The history plays, which emphasize linear time, have a linear and open-ended shape; the tragedies, however, are also linear but closed, moving towards a decisive ending. In the Romances, Shakespeare uses a form that transcends and transfigures the tragic experience by adopting a suprahistorical perspective from the vantage point of the timeless.

Exploring the icon/iconoclastic tensions in Shakespeare's drama, James R. Siemon, *Shakespearean Iconoclasm* (U of California P, 1985), focuses on *H5, JC, Ham.*, and *Lr.*, with a few final comments on *WT*. This book offers a fresh appraisal of the significance of visual images in the plays, underscoring the discrepancy (iconoclasm) that often exists between the characters and their images. Thus, certain features of Shakespeare's drama can be understood as refracting the struggles over imagery and likeness that vexed post-Reformation England. Siemon devotes considerable effort to discussing the iconoclastic movement in the sixteenth-century church.

In *H5* the iconic image of Henry wars with the context of incongruity and dissonance. The use of the iconic in *JC* becomes suspect and alerts us to the elements of figuration at work even in the language. The movement toward myth faces counterthrusts that work to disenchant, to alienate. Far from being an icon of Roman nobility, Brutus after the assassination turns out to have much in common with the opposition. Acts of mutilation in *Ham.* reveal the arbitrariness of what had seemed certain. Hamlet's mutilating treatment of Ophelia concentrates in the nunnery scene; here sign is set against sign. Throughout the play one discerns that all representation amounts to violent usurpation, whether play within the play, the final duel scene, or the larger play itself. The final image in *Lr.*, that of Lear and Cordelia, does not offer a final meaningful emblem of the play's suffering; it sums up the last struggle of a conflict between action and emblem apparent throughout the play. In initially dividing the kingdom, Lear destroys not only a symbol of kingship but also portions royalty itself. We witness several times the iconoclastic fury of Lear. Edgar helps make the Dover Cliff incident profoundly iconoclastic because he creates a grotesque emblem to subdue his father.

Robert N. Watson, *Shakespeare and the Hazards of Ambition* (Harvard UP, 1984), argues that the theme of the "hazards of ambition" unites a number of plays "into a coherent pattern of moral symbolism." The hero attempts to shed his lineal or inherited identity in order to embrace a new identity; but in doing so, he finds himself excluded from the regenerative system he has disdained. In psychoanalytic terms, Watson demonstrates that the hero who assumes a new, artificial identity must struggle to reject the father. In the history plays (*R3, R2, H4,* and *H5*), Shakespeare establishes the Oedipal basis for ambition. *R3,* for example, depicts the protagonist's attempts to forge a new identity by staging a series of rebirths; as a result, Richard's identity becomes something monstrous and artificial. *Mac.* explores Oedipal desire and rejection, implicating the audience in the protagonist's crime. The play exploits the audience's "guilt-ridden urges against authority and even reality." Coriolanus aspires to replace his hereditary identity with an ideal martial one, hoping to become "divine warrior, made of steel, honor and wrath." *Cor.* becomes "a tragically ambivalent morality play," with its hero torn "between the diabolical debasement of bodily pleasures and the god-like exaltation of pure virtue." Leontes in *WT* experiences the hazards of ambition; but unlike the other plays, *WT* allows Leontes safe passage back to regenerative nature.

Jan Kott's *Shakespeare Our Contemporary* (Doubleday, 1966), a book that embraces all the genres, has been highly influential, especially on some theatrical productions—particularly *Lr.* Each generation, Kott argues, must interpret Shakespeare through its own perspective. He sees a "Grand Mechanism" functioning in history, not divine providence. In *R2,* Shakespeare deposes the idea of kingly power, and in *R3* he shows the crumbling of an entire moral order. Kott sees *Ham.* in its political context as a drama of imposed situations. *Tro.* becomes a modern play, a sneering political pamphlet. History in *Mac.,* however, is a nightmare, another metaphor to depict the struggle for power and the crown. The link between *Lr.* and the new theater is a grotesque quality. In his interpretation Kott underscores the absurd nature of the play, making connections to Samuel Beckett's drama. The grotesque, in Kott's view, takes over the themes of tragedy and poses the same fundamental questions. All that remains in the play is the earth—empty and bleeding. The play explores no less than the decay and fall of the world. Kott also examines the darkness of some of the comedies, such as *MND,* which he finds to be the most erotic of Shakespeare's plays, containing a cruel and animal dream. He argues that the ending of *Tmp.* is the most disturbing in Shakespeare's drama, rendering suspect the ideas of reconciliation and forgiveness. The play contains a profound divergence between the greatness of the human mind and the ruthlessness of history and frailty of the moral order. Kott refers to the early comedies as a "bitter Arcadia"; and he suggests that the Sonnets serve as prologue to these plays, confronting the central issue of choice.

SONNETS

Criticism of the Sonnets has been plagued with many attempts to identify the persons to whom the Sonnets are presumably addressed. Many have insisted also that the Sonnets reflect Shakespeare's personal experience. Others have wondered about the sexuality expressed in the poems. Altogether, a large segment of criticism has moved from the poetry to the biography of the poet. Those who argue that the poems tell a "story" have been countered by those who argue that they do not. Shakespeare has been seen in the tradition of the sixteenth-century poets who produced lengthy sonnet sequences. Much of the criticism has centered on an analysis of the themes of the Sonnets. Debate has been going on for some time about the order of the poems, and attempts have been made to create a new order.

A brief review of criticism can be found in A. Nejgebauer, "Twentieth-Century Studies in Shakespeare's Songs, Sonnets, and Poems," *Shakespeare Survey* 15 (1962): 10-18. Barbara Herrnstein, ed., *Discussions of Shakespeare's Sonnets* (Heath, 1964), includes seventeen essays primarily from the twentieth century. Essays, explications of specific Sonnets, a bibliography, and the texts of the Sonnets themselves appear in Gerald Willen and Victor B. Reed, eds., *A Casebook on Shakespeare's Sonnets* (Crowell, 1964). A bibliography that may prove of some help is Tetsumaro Hayashi, *Shakespeare's Sonnets: A Record of Twentieth-Century Criticism* (Scarecrow Press, 1972). It contains three categories: primary sources and editions; secondary sources, books, and articles; and background sources.

An important edition is Hyder Edward Rollins, *The Sonnets,* 2 vols. (Lippincott, 1944), which forms part of the new variorum edition. The first volume presents the text of the Sonnets, textual notes, and commentary; the second volume covers a wide range of subjects, such as text, authenticity of the 1609 text, date of composition, arrangement, question of autobiography, the friend, the dark lady, and the rival poet.

The arrangement of the Sonnets preoccupies Brents Stirling in *The Shakespeare Sonnet Order: Poems and Groups* (U of California P, 1968). The book is difficult to summarize because the argument depends on intricate details, relating one Sonnet to another. Nevertheless, this sophisticated, complicated, detailed argument opts for an order different from the original 1609 quarto text. Stirling's new arrangement derives from internal evidence of style and subject matter, not external, historical matter. In effect he presents here a new "edition" of the poems in the order and sequence that he proposes. Chapter 1 describes the problems that one meets in confronting the order of the Sonnets; chapter 2 offers the new arrangement and commentary about the sequence; and chapter 3 presents sixty pages of verification. Though the Sonnets can be praised for their narrative art, they tell no definable continued story. Stirling also suggests that they have no demonstrable reference to "true" or historical happenings. Needless to say, Stirling's new order has not been altogether accepted, any more than have other proposals for a new arrangement; but he presents a compelling case.

A convenient gathering of traditional information can be found in John Dover Wilson's *Shakespeare's Sonnets: An Introduction for Historians and Others* (Cambridge UP, 1963). This brief eighty-page account discusses the origin and quality of the text, the identity of "W. H." (Wilson argues for William Herbert, earl of Pembroke), and a brief discussion of themes and sources. In his subtitle Wilson has a particular historian in mind—A. L. Rowse, who was at the time making comments about the Sonnets with which Wilson and others disagreed. At the publisher's urging, Wilson put together this little indirect rejoinder.

One of the early standard books is Edward Hubler's *The Sense of Shakespeare's Sonnets* (Princeton UP, 1952). In a thematic approach to the poems, Hubler does not attempt to identify the young man or the dark lady. In fact, he consciously resists the step from poetry to biography and instead focuses on what the Sonnets say. He discusses a number of techniques that Shakespeare uses—word play, puns, structural devices, the couplet (which Hubler thinks often fails). He groups thematic discussion around a chapter on the dark-lady poems (Sonnets 127-52), sections on the young man's beauty, problems of mutability and immortality, "the economy of the closed heart," the knowledge of good and evil, friendship, and fortune. In an appendix Hubler deals with the problem of homosexuality in the poems and with the authorship problem for the plays.

G. Wilson Knight, in *The Mutual Flame* (Macmillan, 1955), reviews the various critical and factual problems connected with the Sonnets; and he finds many, such as the problem of identities, unprovable. Nevertheless, he proceeds to identify Shakespeare the person with the poet in the Sonnets. He views the poems as a semidramatic expression of a clearly defined process of integration, pointing toward the realization of a high state of being. The main attention concentrates on the poet's love for the fair youth. Knight also considers symbolism and finds the rose, king, sun, and gold to be the main symbols related to the theme. He has an extended commentary on the problems of time, death, and eternity in the poems. In a chapter entitled "The Expansion," Knight relates the Sonnets to Shakespeare's dramatic works in a thought-provoking manner.

J. B. Leishman, in *Themes and Variations in Shakespeare's Sonnets* (Hutchinson, 1961), offers primarily a comparative study of Shakespeare's poems with the poetry of other writers according to both style and theme. Basically he observes the resemblance and differences between Shakespeare and other poets. He takes the poems rather literally, suggesting that they do tell a story and that the young man is William Herbert. Leishman considers the Sonnets on love as the defier of Time, and he argues that Shakespeare desires to transcend himself rather than to refashion himself. In love and friendship, Shakespeare finds a compensation for the evils of life.

In *The Master-Mistresses: A Study of Shakespeare's Sonnets* (Chatto & Windus, 1968), James Winny presents a response to the various theories about the Sonnets and a thematic approach to them. The first chapter, in fact, offers a good summing up of the critical and historical theories. Winny denies the validity of the search for the identity of the young man or the dark lady. The Sonnets do not constitute that kind of story; they are fictional but not in the sense of a coherent narrative. Certainly not autobiographical, they do not correspond to anything that we know about Shakespeare's life, and he should not be precisely identified with the persona of the Sonnets. Winny does explore the kind of story that the Sonnets contain—vaguely related groupings of events and ideas. The dark-lady section has even less of a narrative thread because the poet is more absorbed in ideas. Two major themes emerge: truth and falsehood, and increase and procreation. Winny emphasizes the "dualism" of the poems, arguing that the dualistic associations that the poet forms constitute the heart of the sequence.

Making no attempt to pursue a central thesis, Hilton Landry in *Interpretations in Shakespeare's Sonnets* (U of California P, 1963) essentially presents a series of essays on selected Sonnets. He does, however, argue against the conventional grouping of the Sonnets, 1-126 (young man), 127-54 (dark lady); Landry sees no evidence to support this arrangement, which only encourages the fallacy of "story" in the poems. In his discussion Landry places them in their surrounding poetic context. He offers extensive commentary on the following: Sonnet 94, a bridge between 87-93 and 95-96—the octave looks back and the sestet looks forward; 69 and 70, 53 and 54, the problem of the disparity between physical appearance and moral reality; 33-35, 40-42, and 57-58 all suggest a "civil war," first with the young friend (33-35), then aspects of a sexual triangle (40-42), and master-slave relationship, with the speaker in the unhappy role of the slave of love (57-58); 66, 121, and 129 suggest strongly negative feeling, chiefly moral indignation; 123, 124, and 125 define in some essential way the quality of the speaker's love for the person addressed in Sonnet 125.

Murray Krieger's *A Window to Criticism: Shakespeare's "Sonnets" and Modern Poetics* (Princeton UP, 1964), a highly sophisticated, aesthetic, theoretical book, uses the Sonnets to construct an aesthetic theory. Krieger finds in the Sonnets a key to the nature of metaphor, of poetry, and of poetics as well. He focuses on the mirror/window metaphorical system. The mirror of Narcissism and the magical mirror of love appear in the poems; love breaks the enclosure of self-love. The world of self-love in some of the sonnets becomes the world of worms (symbolically); it may also be a political world. The final chapter examines the religious dimension, discussing the miracle of love's eschatology and incarnation. Beginning students may find this book somewhat beyond their reach.

Philip Martin, in *Shakespeare's Sonnets: Self, Love and Art* (Cambridge UP, 1972), does not deal with the traditional problems of the Sonnets, finding those issues largely irrelevant. Instead, he argues that Shakespeare's feeling for selfhood underlies the whole body of the Sonnets, evident in his concern with poetry, with mutability, and above all, with love. This concern for selfhood is uncommon in the love poetry of the age. In the first two chapters, Martin examines what he calls the "sin of self-love," principally the Sonnets on the youth and on the poet himself; these embody characteristics of the whole sequence. Self-love here equals value of the self. Elsewhere Martin explores the whole convention of writing sonnets, trying to answer why so many poets in the sixteenth century were attracted to the form. In one chapter Martin places John Donne and Shakespeare alongside one another for a comparison of their love poetry in order to demonstrate their awareness and use of love conventions and also their criticism of them. The final chapter discusses the immortality of love, an immortality that seems to have its own existence not dependent on the poetry.

In the stimulating book *An Essay on Shakespeare's Sonnets* (Yale UP, 1969), Stephen Booth analyzes how and why we respond to the Sonnets as we do. He notes that the 1609 sequence seems to need interpretation or reorganization, not because of its disorder, but because of its obvious order. Booth demonstrates the various kinds of structural patterns in the Sonnets and the effect of their interaction. One finds a multiplicity of kinds of structure, such as formal, logical, syntactical patterns and "false starts and changes of direction." In all their details the Sonnets set a reader's mind in motion, demanding intellectual energy as they are read; and this effect (the actual experience of passing from word to word for fourteen lines) becomes unusual and valuable.

In a chapter on multiple patterns, Booth discusses rhetorical structure, phonetic structure, patterns of diction, and multiplicity. Like patterns of syntactical units, sound patterns can also evoke a sense of order. He argues later that the style re-creates the experience of paradox, of coping with things in more than one frame of reference, not *for* but *in* the reader. The couplet ties off one set of loose ends and brings the reader's mind back to conceiving of experience in a single system, what Booth calls the "comfort of the couplet." Shakespeare's enlargement of the number and kinds of patterns makes his Sonnets seem full to bursting, not only with the quantity of different actions but also with the energy generated from their conflict. An index of Sonnets discussed helps the reader track down discussion of individual Sonnets. Sonnets 60, 73, and 94 especially get prolonged attention. One could wish that the history of Sonnet criticism contained more such incisive and illuminating discussion.

In a challenging edition that follows his critical study, Stephen Booth, in *Shakespeare's Sonnets* (Yale UP, 1977), presents a modern text side by side with a facsimile of the 1609 Quarto edition of the sonnets. As in his study of the Sonnets, Booth tries in this edition to present the experience of the poems that a Renaissance reader might have had as he moved from line to line and from sonnet to sonnet. Booth's Preface explains (sometimes in witty detail) how he proceeds in the edition and what his editorial principles are. In the commentary notes that follow the presentation of the texts of the Sonnets, Booth seeks to answer *how* the Sonnets work as well as to provide the usual glosses on what the words mean. Some of the commentary is quite extensive, as in the case of Sonnet 116; it always prompts thoughtful reflection about these poems.

A number of important books on the sonnets have appeared in the last few years. Questions of authorship, biographical intention, topical allusion, and the order of the sonnets continue to dominate the criticism. Kenneth Muir in *Shakespeare's Sonnets* (George Allen & Unwin, 1979) and Paul Ramsey in *The Fickle Glass: A Study of Shakespeare's Sonnets* (AMS, 1979) review in detail some of these questions. S. C. Campbell's *Only Begotten Sonnets: A Reconstruction of Shakespeare's Sonnet Sequence* (Bell & Hyman, 1978) analyzes what he considers to be the defective order in the Quarto text and offers "a more coherent order." In *Shakespeare's Dramatic Meditations* (Clarendon, 1976), a more technical and difficult study based on a comparative analysis of word frequency, structural patterns, and themes, Giorgio Melchiori focuses on selected sonnets (20, 94, 121, and 146), which best articulate "Shakespeare's thoughts and feelings."

The sonnets continue to elicit diametrically opposed views. Katharine M. Wilson, in *Shakespeare's Sugared Sonnets* (George Allen & Unwin, 1974), attempts to demonstrate that the sonnets are not serious but parodic. Those sonnets on the dark lady begin with a parody on Sidney's poem and create a travesty of the additional sonnet lady. The poems to the young man are also parodies of prevailing sonnet attitudes: "To say to a man what is commonly said to a woman is itself to parody" (320). Finally, in an appendix entitled "Shakespeare Not Homosexual," Wilson sets out to prove that Shakespeare was not interested in boys. Robert Giroux, in *The Book Known as Q: A Consideration of Shakespeare's Sonnets* (Atheneum, 1982), approaches the sonnets from the point of view of a publisher. Giroux argues that Shakespeare was probably embarrassed, if not horrified, by the publication so late in his career of "these privately circulated and very personal poems." Joseph Pequigney, in *Such Is My Love: A Study of Shakespeare's Sonnets* (U of Chicago P, 1985), offers an unconventional, "homoerotic" reading of the sonnets. He argues that the first 126 sonnets depict an amorous, sexual relationship between the poet and the youth, a relationship that complies with Freud's views on homosexuality. The sonnets, according to Pequigney, form not only a masterly, coherent sequence but also a "grand masterpiece of homoerotic poetry."

In *The Reader and Shakespeare's Young Man Sonnets* (Macmillan, 1981), Gerald Hammond offers a reader-response study of the sonnets. He argues that except for the final twenty-six sonnets, those sonnets addressed to the young man offer an organized, coherent, and developing sequence of poems. The sonnets contain a narrative, but what makes them truly sequential is the reader's developing experience of the nature of love poetry. This interesting, original book posits the existence of a character called "the reader," who through the poems learns how to read sonnets and what to read into them.

An important, challenging book with an intricate argument, Joel Fineman's *Shakespeare's Perjured Eye: The Invention of Poetic Subjectivity in the Sonnets* (U of California P, 1986), follows a post-structuralist strategy and therefore appeals especially to those interested in contemporary critical theory. Fineman argues that in the Sonnets, Shakespeare creates "a genuinely new poetic subjectivity," "a new poetics," and "a new first-person poetic posture" out of outmoded forms. Focusing on differences, paradoxes, and oppositions, Fineman examines, among other things, the relation between the tradition of visionary language of praise and the representation of the poetic persona, the relation between the sonnet sequence addressed to the youth and those sonnets addressed to the Dark Lady, and the larger implications of his argument for Shakespeare's dramatic works.

STUDIES OF GROUPS AND MOVEMENTS

THE HISTORY OF CRITICISM

Students may be involved with research that includes some study of the history of Shakespearean criticism; if so, several works can prove helpful. Surveys of some of the problems can be found in three essays: Kenneth Muir, "Fifty Years of Shakespearean Criticism: 1900-1950," *Shakespeare Survey* 4 (1951): 1-25; Hardin Craig, "Trends of Shakespeare Scholarship," *Shakespeare Survey* 2 (1949): 107-14; M. C. Bradbrook, "Fifty Years of the Criticism of Shakespeare's Style," *Shakespeare Survey* 7 (1954): 1-11.

One of the standard works available on the history of criticism is Augustus Ralli, *A History of Shakespearean Criticism*, 2 vols. (Oxford UP, 1932). This monumental compilation of criticism ranges from the beginning to 1925. It covers criticism in England, Germany, and France (it is interesting to observe that the only American critic deemed worthy of noting was Stoll). Ralli summarizes and evaluates scores of critics, arranged by nationality, for specific time periods. The discussion proceeds critic by critic. The author also sums up at the end of each section. Students may find the book cumbersome to use and the author's sometimes inflated style objectionable.

Easier to use, Frank Kermode's *Four Centuries of Shakespearian Criticism* (Avon, 1965) is an anthology of criticism ranging from Francis Meres's (1598) to items published in the early 1960s. The material centers on general criticism, comedies, histories, tragedies, and essays on the four major tragedies. Paul N. Siegel's *His Infinite Variety: Major Shakespearean Criticism since Johnson* (Lippincott, 1964) makes its selections on the basis of value rather than historical significance. Topics include general characteristics, history plays, romantic comedies, satiric comedies, tragedies, and tragi-comic romances. Siegel also includes an extensive bibliography.

F. E. Halliday, in *Shakespeare and His Critics* (Duckworth, 1958, rev. ed.), presents a forty-page historical survey of the major figures and movements in Shakespearean criticism; then he gives examples of criticism from 1592 to 1955, which move from play to play and include the nondramatic poetry. A major book that analyzes developments in criticism is Arthur M. Eastman, *A Short History of Shakespearean Criticism* (Random House, 1968), a 400-page review of major critics. The first chapter concentrates on the first 150 years; subsequent chapters survey such critics as Johnson, Schlegel, Coleridge, Lamb, Hazlitt, Dowden, Shaw, Bradley, Stoll, Knight, Spurgeon, Tillyard, Harbage, Granville-Barker, and Northrop Frye. Eastman presents his analysis of their work with generous quotations from their criticism. One might quarrel with Eastman's selection, which elevates certain critics to importance while overlooking others; but such is the plight of any such assessment. Those whom he does discuss, however, reveal diverse critical approaches.

Norman Rabkin's *Approaches to Shakespeare* (McGraw-Hill, 1964) specifically aims at offering information on different types of criticism and contains a collection of twenty previously published essays, representing different approaches to Shakespeare, such as textual, stage production, biographical imagery, Christian. Patrick Murray, in *The Shakespearean Scene: Some Twentieth-Century Perspectives* (Longmans, 1969), analyzes several of the twentieth-century critical approaches to Shakespeare. He discusses the idea of character—its importance, the nature of Shakespeare's characters, and the psychological treatment of the characters. Another point focuses on dramatic imagery—how this approach ties in with themes and character. Murray also comments on the religious quality and offers specific analysis of *Lr., Ham.*, and *MM*. From the historical perspective Murray cites the awareness of Elizabethan times and dramatic conventions. Throughout, Murray usually indicates how and where earlier critics may have taken any of these particular critical approaches and how they might have prepared the way. The book concentrates on the theory of a particular type of criticism, its assumptions, its contributions, and its weaknesses, offering evidence from the practitioners.

The importance of Coleridge as a critic has already been emphasized; the standard edition of his criticism is Thomas M. Raysor, ed., *Coleridge's Shakespearean Criticism*, 2 vols. (Constable, 1930). Raysor presents a lengthy introduction and then a text of the criticism from lectures, reports on lectures, and parts of essays. But this edition has come under recent questioning, at least the text for the lectures of 1811/12. R. A. Foakes, in *Coleridge on Shakespeare: The Text of the Lectures of 1811-12* (UP of Virginia for the Folger Shakespeare Library, 1971), has reedited J. P. Collier's diary, which includes transcripts of Coleridge's lectures. The variations from the accepted text of Raysor raise new problems about the reliability and accuracy of the Coleridge text as it has come down to us. Students will find handy the selection of Coleridge's writings available in the book edited by Terence Hawkes, *Coleridge's Writings on Shakespeare* (Capricorn, 1959).

A narrative account of Shakespeare's reputation appears in Louis Marder's *His Exits and His Entrances: The Story of Shakespeare's Reputation* (Lippincott, 1963). This book offers a wide range of information, including discussion of the idolatry of Shakespeare, frauds and forgeries, Stratford and Stratford festivals, Shakespeare in the schools as a subject, Shakespeare's popularity in American theater, and a brief glance at Shakespeare's reputation in other parts of the world: Germany, Scandinavia, Russia, and the Orient. A useful source book on reputation is *The Shakespeare Allusion Book: A Collection of Allusions to Shakespeare from 1591 to 1700* (Oxford UP, 1932), compiled by C. M. Ingleby, L. Toulmin Smith, and F. J. Furnivall; revised by John Munro (1909), with a new preface by E. K. Chambers. This work emanated from one of the nineteenth-century Shakespeare societies. Volume 1 includes an extensive introduction and the chronological listing of allusions from 1591 to 1649; volume 2 covers 1650 to 1700.

SHAKESPEARE'S LANGUAGE

Considerable attention has focused on matters of Shakespeare's language, especially in modern criticism. (See also the items on language included in the section on reference books earlier in this chapter.) One dimension of language study has been the emphasis on dramatic imagery. One of the most influential books has been Caroline Spurgeon's *Shakespeare's Imagery and What It Tells Us* (Cambridge UP, 1935). This pioneering study is statistical and quantitative, complete with charts and graphs. Regrettably, a large part of the book compiles information that portrays Shakespeare the man, not the artist; Spurgeon sums up his likes and dislikes and sees him as basically "Christ-like." Though she does understand the importance of imagery for our perception of the drama, she does not seem to know quite what to do with it. She perceives themes of iterative imagery and classifies them. Clearly she pointed a new direction in Shakespearean criticism; many others have built on her study.

Working independently at the same time, Wolfgang Clemen in 1936 published a book in German, later revised and translated as *The Development of Shakespeare's Imagery* (Methuen, 1951). Clemen describes the development of the language of imagery and its functions. He detects a pattern of evolution and growth in Shakespeare's use of imagery as the dramatist little by little discovered the possibilities that imagery offered him. Clemen focuses on imagery of the early and middle period, of the great tragedies, and of the Romances. Shakespeare reaches a certain level of skill, as in the tragedies, and then there are variations of style, rather than evolution. Clemen argues that growth in the use of imagery corresponds to increased dramatic skill; thus, later images integrate fully into the plays.

Studying Shakespeare's use of rhetoric, Sister Miriam Joseph, *Shakespeare's Use of the Arts of Language* (Columbia UP, 1947), presents a sophisticated, scholarly study of the formal art of rhetoric in the Renaissance and the evidence found in Shakespeare's plays and poems of his knowledge and use of various compositional devices. The author surveys the theory of composition and of reading in Shakespeare's England, then explores Shakespeare's use of the theory—grammar, rhetoric, and logic. Shakespeare's formal devices contribute to the power and richness of his language, as they also account for some of its peculiarities. A different language approach is provided by Hilda M. Hulme, *Explorations in Shakespeare's Language* (Longmans, 1962). This linguistic study examines in part the traditions that contributed to Shakespeare's language: for example, proverbs, Latin, bawdy. The author also discusses Shakespeare's spelling habits and variants in pronunciation, examining evidence from contemporary Stratford. Hulme explores the meanings of some of the words and phrases in the plays and provides a helpful index.

Several books make practical application of language studies. Ifor Evans, in *The Language of Shakespeare's Plays* (Methuen, 1959; originally 1952), offers no all-encompassing thesis but, rather, individual essays covering almost the entire canon, beginning with an analysis of language in *LLL*. Generally in the early comedies, Shakespeare had no overriding loyalty to the story if wit and invention tempted him. But the histories posed the need for a new kind of discipline. Evans finds that nowhere were Shakespeare's intentions in language more complex and his success more complete than in *Lr.*

A rich book that investigates language is M. M. Mahood's *Shakespeare's Wordplay* (Methuen, 1957). Mahood explores Shakespeare's language through the device of the pun, but the book also examines many subtleties in Shakespeare's use of words. Mahood discusses in some depth *Rom., R2, Ham., Mac., WT,* and the Sonnets. Wordplay becomes one of the most effective means toward the ironic interchange between character and creator. The Sonnets reveal examples of a consciously used, hardworked rhetorical device of wordplay, as well as more unintentional, involuntary examples. In the final chapter the author surveys Shakespeare's attitude toward language, his world of words. In a relatively brief book, *Redeeming Shakespeare's Words* (U of California P, 1962), Paul A. Jorgensen explores the fullest possible explication of words that are either thematic or significant in certain plays; as, for example, the use of "honesty" in *Oth.,* "noble" in *Cor.,* "redeeming time" in *H4.* Jorgensen also discusses *Ado* and *Ham.*

Brian Vickers, in *The Artistry of Shakespeare's Prose* (Methuen,

1968), traces and analyzes the dramatist's use of prose throughout the canon, watching the quantity of prose peak in *Wiv.* Prose is largely the vehicle of comedy and the comic parts of the histories; at the same time, the prose of the tragedies is in some ways Shakespeare's greatest achievement, Vickers suggests. Prose is also the typical medium for the subplots. Investigation of the prose style centers on imagery, linguistic structure, and rhetorical structure. In order to analyze Shakespeare's development in the use of prose, Vickers proceeds chronologically through the canon. Thus, for example, *MND* can be seen as an improvement over *LLL* by its consistency and economy. Shylock's prose, Vickers observes, is the great innovation in *MV.* Vickers devotes much attention to Falstaff. The prose of *TN* is largely given to the lower orders of society and to the upper-class representatives when they come in contact with the servants. Iago dominates the prose in *Oth.* and uses it as a medium for dissembling and mounting his intrigue against Othello. Increasingly the tragedies' prose fulfills its functions for clowns and madmen, witness the Fool and Lear in *Lr.* Vickers finds more energy in the prose of *WT* than in the other Romances. One obvious point: Shakespeare applies to a tragic purpose the prose techniques that he evolved in his comedies.

In a book that concentrates on the tragedies, Madeleine Doran in *Shakespeare's Dramatic Language* (U of Wisconsin P, 1976) explores connections between language and dramatic style, as she outlines in the opening chapter the essential elements of style. What follows are discrete essays on six tragedies. Doran notes, for example, that in Hamlet's style the range and intensity together are the key to his extraordinary vitality. In *Oth.*, she examines the conditional and subjunctive statements as indicators of character and action. The interplay of association and negation gives dramatic life and sensibility to the plot; here syntax informs the larger dramatic structure. In a grammatical and rhetorical analysis of *Lr.*, Doran explores the uses of command, question, and assertion. Again, the emphasis is on syntax. Subsequent chapters analyze the importance of proper names in *JC,* the language of hyperbole in *Ant.,* and the language of contention in *Cor.*

In a historical study of language, Jane Donawerth in *Shakespeare and the Sixteenth-Century Study of Language* (U of Illinois P, 1984) explores the language texts that Shakespeare could have known and what use he made of them. The book's initial chapters provide information about what was known about language study in the sixteenth century, limiting the investigation to topics relevant to Shakespeare's art. Shakespeare makes use of language controversies in his plays. Donawerth analyzes in detail the language of five plays: *LLL, Jn., MV, AWW,* and *Ham.* She notes, for example, that in *LLL* the controlling conception of language is of an ordered system of rational symbols through which their speakers generate meaning. Ideas about language in this play help distinguish the major groups of characters. With the entrance of Marcade into the play, the dominant ideas about language—the grammar book units of letter, syllable, and word, the concept of language as an ordered system of rational symbols—are transformed as well. Ideas about language in *AWW* derive mainly from the humanists' distinction between words and things. In *Ham.,* men and women define themselves by their attitudes toward language, demonstrating Shakespeare's consummate ability to use language.

TEXTUAL CRITICISM

If a student should want to investigate the somewhat complicated area of textual studies, several books can prove quite useful. Philip Gaskell's *A New Introduction to Bibliography* (Clarendon, 1972), which updates and revises the much earlier *An Introduction to Bibliography* (1928), by R. B. McKerrow, provides much information about the whole process of book production of the Renaissance period. Gaskell covers such topics as book production, printing type, composition, paper, imposition, presswork, binding, patterns of production, and the English book trade to 1800. In addition, Gaskell deals with the machine-press period, 1800-1950. He also discusses textual bibliography and includes an extensive reference bibliography.

A helpful guide to the increasing number of textual studies is T. H. Howard-Hill, *Shakespearean Bibliography and Textual Criticism: A Bibliography* (Clarendon, 1971). In this 180-page bibliography, Howard-Hill first defines the limits and explains the arrangement of the bibliography, which has three broad categories: general bibliographies of and guides to Shakespearean literature;

works (collected works, collections and libraries, quartos, folios); and textual studies (handwriting, individual texts arranged alphabetically). The entries proceed chronologically from earliest to latest.

A valuable summing up of the world of textual criticism may be found in F. P. Wilson, *Shakespeare and the New Bibliography* (Clarendon, 1970), revised and edited by Helen Gardner. This book was originally written in the 1940s and is an excellent analysis of where textual criticism stood up to that point, now updated by Gardner. It records a history of the years in which the distinctive problems involved in the handling of printed texts were first clearly defined and investigated. The essay also serves as a valuable introduction for anyone embarking on a study of the problems of establishing Shakespeare's text. The book covers such topics as the beginnings to 1909, publication of plays, printing of plays, dramatic manuscripts, copy for the quartos and folios, and principles of textual criticism.

In a collection of essays, Fredson Bowers, *On Editing Shakespeare* (UP of Virginia, 1966), probes the following topics: the texts and their manuscripts, the function of textual criticism and bibliography, the method for a critical edition, what Shakespeare wrote, today's Shakespeare texts, and tomorrow's. Three basic questions govern the first half of the book: (1) the nature of the lost manuscript that served as the printer's copy, (2) the nature of the printing process itself and its implications for the texts, and (3) the relationship between all preserved examples of the text and the relative degrees of authority. The final chapter comments on past editions back to the Globe one of 1864 and on what remains to be done. Bowers assigns prime importance to the need for a complete old-spelling edition of Shakespeare.

In what has become one of the standard books on such matters, W. W. Greg, *The Shakespeare First Folio: Its Bibliographical and Textual History* (Clarendon, 1955), presents an authoritative summing up of what was known in the mid 1950s about the textual problems of the Folio. Greg initially discusses how the Folio as a collection of Shakespeare's plays came about; he also deals with questions of copyright. The bulk of the book surveys the many kinds of editorial problems apparent in the Folio. To do so Greg systematically goes through the canon play by play and discusses scholarly opinion on the nature of the text. Greg also considers those plays that had earlier quarto texts and their relationship to the Folio. A final chapter deals with the printing of the Folio, now superseded by Hinman's work. But this book, written by one of the leading authorities in the field of textual criticism, makes a handy and indispensable reference for checking on the nature of the texts.

Alice Walker also deals with some of these problems in *Textual Problems of the First Folio* (Cambridge UP, 1953). She focuses on what lies behind the Folio texts of *R3, Lr., Tro., 2H4, Ham.,* and *Oth.* She argues that once we recognize conflation and contamination in these Folio texts, it is much easier to determine the character of the manuscripts that lie behind them. The book seeks to determine what lay between Shakespeare's manuscript and the Folio texts of these six plays and what the editorial implications are for the use of corrected quartos as Folio copy.

A very difficult work for undergraduate students but nevertheless one of the most significant is Charlton Hinman's *The Printing and Proof-reading of the First Folio of Shakespeare,* 2 vols. (Clarendon, 1963). This is a highly technical survey of the process involved in the printing of the Folio—the nature of the Jaggard print shop, edition size and speed of production, standard printing-house procedures, and so on. Hinman makes an extensive study of the type used in the Folio and what it reveals. In his analysis of the compositors who set the type, Hinman identifies five different compositors by their characteristic habits, indicating which portions of the text they set. And of course, he discusses the process of proofreading. Volume 2 offers a detailed analysis of the printing in the Folio—histories, tragedies, and comedies—and also presents a review. Though parts of the argument are being challenged and modified, especially the identification of the compositors, it is unlikely that anyone is going to match the scholarly fortitude and endurance of Hinman.

E. A. J. Honigmann's *The Stability of Shakespeare's Text* (Edward Arnold, 1965) runs somewhat counter to the general drift of the textual critics. The real subject of the book is the "instability" of Shakespeare's texts. Honigmann raises the unsettling prospect that variants of the same substantive text may represent not errors but Shakespeare's two different versions. Such a theory goes somewhat against the "new bibliography" school, at which Honigmann takes several good swats. He finds more reason for skepticism about the nature and condition of Shakespeare's texts than for the optimism that geneally emanates from the new bibliographers. Honigmann has a keen distrust of their "facts." His final chapter deals with editorial policy in light of his argument. Though not the only challenge to the prevailing winds of textual criticism, this book reveals the vitality of textual criticism.

In what were initially lectures, Stanley Wells in *Re-Editing Shakespeare for the Modern Reader* (Clarendon, 1984) examines the problems facing an editor of Shakespeare today; many of these insights have come fron Wells's involvement with the Oxford Shakespeare edition. He outlines the arguments about old versus modern spelling, argues the case for emending Shakespeare's text, and discusses editorial treatment of stage directions. Many examples support the discussion. Wells closes with a detailed analysis of Act I of *Tit.*, illustrating how editorial theories work in practice. One of the basic assumptions underlying the critical principles for editing is that the texts are open to different kinds of editorial treatment according to the varying needs of those who read them: there is no single "right" way to edit Shakespeare.

THEATRICAL CRITICISM

"Theatrical" can cover a wide range of studies, including details of the Elizabethan theater, its acting companies, specific actors, its repertory, its buildings and their physical qualities, the nature of Elizabethan acting; developments in drama, both in staging and in the construction of the dramas themselves; stage history from earliest to latest productions; and more recently, Shakespeare on film. Any student seeking to work in this area has much to choose from; what follows attempts to call attention to some of the basic resources.

A convenient and helpful bibliography is Philip C. Kolin and R. O. Wyatt, "A Bibliography of Scholarship on the Elizabethan Stage since Chambers," *Research Opportunities in Renaissance Drama* 15-16 (1972-73): 33-59. This list of some 360 items covers the scholarship since 1923 on the physical characteristics of the Elizabethan stage. A review article is Allardyce Nicoll's, "Studies in the Elizabethan Stage since 1900," *Shakespeare Survey* 1 (1948): 1-16. M. St. Clare Byrne's "Fifty Years of Shakespearean Production: 1898-1948," *Shakespeare Survey* 2 (1949): 1-20, reviews production. A valuable collection of essays on the theater is G. E. Bentley, *The Seventeenth-Century Stage: A Collection of Critical Essays* (U of Chicago P, 1968). This includes documents of the early seventeenth century and modern discussions of theaters and productions, mostly in the reigns of James I and Charles I; additional essays deal with actors and acting of the period.

An impressive mass of material appears in the authoritative work by E. K. Chambers, *The Elizabethan Stage*, 4 vols. (Clarendon, 1923). Not a narrative that one might read straight through, this study contains a compendium of vast amounts of material arranged as follows: volume 1, the court, control of the stage; volume 2, the companies: boy companies, adult companies, international companies; actors; playhouses: public and private; volume 3, staging, at court and in the theaters; plays and playwrights; volume 4, anonymous work: plays, masques, entertainments; also appendixes and indexes. Here one might find all the information, for example, on a particular actor or the facts about a particular play. Chambers's cutoff date is 1616.

Equally impressive and thorough is the continuation of Chambers by G. E. Bentley, *The Jacobean and Caroline Stage*, 7 vols. (Clarendon, 1941-68). This work is also a source of primary records and other materials pertinent to the stage, 1616-42. The subjects proceed as follows: volume 1, acting companies; 2, players; 3-5, plays and playwrights; 6, private theaters, public theaters, and theaters at court; 7, appendixes to volume 6 and a general index to volumes 1-7. Building on this research, Bentley has also written two books that pursue some theater topics in detail: *The Profession of Dramatist in Shakespeare's Time, 1590-1642* (Princeton UP, 1971) and *The Profession of Player in Shakespeare's Time, 1590-1642* (Princeton UP, 1984).

An important recent study, still in process of completion, on the development of theatrical production and related matters is Glynne Wickham, *Early English Stages: 1300 to 1600*, 4 vols. (Routledge & Kegan Paul; Columbia UP, 1959-81). Concerned primarily with theatrical history and matters of staging, Wickham in volume 1 deals principally with medieval stagecraft: the open-air entertainments (miracle plays, pageant theaters), indoor entertainments (morals, interludes), medieval dramatic theory and practice. In volume 2, part 1, Wickham notes how medieval dramatic tradition carried on into the Renaissance; he also examines state control of the drama. He emphasizes the emblematic tradition (nonrealistic) in the playhouses of the Renaissance. In volume 2, part 2, Wickham discusses the Privy Council order of 1597 for the destruction of London's playhouses and how it was circumvented. Mainly he deals with the playhouses, the recognized theaters, some of the inns with a theatrical tradition, and stage conventions. More than most theater historians, Wickham emphasizes the place of festivals, pageants, and entertainments in the development of a dramatic tradition. Volume 2, part 2 (pp. 3-8), offers a good summary of where Wickham's argument stands. The 1981 volume explores drama and occasion, emblems of occasion, and English comedy and tragedy from their origins to 1576.

M. C. Bradbrook, in *The Rise of the Common Player: A Study of Actor and Society in Shakespeare's England* (Chatto & Windus, 1962), examines both social and dramatic history. Part 1 gives the social history of the public theaters and of the acting companies who played there. Part 2 focuses on typical individuals, such as Richard Tarlton, the first great star of the English stage, and Edward Alleyn, the greatest tragic actor of his time. Further, in part 2, Bradbrook discusses the household players and the rise and fall of choristers' theaters in London, 1574-1606. In the final part the author illustrates something of the general dramatic sports of the age, the common life that gave rise to many occasions for dramatic entertainment. Bradbrook also includes consideration of performances at the universities; thus the book traces the rise of actors from positions of insecurity and no social standing to places of considerable prominence.

Arguing that Shakespeare's drama is unthinkable without the popular dramatic tradition, Robert Weimann, in *Shakespeare and the Popular Tradition in the Theater,* edited by Robert Schwartz (Johns Hopkins UP, 1978), explores various traditions from medieval times to Shakespeare's own era. Weimann emphasizes the structure and function of the popular tradition rather than influence. Only when Elizabethan society, theater, and language are seen as interrelated does the structure of Shakespeare's dramatic art emerge as fully functional. An underlying assumption is that Shakespeare's theater helped create the specific character and transitional nature of his society. One way of understanding that force is to perceive the power of popular dramatic traditions.

The dramatic integration of varied social values and cultural elements makes the structure of the plays so balanced and the poetic perspective of experience so satisfying. Through many references to the plays, Weimann illustrates the ways in which Shakespeare appropriates aspects of the popular tradition. Certainly this theater history charts a rather different course in criticism by emphasizing the function of theater in society.

Students will find helpful books that offer a summing up of the general ideas about the theater of Shakespeare's time. A. M. Nagler, in *Shakespeare's Stage* (Yale UP, 1958), provides a brief survey of the general topics associated with Shakespeare's theater: the London theaters, qualities of the stage, staging of *Rom.*, actors and style of acting, Blackfriars Theater, and audience. *Shakespeare and His Theatre*, G. E. Bentley (U of Nebraska P, 1964), fulfills a similar function. This brief, readable book deals with some of the main points about the theater, such as Shakespeare and his dramatic company, the Globe Theater, Blackfriars Theater, and the condition of the theater after Shakespeare, especially the audience.

Much more extensive is Andrew Gurr's *The Shakespearean Stage, 1574-1642* (Cambridge UP, 1970; rev. ed., 1980). Gurr explores five topics: the companies, the players, the playhouses, staging, and audiences. His work derives from materials compiled by Chambers and Bentley, but the book is more than a redaction of their work. Gurr hopes by providing this background to minimize our misunderstandings about the theater and related matters in the period 1574-1642—that is, from the first royal patent granted to a group of actors to the closing of the theaters by Parliament in 1642. This material can enlarge the dimensions of our understanding of any play of the period. We learn, for example, about the composition of the acting companies, how many there were, the nature of their repertory, the kinds of buildings they performed in, the economics of the theater, and techniques of staging. This well-documented book makes a contribution to scholarship, and students will find it especially valuable.

Understandably there have been a number of studies on the nature of the playhouse itself. One must remember that all of these theories are largely conjectural, there being little in the way of hard evidence. One of the first studies that became widely accepted is John Cranford Adams, *The Globe Playhouse: Its Design*

and Equipment, 2d ed. (Barnes & Noble, 1961; originally 1942).
The book aims to reconstruct as fully as possible the design and
equipment of the Globe. Such a study prepares the way for a
fuller understanding of Shakespeare's plays. Adams's study follows two assumptions: that the requirements of Elizabethan plays
reflect design and available equipment, and that all the evidence
should be taken into account—pictorial, stage directions, and
so on. Adams presents extensive discussion about the location
of the Globe, the playhouse frame, the auditorium, platform
stage, tiring house, and superstructure. His quite traditional approach is now questioned, especially the notion of the inner
stage and the third-level upper stage. But most "models" of the
Globe adhere to Adams's theory. Irwin Smith essentially follows
Adams in *Shakespeare's Globe Playhouse* (Scribner's, 1956). He discusses the same topics as Adams does, but includes fifteen scale
drawings of their reconstruction of the Globe (the model of
which now resides at the Folger Library).

C. Walter Hodges counters some of the earlier views of the
theater in *The Globe Restored: A Study of the Elizabethan Theatre,*
2d ed. (Oxford UP, 1968; originally 1953). Hodges argues that
we must recognize the uncertainties involved in attempting to
reconstruct the Globe. He discusses the problems involved, such
as the scaffold (platform stage) and the nature of the tiring house.
The Globe ought to be rebuilt only for the purpose of reestablish-
ing, as the proscenium theater cannot, the intimate, vital relationship between actor and audience. Hodges includes many
illustrations.

In a searching analysis of evidence of many kinds, John Orrell
in *The Quest for Shakespeare's Globe* (Cambridge UP, 1983) seeks
to understand the physical dimensions of the Globe Theater.
Examining pictorial evidence, Orrell applies mathematical form-
ulas to determine the accuracy of drawings of London, such as
those seventeenth-century ones by Visscher and Hollar. The
theater that emerges from this study is a larger, less intimate house
than was once thought likely, capable of holding 3,000 spectators
and requiring a wide range of abilities from its actors. Orrell moves
from the evidence of the contract for building the Fortune Theater to its implications for the Globe. He wonders about the
sound in the Globe and about the significance of its site place-
ment—about the latter he observes that the Globe faced the exact

point of midsummer sunrise. Accepting Orrell's scientific and persuasive proof, we have reason to be confident about the exterior details of the Globe as a building.

Other studies have more specifically examined the relationship of the stage to actual production of Elizabethan plays. In a valuable book *Shakespeare at the Globe, 1599-1609* (Macmillan, 1962), Bernard Beckerman focuses on staging demands at the Globe. Topics covered include repertory, dramaturgy (climax, finale, scene structure, dramatic unity), stage (parts, design), acting (influences on acting style), and staging (stage illustration). The book deals only with plays produced at the Globe, 1599-1609, the first decade of its existence. Beckerman argues against the conventional idea of the "inner stage" and finds little evidence to support the idea of this as a permanent feature of the tiring-house façade. He emphasizes the importance of dramatic illusion. And he believes that the actual production of a play relied less than we had thought on specific parts of this stage. Instead, the style in staging inhered in the dramatic form, not in the stage structure.

J. L. Styan offers a guide with which to explore stagecraft in *Shakespeare's Stagecraft* (Cambridge UP, 1967). Styan explores the theater equipment—stage, staging and acting conventions; Shakespeare's visual craft—the actor and his movement, grouping on the open stage, and the full stage; Shakespeare's aural craft—speaking the speech, orchestration of speech. While Shakespeare's text gave the actor precise instructions about how certain things were to be done, it also allowed for flexibility and some improvisation. Overall, this is a rather practical approach to staging.

Examining Shakespeare's theatrical techniques, Jean E. Howard in *Shakespeare's Art of Orchestration: Stage Technique and Audience Response* (U of Illinois P, 1984) argues that Shakespeare carefully controls and shapes what an audience hears, sees, and experiences and that this verbal and visual orchestration is central to the effectiveness and meaning of the plays. Howard identifies a group of techniques by which Shakespeare implicitly prepared his plays for effective stage presentation: aural, visual, and kinetic effects. Evidence suggests that Shakespeare thought a good deal about potential response from audiences. Howard analyzes Shakespeare's management of verbal diversity, the technique of counterpoint, the note of silence, the orchestration of bodies, and the effect of orchestration on the play's theatrical structure and the audience's total experience. In the chapter on silence, for example, Howard explores the varying functions of such silence, from denoting closure of an action to dumb shows to creating tension; her examples range across a number of plays, such as *Ham.*, *Oth.*, *Lr.*, and *Ant.* The final scene in *Lr.* also illustrates the effect of choreography: the visual coming together of the play's chief characters ironically casts our minds back to the earlier scene in which Lear wanted to stand in command of such a gathering. A full discussion of *TN* closes the book; this play illustrates the intimate relationship between Shakespeare's stage technique and meaning for the audience.

Concentrating on visual language in the plays, David Bevington in *Action Is Eloquence: Shakespeare's Language of Gesture* (Harvard UP, 1984) examines Shakespeare's attitude toward stage gesture and image. He perceives a duality: the power of these gestures and the potentially misleading nature of this visual language. Bevington attempts to develop a contrastive vocabulary of visual signals in a number of plays; he explores costume and hand properties, gesture and expression, theatrical space, and the language of ceremony. A final chapter analyzes *Ham.* Costuming symbolized an ordered world of hierarchical rank and also celebrated a festive world of release from constraints. Shakespeare's characters find something invaluably normative in the gestural language of emotion. He inherited the symbolic stage façade and formalized spatial relationships of actors; but he also used the stage space to frame a world of illusion, escape, and rebellion against authority. Drawing on other critics, Bevington argues that universal role playing in Elizabethan society provided the dramatists with a significant model for their portrayal of characters. Ceremony in the plays often serves as a focus of dramatic conflict; it may affirm meaning or threaten it. Bevington suggests that the many disruptions of ceremony call into question the very language of visual signs. Throughout this richly documented book, Bevington pursues his dialectic of seemingly fixed meaning and ambiguous transformation as seen in the visual language of Shakespeare's theater.

More historically oriented is T. J. King's *Shakespearean Staging, 1599-1642* (Harvard UP, 1971), which surveys the theatrical requirements for 276 plays first performed by professional actors in the period 1599-1642, providing a clear picture of how the plays of Shakespeare were acted by his contemporaries. King seeks positive correlations between the external evidence, architecture and pictures of early English stages, and the internal evidence, as provided by the texts. He specifically evaluates stage requirements: entrances and large properties, above the stage, doors or hangings, below the stage. There is an extended study of the staging of *TN* at the Middle Temple. Appendix A offers a valuable review of major scholarship since 1940.

Not so much historical as practical is Harley Granville-Barker's influential *Prefaces to Shakespeare*, 2 vols. (Princeton UP, 1947), which examines production problems and techniques for ten plays—three comedies and seven tragedies. In an introductory essay in the first volume the author deals with matters of Shakespeare's stagecraft, the convention of place, the speaking of the verse, the boy-actress, the soliloquy, and costume. The author focuses throughout on how a modern director or producer must solve the staging problems inherent in the text.

B. L. Joseph examines techniques of acting in *Elizabethan Acting*, 2d ed. (Oxford UP, 1964; originally 1951). This brief study provides what is known about acting in the period and Joseph's own inferences from available material. He discusses external action, speech habits, gestures, and development of character. Joseph argues that the actors were able to seem to be the very person whom they represented in performance. The speaking suited both character and style. Appearance and movement served the same two purposes simultaneously: communicate naturally what is within the imaginary character and become the creative instrument ideally suited to the needs of Elizabethan plays and audiences.

Alfred Harbage, in *Shakespeare's Audience* (Columbia UP, 1941), responds to another aspect of the theater experience. Harbage explores the kinds of evidence available that accurately reflect information about the audiences. He discusses the likely size of the audiences at the theaters, the kind of people, and their behavior. He also evaluates the scholarship on this subject. In his view the audience represented a cross section of the London population, predominantly a working-class audience. At points Harbage paints a somewhat romantic portrait of the audience, but this is a valuable book for the information gathered about economics and society.

Responding to Harbage and others, Ann Jennalie Cook, *The Privileged Playgoers of Shakespeare's London, 1576-1642* (Princeton UP, 1981), counters with a view of theater audiences as being dominated by members of the privileged class because only they had sufficient money, time, and interest to frequent the theaters regularly. Thus, the playgoers, in Cook's view, came chiefly from the upper levels of the social order. Cook offers an impressive gathering of historical facts and social analysis to establish her case. She reminds us of the privileged society's involvement with drama through education and the system of patronage. Other ways indicate how much the professional drama slanted its enterprise toward an affluent, educated, leisured clientele. Thoroughly documented, this book offers a necessary corrective to the view of theater audiences as made up of a democratic cross section of the population. Whether privileged playgoers dominated the audience, as Cook claims, remains problematical.

Other books have brought the matter of stage history up to more recent times. A standard source is George C. D. Odell's *Shakespeare from Betterton to Irving*, 2 vols. (1920; rpt., Benjamin Blom, 1963), which treats two and a half centuries of staging practices, from 1660 to the beginning of the twentieth century. Volume 1 proceeds through Garrick (1742-76). This study includes a history of the theaters but mainly emphasizes stage presentation. Arthur Colby Sprague, in *Shakespeare and the Actors: The Stage Business in His Plays (1660-1905)* (Harvard UP, 1945), deals with stage history arranged as follows: comedies, histories, *Ham., Oth., Mac.,* and the other tragedies.

J. C. Trewin, in *Shakespeare on the English Stage, 1900-1964* (Barrie & Rockliff, 1964), presents a selective survey of Shakespearean productions in the British theater since 1900. Trewin outlines theories and experiments, changes and chances. The appendixes list all Shakespeare productions for West End, 1900-1964; Old Vic, 1914-64; and Stratford, 1879-1964. The book contains a generous selection of photographs of productions and of actors.

In *Shakespeare and the Film* (J. M. Dent, 1971; rev. ed., A. S. Barnes, 1979), Roger Manvell describes and discusses the principal sound films that have been adapted from Shakespeare's plays and comments on the modification of the plays in order to make them effective films. Separate chapters examine Laurence Olivier, Orson Welles, Russian adaptations, adaptations of *JC*, Italians and Shakespeare, and theater into film. The book includes many illustrations. Though revised and updated for the 1979 paperback publication, Manvell's book does not discuss any film appearing after 1971.

In an opening chapter, Jack J. Jorgens in *Shakespeare on Film* (Indiana UP, 1977) explores the problems that beset any film maker trying to move from the text to the screen. Part of the film maker's task is to balance the "horizontal" movements (good plots, developing characters) with powerful "vertical" moments (resonant images, penetrating meditations, complex poetic patterns). Camera angles, choice of music, use of sound effects, visual spectacle, and how the verse should be spoken are all matters that the film maker must resolve. The remainder of Jorgens' book examines some major Shakespeare films, where, for example, one can gain an assessment of the success and limitations of Franco Zeffirelli's *Rom.*, the most commercially successful Shakespeare film. Peter Hall, Laurence Olivier, Orson Welles, Roman Polanski, and Grigori Kozintsev are among the prominent film makers whose work is analyzed.

FEMINISM AND GENDER STUDIES

In 1980 an important collection of essays in feminist criticism appeared, entitled *The Woman's Part: Feminist Criticism of Shakespeare,* edited by Carolyn Ruth Swift Lenz, Gayle Greene, and Carol Thomas Neely (U of Illinois P, 1980). Seventeen essays by different critics examine a wide range of topics and plays. The Introduction by the editors offers a fine summary of where feminist criticism was by the beginning of the 1980s. The editors suggest that the authors of these essays liberate Shakespeare's women from the stereotypes to which they have too often been confined; they examine women's relations to each other; they analyze the nature and effects of patriarchal structure; and they explore the influence of genre on the portrayal of women. Not only are the essays valuable but so, too, is the concluding bibliography on "Women and Men in Shakespeare." One should also consult two special issues of *Women's Studies,* vol. 9, nos. 1-2 (1981-82); both have as their topic Feminist Criticism of Shakespeare and include an assessment and categorization of feminist criticism of Shakespeare.

Believing that the drama from 1590 to 1625 was essentially feminist in sympathy, Juliet Dusinberre in *Shakespeare and the Nature of Women* (Macmillan, 1975) argues for the powerful influence of Puritanism in shaping new ideas about the position of women in society. Dusinberre sees this influence throughout the drama. She therefore asserts that Shakespeare's feminism lies in his skepticism about the nature of women; that is, Shakespeare in his drama questions received ideas about women. Dusinberre explores such major topics as the idea of chastity, the problem of equality, gods and devils, and feminity and masculinity, with some examination of the authority of women and their education. Dusinberre does not focus on individual plays for extensive treatment but rather connects appropriate parts of plays with the ideas being analyzed. Her basic idea is that the Elizabethan and Jacobean periods bred the conditions of a feminist movement, sparked by the breakdown of old ideas in religion and politics and the spirit of independence fostered by the Puritans. This important book helped define a number of issues to be confronted by other feminist critics.

Lisa Jardine, in *Still Harping on Daughters: Women and Drama in the Age of Shakespeare* (Harvester, 1983), sets out to counter an emerging orthodoxy in feminist studies, and she specifically takes aim at Dusinberre's optimistic assessment of woman's situation in the Shakespearean era. To some extent, this book is, like Dusinberre's, a historical study, trying to sketch the actual position of women, with attention also given to the fictional women in drama and elsewhere. Jardine argues that the steady interest in women in the drama does not reflect newly improved social conditions and greater possibility for women; rather, it reveals patriarchy's unexpressed worry about the great social changes that were occurring in this period. In one chapter in particular, Jardine analyzes the presumed liberating possibilities for women: Protestantism, humanist education, and marital partnership. She finds a bleaker picture than had Dusinberre, believing that little change had actually occurred in attitudes about women. Jardine's study helps make clear the difficulties of learning precisely what position women occupied in Renaissance society.

In her *Women in Shakespeare* (Harrap, 1980), Judith Cook surveys most of Shakespeare's female characters, with some emphasis on how actresses have portrayed them on the stage. Similarly,

Angela Pitt, in *Shakespeare's Women* (David & Charles, 1981), ranges through the canon, commenting on the female characters. Neither book has an all-encompassing thesis, but both have excellent illustrations. Pitt has a final chapter on Shakespeare's women on stage.

In her study of the plight of women in a patriarchal society, Irene G. Dash in *Wooing, Wedding, and Power: Women in Shakespeare's Plays* (Columbia UP, 1981) focuses on *LLL, Shr.* (Courtship); *Rom., Oth.,* and *WT* (Sexuality); and *H6-R3* tetralogy and *Ant.* (Power). Dash observes, for example, that *Shr.* questions accepted premises and offers a remarkably mature affirmation of the potential for understanding between a man and a woman. Dash's study obliges critics to abandon some stereotypical notions about the position of women in the plays, thereby opening the plays to a fresh examination and showing the multifaceted portraits of women.

Concerned with the process of maturation, social integration, self-knowledge, and various rites of passage, Marjorie Garber in *Coming of Age in Shakespeare* (Methuen, 1981) ranges across Shakespeare's canon, exploring the characters' processes of achieving maturity. Garber moves from the experience of childhood to matters of death and dying. In between she explores other rites of passage, such as sexual development, language acquisition, and marriage. Shakespeare reminds us, Garber argues, that the players are merely men and women, like ourselves, with similar stresses in development and maturation.

Marilyn French's *Shakespeare's Division of Experience* (Summit, 1981) is a feminist approach to the plays, spanning the entire canon. According to French, two gender principles govern all experience and literature: masculine and feminine. The extreme of the masculine side is the ability to kill; that of the feminine side, the ability to give birth. The masculine principle pursues power in the world and is associated with prowess and ownership, physical courage, authority, legitimacy. The masculine principle is also linear, temporal, and transcendent, attempting to construct something in the world and within time that will enable the individual to transcend nature. By contrast, the feminine principle embraces acceptance of simple continuities and identifies itself with nature. This principle also has two subprinciples: inlaw and outlaw. The outlaw category is associated with darkness, chaos, flesh, and above all, sexuality. This principle is subversive because it would undermine the masculine principle, eradicating its established structures. The inlaw feminine principle, on the other hand, focuses on the benevolent qualities of nature; founded on the ability to give birth, it includes compassion, mercy, and the ability to create felicity.

French argues that Shakespeare's comedies are feminine and the tragedies, masculine. Literature concerned with the feminine principle is circular in structure, while masculine literature is linear. Shakespeare's history plays are primarily masculine because their subject is power in the world. In the last plays the feminine principle seems to triumph. Analyzing the plays, French explores such issues as power, marriage, constancy, money, emotion, and chaste constancy in the comedies and early histories. Thus, for example, French suggests that *Shr.* concludes with a harmonious synthesis of unabused masculine and inlaw feminine principles; but it celebrates the outlaw aspect, defiance and rebellion. In the problem plays, Shakespeare scrutinized his two main ideals— female chaste constancy and male legitimacy—and found them both in some way wanting. *Tro.* and *Mac.* illustrate a world in which the inlaw feminine principle is eradicated because of devaluation. In *Lr.*, French finds Edmund, Goneril, and Regan to be "masculine" and argues that Lear himself moves from "masculinity" to "femininity." *Ant.* is unique in the canon because it presents in a positive way the outlaw feminine principle embodied in a powerful female. The Romances reassert the feminine principle; and their structures combine the linear, plotted form of the tragedies with the circular, associational form of the comedies. In these last plays powerful males learn by suffering the limits of worldly power.

Locating feminism in the critic rather than in the author or his work, Linda Bamber in *Comic Women, Tragic Men: A Study of Gender and Genre in Shakespeare* (Stanford UP, 1982) concentrates on the connection between gender and Shakespeare's different genres. She examines in detail *Ant., Ham., Mac., Cor.,* several comedies and histories, and *Tmp.* Bamber designates the feminine principle as "Other"; therefore, according to her, Shakespeare privileges the Self in tragedy and the Other in comedy—hence tragic men and comic women. In every genre the possibilities of the masculine Self and the nature of the feminine are functions of one another. Whether or not consistently a feminist, Shakespeare as author responds to the centrality of the feminine in his work. As self-judgment is the prerogative of the Self in tragedy, self-acceptance is the prerogative of the Other in comedy. The Other in Shakespeare, Bamber argues, exists for the most part as a form of external reality, an embodiment of the world and not merely a vessel for what the psyche rejects.

One dimension of Cleopatra's character, for example, views her as the Other against Antony's representation of the Self. Cleopatra is, like Shakespeare's women, a finished product, not a divided self. Her style of confronting Nature, Bamber suggests, functions from her gender. In contrast, *Mac.* and *Cor.* offer no clear example of Other, for the principal female characters are not Other to the hero. In Shakespeare's comedies, and only in his comedies, we see the feminine Other face to face; therefore, our response to the comic heroine is direct and unmediated by her father, lover, or husband. The confidence that permeates the world of the comedies derives from genre and grows out of the avoidance of a choice between serious meaning and frivolousness. Another feminine privilege in comedy avoids change and development. Bamber traces an evolutionary development of women in the histories from second-class citizen in the world of men toward a separate identity in a movement toward tragedy. In Shakespeare's last plays, the feminine Other is lost and found or dies and is reborn. But Bamber sees *Tmp.* as *postsexual;* that is, Prospero is not only bereft of the Other, he is also free of the Other. He renounces sexuality and takes control of everything.

Focusing on selected plays that span Shakespeare's canon, Marianne Novy in *Love's Argument: Gender Relations in Shakespeare* (U of North Carolina P, 1984) examines the conflict between mutuality and patriarchy and the conflict between emotion and control. Both conflicts involve the politics of gender. In the comedies and Romances, Shakespeare creates images of gender relations that keep elements of both patriarchy and mutuality in suspension, and the Romances in particular portray female resilience. Comedies, such as *Ado, AYL,* and *TN,* illustrate the mutual dependence in male/female relationships, a dependence reinforced by imagery, structure, and characterization. In these comedies, Novy argues, women's gestures of submission often balance similar gestures from the men. She explores the theme of patriarchy and play in *Shr.*, observing that Kate's behavior is a dramatically heightened version of the kind of compromise that keeps a society going. Novy finds in *MV* a criticism of the ideal of self-denial in favor of the comprehensive attitude of Portia, who is not only more assertive than Antonio but also more accepting of sexuality.

Women in the tragedies occupy a problematic position, often confined to serving as audience to the hero—*Ant.* being an exception. Men in the tragedies often have to define their masculinity by violence. *Rom.* and *Tro.* show women set in a society that deems them weak. In a tragedy like *Oth.* the combination of patriarchy and mutuality breaks down and cannot be restored. In loving Desdemona, Othello has ventured outside the man's world of war and thus become vulnerable, in danger of being ruled by emotions. *Lr.*, Novy suggests, implies criticism of the prerogatives of the father and an exploration of some behavior that patriarchy fosters. In contrast to the tragedies, the Romances illustrate the inadequacy of the traditional masculine stereotype because the male figures express their insecurity, are sometimes passive, and are more concerned about their own and others' children. The power of generation informs all the Romances, and the men uncharacteristically respond to this force of procreation. In a word, at the heart of the Romances exists a man's need for his family. In a final chapter, Novy examines how Shakespeare's use of gender and cross-gender imagery changes significantly from the comedies through the tragedies to the Romances.

Using psychoanalytic theory, Coppélia Kahn in *Man's Estate: Masculine Identity in Shakespeare* (U of California P, 1981) sets out to define the dilemmas of masculine selfhood as seen in two major problems: man's relationship to women and the problem of patriarchy, which paradoxically gives men power over women and makes them therefore vulnerable to women. Kahn proceeds chronologically, not through the Shakespeare canon, but through the ages of man from adolescence to fatherhood. Thus she ranges from *Ven.* through the history plays, to problems of marriage in *Rom.* and *Shr.*, to psychosocial meanings of cuckoldry as in *Ham.*, through incomplete men such as Macbeth and Coriolanus, and finally to the masculine quest for selfhood in the context of the family and the life cycle, epitomized in *WT.*

Shakespeare, Kahn argues, questioned matters of sexual identity, not providing neat answers but rather documenting and illustrating the struggle. Kahn's illuminating analysis underscores the importance of how the artist defined masculinity.

By examining in detail *AYL, H5, Ham., Oth., Lr., Ant.,* and *WT,* Peter Erickson's *Patriarchal Structures in Shakespeare's Drama* (U of California P, 1985) documents the pervasive social and political structure of patriarchy and its implications for the position of women. Erickson observes that male characters in the early plays powerfully resist women; there is, however, a gradual shift eventually toward a possible accommodation with women, accompanied by struggle and anguish. This shift results in part from the need to marry and establish families. The *Ham./Oth./Lr.* sequence is crucial for demonstrating the lessening of male bonding and a corresponding increase in attention focused on the male hero's bond with women. In *Ant.,* boundaries blur, and *WT* enacts the disruption and revival of patriarchy. This valuable book offers the fullest treatment of the dominant social structure in the fictional and real worlds of Shakespeare.

Examining how marriage, achieved or broken, influences the themes and structures of the plays, Carol Thomas Neely in *Broken Nuptials in Shakespeare's Plays* (Yale UP, 1985) explores in detail *Ado, AWW, Oth., Ant.,* and *WT.* Taken together, these plays encompass the whole process of wooing, wedding, and repenting; they also embody the conflicts attendant on marriage by the incorporation of broken nuptials. Neely briefly sketches marital patterns and customs in the Renaissance, and she explores fully the intricately interwoven contexts that define the meaning of women's actions in the plays. Throughout the comedies, broken nuptials counterpoint the festive wedding ceremonies. By examining several comedies, Neely shows how *Ado* extends earlier uses of the broken-nuptial motif and anticipates its darker configurations in the problem comedies and tragedies. Neely notes, for example, that male power in *Ado* remains tame and diffused. In the problem plays, women fulfill a different function: they temper the skepticism and cynicism of the plays. Sexuality in these plays—for example, *AWW*—frequently dissociates itself from marriage and procreation, as manifested in seduction, prostitution, aggressive lust, promiscuity, and adultery. The conclusion of *AWW* shows marriage not as a happy ending but as an open-ended beginning. *Oth*. illustrates the idealization and degradation of sexuality, the disintegration of male authority and loss of female power, the isolation of men and women, and the association of sexual consummation with death. Neely discusses the interaction between gender and genre in *Ant.*, with its generic boundaries expanded. The gender roles polarize sexually, emotionally, and socially within a patriarchal framework. In *Ant.* marriage loses its comic purpose of rejuvenation and its tragic status as a catalyst to self-knowledge and self-destruction. Neely analyzes the problem of incest and issue throughout the Romances, focusing on *WT*. Daughters in these plays are responsible both for protecting their chastity and choosing their own husbands. Neely sees birth as the central miracle of *WT*, a birth that leads to a restoration achieved by the rich presence and compelling actions of women. Perdita, for example, exhibits healthy relationships and helps transform the corruption of Sicily, a function that Paulina also assists.

In *Shakespeare's Restorations of the Father* (Rutgers UP, 1983), David Sundelson explores the nature and consequences of patriarchy in certain plays, ones that present the central Shakespearean pattern: not just the fall of fathers, but also their restoration; not only death and absence, but also revival and return. Sundelson also seeks to answer what makes the father's restoration so necessary. What is the larger psychological context in which the father's return plays so important a part? Sundelson concentrates on history plays (*R2* to *H4*), *MV*, *MM*, and *Tmp*. Appearance, disappearance, reappearance: this rhythm recurs throughout Shakespeare's work concerning fathers. Closeness without kinship and familiarity but not family pervade a play such as *H5*. If history is for Shakespeare an almost exclusively male affair, the comedies focus on women, an exploration of their nature, their search for selfhood and attachment. But in *MV*, fathers may be absent or feeble, defeated by law or circumstance, or simply dead; still their power is difficult to escape. At the heart of *MM* reside grave fears about the precariousness of male identity and fears about the destructive power of women. Ferdinand will marry Miranda in *Tmp.*; but the central attachment, Sundelson argues, remains between the father and daughter.

Sarup Singh, in *Family Relationships in Shakespeare and the Restoration Comedy of Manners* (Oxford UP, 1983), offers a general portrait of actual family structures as well as fictional ones, examining, for example, the changing patriarchal structure in the Renaissance. One distinguishing feature of Shakespeare's plays, Singh observes, is the open rebellion of daughters against fathers—fathers who are not willing to tolerate disobedience. Prospero's relationship with Miranda is exceptional. Generally, Shakespeare recognizes the urges of youth and the traditional role of old age, even as he reflects the inherent tensions in a patriarchal society. Examining Shakespeare's comedies, Singh concludes that Shakespeare endeavored to reconcile love and marriage. This book further explores how the later seventeenth-century drama corresponds to or differs from Shakespeare's treatment of family relationships.

Simply put, Diane Elizabeth Dreher, in *Domination and Defiance: Fathers and Daughters in Shakespeare* (UP of Kentucky, 1986), explores the complex relationship between Shakespeare's fathers and daughters in terms of its psychological tensions and the changing concepts of marriage and family during the dramatist's time. Thus, one chapter examines the historical background of family relationships in the Renaissance. Dreher also discusses the psychological perspective of these familial bonds. Essentially, Dreher argues that the conflicting tensions in Shakespeare's father/daughter relationships resolve in comedy, explode in tragedy, and transform in romance. For examples of dominated daughters, Dreher turns to Ophelia, Hero, and Desdemona—the last conforms to a static and fatal ideal of feminine behavior. But Desdemona is also defiant and therefore figures in the discussion of those daughters who resist and defy their fathers, such as Hermia, Imogen, Jessica, and Cordelia. All leave behind traditional filial obedience, affirming something new in its place. The plays uphold intelligence and assertiveness as admirable qualities in women, and Dreher examines such qualities in a chapter on androgynous daughters—Portia, Viola, and Rosalind, for example. Shakespeare's final plays emphasize the need of the fathers for balance and integration, and the daughters in these Romances serve a symbolic function in helping bring about desired harmony.

POSTSTRUCTURALISM AND NEW HISTORICISM

Two movements in criticism are having an increasing impact on Shakespeare studies: poststructuralism and new historicism (both discussed in chapter 1, the first under Analyses of Language and Imagery and the second under Historical Criticism). A collection of essays that brings together discussion of several plays from different and newer critical perspectives is *Shakespeare and the Question of Theory*, edited by Patricia Parker and Geoffrey Hartman (Methuen, 1985). The three principal critical areas are language (including deconstruction), feminism, and new historicism (with a dash of psychology). The editors also add several essays on *Ham*. The editors seek to raise for debate a whole range of central issues that reflect current critical thinking. The British equivalent of the Parker-Hartman volume is *Alternative Shakespeares* (Methuen, 1985), edited by John Drakakis. This collection of essays seeks to accelerate the break with established canons of Shakespearean criticism, offering a variety of essays that include deconstruction, new historicism, Marxism, feminism, cultural materialism, and psychoanalytic criticism. A forthcoming volume of essays, *Shakespeare and Deconstruction*, edited by David M. Bergeron and G. Douglas Atkins (Peter Lang), examines this mode of criticism, ranging across the canon. One should also refer to Joel Fineman's book on the Sonnets, reviewed earlier in this chapter, as another example of poststructuralist criticism.

Norman Rabkin, in *Shakespeare and the Problem of Meaning* (U of Chicago P, 1981), explores from a poststructuralist perspective the question of meaning. Rabkin argues that much criticism seems unsatisfactory because it seeks univocal and unequivocal meaning in Shakespeare and ignores the welter of often contradictory responses. Instead, Rabkin suggests, the critic should seek divergent and multivalent responses. According to Rabkin, meaning depends on "complementarity"—a paradox in which "radically opposed and equally total commitments to the meaning of life coexist in a single harmonious vision" (113). Meaning encompasses both the paradigm that invites us to reduce our experience and the elements that undercut the paradigm. *MV*, for example, asks us to establish a thematic center but simultaneously undermines that very center.

Although unequivocal readings deny divergent responses, they can help us understand the complexities of Shakespeare's drama by calling attention to what the critics have left out. Reductive readings of *H5* distort the play's meaning and ignore Shakespeare's recognition of the irreducible complexity of things. *H5* suggests radically opposed, contradictory responses to a historical figure about whom we expect the simplest of views. Similarly, Rabkin examines several eighteenth-century imitations and adaptations of Shakespeare's tragedies and argues that such versions, which can be seen as critical interpretations of Shakespeare's drama, attempt to offer single meaning and are, therefore, reductive. They simplify, reduce, depoliticize the original, offering clearcut choices; as a consequence, they unwittingly underscore the significant and irreducible multivalence of Shakespeare's tragedies. Finally, Rabkin argues that the Romances exhibit a different problem of meaning. Unlike the other plays, they do not tempt us to *choose* between contradictory responses but, rather, to *accept* an overlay of paradoxically contradictory patterns.

Stephen Greenblatt's several essays and his book, *Renaissance Self-Fashioning: From More to Shakespeare* (U of Chicago P, 1980), have had major influences on many new historical studies. Though not focused exclusively on Shakespeare, this book exam ines the poetics of culture and sees in Shakespeare the historical pressure of an unresolved and continuing conflict. Greenblatt finds in Shakespeare a condition of subversive submission toward the state. Also exploring the relationship of artists to the state, Jonathan Goldberg, in *James I and the Politics of Literature: Jonson, Shakespeare, Donne, and Their Contemporaries* (Johns Hopkins UP, 1983), argues that language and politics are mutually constitutive, that society shapes and is shaped by the possibilities in its language and discursive practices. Goldberg studies the relationships between authority and its representations in the Jacobean period. For Goldberg, the theater is the place in which the royal style could be most fully displayed. His focus on Shakespeare is primarily on *MM*. In the Duke, Shakespeare represents his powers as playwright as coincident with the powers of the sovereign—the clearest emblem for the relationship between literature and politics in the Jacobean period. A most helpful analysis of the movement in new historicism is Jean Howard's essay "The New Historicism in Renaissance Studies," *English Literary Renaissance* 16 (1986): 13-43.

In *Radical Tragedy: Religion, Ideology and Power in the Drama of Shakespeare and His Contemporaries* (U of Chicago P, 1984), Jonathan Dollimore explores the connections between Jacobean tragedy and its social context. Seeking to undermine religious and political orthodoxy, the Jacobean theater submitted institutions and all means of "ideological legitimation" to "sceptical, interrogative and subversive representations." The theater employs "subliteral encoding," namely parody, dislocation, and structural disjunction, to by-pass censorship. Dollimore focuses on a number of non-Shakespearean tragedies, in addition to *Tro.*, *Lr.*, *Ant.*, and *Cor.* He discusses political, social, and ideological contradictions in *Tro.*, a play that offers a prototype of the "modern decentred subject." *Lr.* is, above all, a play about power, property, and inheritance. Rejecting both the Christian and the humanist interpretations of this play, Dollimore argues that *Lr.* shows man decentered. The play also rejects pity as a means for man to redeem himself, ultimately denying closure and recuperation. *Ant.* and *Cor.* both question the "martial ideology" and expose the contradictions inherent in this ideology. A collection of eleven essays in *Political Shakespeare: New Essays in Cultural Materialism* (Cornell UP, 1985), edited by Jonathan Dollimore and Alan Sinfield, points the way to an interpretation of Shakespeare that emphasizes politics and power—the problems for the state of containment, subversion, and consolidation and what role literature plays in these sociopolitical events. Such an approach ranges across all parts of the canon, not just history plays.

Concerned with how Shakespeare represents power, Leonard Tennenhouse, in *Power on Display: The Politics of Shakespeare's Genres* (Methuen, 1986), demonstrates ways in which a new historicist approach may reinterpret the drama. Simply put, he argues that the plays participated in the political life of Renaissance England; thus, political imperatives were also aesthetic imperatives. Rather than merely reflecting political life, the theater, Tennenhouse suggests, was a place where political events occurred and where history was produced, giving rise to spectacles of power. To write about courtship and marriage, as in the early comedies, was to take up a political argument. *MND* declares that the theater has the power to create the illusion of a community out of the contradictory bodies of authority. The final scene in *Shr.* gives Kate real political power for the first time. *MV* demonstrates the political importance of writing. These early comedies transfer power to the aristocratic female. *TN* presents another variation. Tennenhouse explores how the carnival spirit helps bring about change and reveals a struggle for power.

The author uses both *H8* and *Ham.* to show that the figures organizing materials for the stage also shaped policies of state. This intention leads Tennenhouse into a discussion of some history plays, such as *R2* and *R3*. Indeed, the history plays turn on the use of materials of carnival, and they demonstrate that power rests with those who can seize the symbols and signs that legitimize authority. With *Ham.* the Elizabethan strategies for authorizing monarchy become problematic. Analyzing *Lr., Mac., Oth.,* and *Ant.,* Tennehouse focuses on the determinant components of Jacobean drama: kingship versus kinship; natural versus metaphysical bodies of power; the signs and symbols of state versus the exercise of state power. In some of these plays, Shakespeare takes the signs and symbols of legitimate authority and inverts them. In the Romances the paternally organized family provides the occasion not for resistance but for spectacular displays of patriarchal authority. Tennenhouse provides much historical background and also examines a number of plays by Shakespeare's contemporaries.

INTERDISCIPLINARY STUDIES

MUSIC

In the past two decades scholars have paid increasing attention to the relationship between music and Shakespeare's drama. Some studies have dealt with the specific use of song in the plays, whereas others have tried to locate sources of the songs or find the original settings. As a result, we have considerably more information about the music in Shakespearean drama. F. W. Sternfeld reviews twentieth-century scholarship on music in his part of the larger essay "Twentieth-century Studies in Shakespeare's Songs, Sonnets, and Poems," *Shakespeare Survey* 15 (1962): 1-10. Another interesting essay is D. S. Hoffman's "Some Shakespearean Music, 1660-1900," *Shakespeare Survey* 18 (1965): 94-101.

The earliest studies only hinted at what has eventually become known about the music. Edward W. Naylor, in *Shakespeare and Music,* rev. ed. (1931; rpt., Da Capo & Blum, 1965; originally 1896), discusses technical musical terms of the period, as well as instruments, musical education, songs and singing, dances, music of the spheres, and the use of musical stage directions. This elementary book has a descriptive rather than an analytic approach to the function of music in the drama. Of a different order, Richmond S. Noble's *Shakespeare's Use of Song, with the Text of the Principal Songs* (Oxford UP, 1923) presents the word-text and extensive information on each song in the plays but includes no music. He credits Shakespeare with most of the songs.

One of the principal contributors to a study of music is John H. Long, whose three books have added much information to our knowledge of music in the drama. His first book, *Shakespeare's Use of Music: A Study of the Music and Its Performance in the Original Production of Seven Comedies* (U of Florida P, 1955), briefly surveys songs and instrumental music in Elizabethan drama and offers discussion of *TGV, LLL, MND, Ado, AYL, MV,* and *TN.* Music as a dramatic device not only intensifies the impact of language; it also forwards the action, the portrayal of character, delineation of settings, and creation of atmosphere. Long sees three phases in these comedies: (1) music signals the presence of critical or climactic situations; (2) it serves as sedative, countering intense (tragic) moments (*MV, Ado*); and (3) it experiments, weighing the advantages of stylistic use of music and its naturalistic use. In this and the other two books, Long incudes a bibliography.

In *Shakespeare's Use of Music: The Final Comedies* (Florida, 1961), Long deals with *Shr., Wiv., AWW, MM, Per., Cym., WT,* and *Tmp.* Again he seeks to determine the functions of the performed music, the manner of performance, the original musical scores (where possible), and significance. The music in these plays underscores crucial scenes, makes the supernatural perceptible, and synthesizes abstract or psychological ideas.

The final volume, *Shakespeare's Use of Music: The Histories and Tragedies* (Florida, 1971), examines all of the history plays except *Jn.,* all of the tragedies, and *Tro.* The histories use music primarily in its public, social, and ceremonial vein; hence the music is largely instrumental. Vocal music in the tragedies consists almost entirely of bits of ballads or parts of old popular songs, in contrast to the comedies, which generally have art songs or complete lute songs. Long argues that the use of music in the tragedies suggests that Shakespeare saw tragedy as an intense vision of inner conflict and mental and physical destruction.

A major study that focuses on the tragedies, F. W. Sternfeld's *Music in Shakespearean Tragedy* (Routledge & Kegan Paul, 1963) contains a critical discussion and facsimile reproductions of available songs or likely ones (scores of the original songs). He discusses the tradition of vocal and instrumental music in tragedy, including mainly the non-Shakespearean drama. Two chapters deal specifically with the complexity of Desdemona's "Willow Song" and with Ophelia's songs. Sternfeld believes that Robert Armin was the principal musician-actor in the dramatic company. Two chapters deal extensively with instrumental music. Chapter 10 has a "retrospect of scholarship on Shakespeare and music" (up to about 1960). This book includes an extensive bibliography and helpful indexes—for example, the index of lyrics and a dictionary catalogue of the songs in all of Shakespeare's plays.

Peter J. Seng's *The Vocal Songs in the Plays of Shakespeare* (Harvard UP, 1967) serves basically as a reference book that endeavors to bring together all the relevant material on the vocal songs in the plays. The material proceeds as follows: (1) headnote giving the source of the text (Folio or quarto) and the song's location in that text, as well as act, scene, and line number in modern editions; (2) the text of the song exactly reproduced from the earliest authoritative edition; (3) general critical commentary arranged according to date (what critics have said about it); (4) textual commentary (glosses with comments from various scholars as to the meaning); (5) information about music for the song (earliest known source if any); (6) information about sources for the song or any analogues to the particular song (words, not melody); (7) observations about the dramatic function in the play. A bibliography of both primary and secondary sources appears at the end of the book.

Several books examine more generally music in the Renaissance and may be of interest to researchers. Bruce Pattison, in *Music and Poetry of the English Renaissance* (Methuen, 1948), demonstrates the relationship between the lyric and poetry; he defines the various musical forms—madrigal, air, ballad, and so on. John Stevens, *Music and Poetry in the Early Tudor Court* (Methuen, 1961), provides good background material. This book focuses principally on the early sixteenth century; one chapter deals with music in ceremonials, entertainments, and plays. Gretchen L. Finney's *Musical Backgrounds for English Literature: 1580-1650*

(Rutgers UP, 1962) approaches music as a philosophical concept (speculative music). Wilfrid Mellers, in *Harmonious Meeting: A Study of the Relationship between English Music, Poetry, and Theatre, c. 1600-1900* (Dobson, 1965), includes two chapters specifically on Shakespeare: "Music in the Shakespearean Theatre" and "Masque into Poetic Drama," which deals with *Tmp.*

CULTURE

Several types of interdisciplinary studies can be gathered under the heading of "culture," including investigations into the philosophy of the period and cultural and political history. E. M. W. Tillyard's *The Elizabethan World Picture* (Chatto & Windus, 1943) has become one of the classic summaries of the intellectual milieu. In this brief book Tillyard outlines common beliefs of the Elizabethan period, demonstrating that the English Renaissance was not so much a reaction against medieval ideas as a subsuming and appropriation of them. Tillyard emphasizes the hierarchical, ordered universe, illustrated from the works of many different kinds of writers and thinkers. The Elizabethans, according to Tillyard, perceived order in three forms: the Chain of Being (a design of order stretching from God through inanimate objects), a series of corresponding planes (macrocosm/microcosm, body politic/macrocosm, and so on), and a Cosmic Dance. Tillyard's assessment emphasizes this optimistic, ordered world to the exclusion of the new, contrary voices becoming prevalent at the end of the sixteenth century.

Similarly, Hardin Craig, in *The Enchanted Glass: The Elizabethan Mind in Literature* (Oxford UP, 1936), analyzes the philosophical background of the Elizabethan period. He establishes the cosmology and identifies man's position in it, emphasizing the importance of reason. Craig attempts to define the characteristic reactions of the Elizabethan mind, the discussion of which reveals the problem of interpreting Elizabethan literature.

Theodore Spencer shows something of the other side of the coin in *Shakespeare and the Nature of Man,* 2d ed. (Macmillan, 1961; originally 1942). In the first two chapters, especially relevant for the intellectual background, Spencer describes the ideal picture of man, the optimistic theory of order and hierarchy, based on the concept of universal order and law, with man the center of such a world. Opposing voices existed; and Spencer traces them to three general areas: new science, Copernicus, and others; new politics, epitomized in Machiavelli; and new morality, apparent in the writings of Montaigne. All of these forces question the premise of universal order. The remainder of the book offers interpretations of various plays, viewing them, partly, in light of the Renaissance intellectual conflict as they come to terms with the nature of man.

These new matters of conflict receive extensive treatment in Hiram Haydn's *The Counter-Renaissance* (Scribner's, 1950), a lengthy intellectual history of the movement that ran counter to the received, medieval world view of the ordered, hierarchical world. The counter-Renaissance originated as a protest against the basic principles of the classical Renaissance, as well as against those of medieval Scholasticism. All of its strands, whether science, morality, or politics, argued for a repeal of universal law; it was relativistic and pragmatic. Haydn discusses the various manifestations of this collective movement and assesses the Elizabethan reaction to it; he sees them as much more responsive and attuned than Tillyard does. In a final chapter Haydn specifically examines Shakespeare, focusing on *Ham.* and *Lr.* He finds Shakespeare very aware of this countermovement, as he used a number of its ideas for dramatic purpose, whatever Shakespeare's personal beliefs may have been. C. S. Lewis, in *The Discarded Image: An Introduction to Medieval and Renaissance Literature* (Cambridge UP, 1964), defines common philosophical beliefs of the medieval period, their derivation, and their perpetuation into the Renaissance. In his final chapter Lewis assesses the influence of this model of the ideal world.

Believing Scholasticism and Neoplatonism to be the two dominant Renaissance approaches to philosophy, Walter Clyde Curry in *Shakespeare's Philosophical Patterns* (Louisiana State UP, 1937) discusses both. He interprets *Mac.* in light of the former and *Tmp.*, the latter. Though not a systematic philosopher, Shakespeare does seem to have possessed a comfortable and accurate knowledge of the basic principles of the two philosophical systems dealt with here. This book concerns itself with the reconstruction of philosophical traditions and with Shakespeare's use of them. Roland M. Frye discusses religious philosophy more explicitly in *Shakespeare and Christian Doctrine* (Princeton UP, 1963).

Frye first deals with the contrasting critical approaches to Shakespeare: theological analysis (epitomized by G. Wilson Knight) and secular analysis (A. C. Bradley). (Frye's focusing on Knight has been justly criticized.) Part 2 of the book concerns the historical background of sixteenth-century theology in order to give a more precise view of the theological inheritance of Shakespeare. The final part analyzes the dramatist's theological references, arranged by topics. Frye attempts to steer a course between the excesses of either side, both of which he finds to be basically uninformed about historical theology. He especially takes to task, for excesses in the "Christian" approach, J. A. Bryant, Jr., *Hippolyta's View: Some Christian Aspects of Shakespeare's Plays* (UP of Kentucky, 1961). Frye's book functions by and large as a sensible corrective.

Several books will give students a sound introduction to the political and cultural history of the period. Two volumes in the Oxford History of England series are appropriate. J. B. Black, in *The Reign of Elizabeth, 1558-1603,* rev. ed. (Clarendon Press, 1959; originally 1936), focuses on the political and social history of the Elizabethan period and includes a chapter on "Literature, Art and Thought"; he includes an extensive bibliography. In a companion volume, *The Early Stuarts, 1603-1660,* 2d ed. (Clarendon, 1959; originally 1937), Godfrey Davies discusses political and constitutional history, as well as social and economic history. He also includes separate chapters on the arts and on literature, with a bibliography.

Two books by A. L. Rowse specifically concern cultural history. *The Elizabethan Renaissance: The Life of the Society* (Macmillan, 1971) contains chapters on the court, the role of the gentry, class and social life, food and sanitation, sex, custom, witchcraft, and astrology. And in *The Elizabethan Renaissance: The Cultural Achievement* (Macmillan, 1972), Rowse portrays the cultural life of the age with chapters on drama, language, literature, and society; words and music; architecture and sculpture; painting; domestic arts; science and society; nature and medicine; and mind and spirit (philosophical).

SOURCES

Another area that brings one into the realm of interdisciplinary or intercultural studies is that of Shakespeare's likely sources or major influences from various literatures and cultures. Such an investigation involves not only source hunting but also a consideration of how the dramatist used these likely sources for dramatic purposes. Certainly one measure of Shakespeare's artistic achievement derives from setting his source alongside the drama to see how they differ.

For students doing research in Shakespeare's sources, the major work of scholarship that must be consulted is the eight-volume *Narrative and Dramatic Sources of Shakespeare* (Routledge & Kegan Paul; Columbia UP, 1957-75), compiled by Geoffrey Bullough. This monumental work includes an extensive introductory essay on the sources and then the texts of the possible or probable sources and analogues where appropriate. The volumes proceed as follows: 1, early comedies, poems, and *Rom.;* 2, comedies, 1597-1603, through *MM;* 3, earlier English history, *H6, R3,* and *R2;* 4, later English history, *Jn., H4, H5,* and *H8;* 5, Roman plays; 6, other "classical" plays, *Tit., Tro., Tim.,* and *Per.;* 7, major tragedies, *Ham., Oth., Lr.,* and *Mac.;* 8, the Romances, *Cym., WT,* and *Tmp.* Bullough adds a useful bibliography in these volumes.

Several books designed primarily for students provide source materials for selected plays. For example, Alice Griffin, ed., *The Sources of Ten Shakespearean Plays* (Crowell, 1966), includes the source texts for *Rom., Shr., H4, H5, JC, TN, Oth., Mac.,* and *Ant.* The texts use modernized spelling and punctuation. Joseph Satin, ed., *Shakespeare and His Sources* (Houghton Mifflin, 1966), offers modernized texts of the sources for *R3, R2, MV, H4, H5, JC, TN, Ham., Oth., Lr., Mac.,* and *Ant.* Richard Hosley's edition *Shakespeare's Holinshed* (Putnam's, 1968) deals with one particular source: the 1587 text of Holinshed's *Chronicles* for all the history plays and *Lr., Cym.,* and *Mac.* Hosley cites not only the page number from Holinshed but also the appropriate section from the plays, cited by act, scene, and line number.

In *Shakespeare's Sources: Comedies and Tragedies* (Methuen, 1957), Kenneth Muir interprets Shakespeare's use of sources. Muir finds no discernible pattern about how Shakespeare worked or used his sources throughout the comedies and tragedies; the dramatist seems, instead, to have come to each play individually. In all, Muir considers twenty plays, discussing the likely sources, Shakespeare's use of them, parallels, and comparisons.

Believing that the study of the use of sources provides an invaluable clue to Shakespeare's art and thought, Virgil Whitaker, *Shakespeare's Use of Learning: An Inquiry into the Growth of His Mind and Art* (Huntington Library, 1953), pursues the argument throughout the canon. Whitaker argues that Shakespeare grew in learning while he developed as a playwright, and this progress as a dramatist depended to a considerable extent on his increased learning. The attempt to understand the growth of the dramatist's mind focuses on his use of sources. The methodology examines first the plays that have a clearly defined source and then looks for occurrences of allusions to the learning of his day and their importance to the play. The intellectual development apparently led to a fundamental change in his method of building his plays from his sources: first he followed rather closely the source, and then he reshaped drastically in order to make the action reveal characters that illustrate or conform to philosophic concepts (for example, *Mac.* and *Lr.*). One may not want to go quite as far as Whitaker's argument, but this imposing study reminds us again of Shakespeare's apparently immense learning.

A number of scholars have been especially concerned with the dramatist's dependence on or knowledge of classical literatures and traditions. An edition of one source can be found in T. J. B. Spencer's *Shakespeare's Plutarch* (Penguin, 1964). This text follows the 1595 folio edition of Plutarch's *Lives* as translated by North. Spencer presents here the lives of Julius Caesar, Marcus Brutus, Marcus Antonius, and Martius Coriolanus. The notes at the botton of the pages make the links to the plays.

J. A. K. Thomson, in *Shakespeare and the Classics* (Allen & Unwin, 1952), argues for the two greatest classical sources: Plutarch's *Lives* and Ovid's *Metamorphoses,* familiar to Shakespeare through Elizabethan translations. Thomson sees in Plutarch, in fact, a model for Shakespeare's tragic form. He discusses the poems and plays individually and their indebtedness or treatment of classical story. Without an index, this book remains somewhat difficult to use.

In her study *Shakespeare and the Greek Romance: A Study of Origins* (UP of Kentucky, 1970), Carol Gesner deals with the Greek romances and their tradition and with Shakespeare's use of them, culminating in the full-fledged use of Heliodorus and *Apollonius of Tyre* in the final Romances. In *Per.*, *Cym.*, *WT*, and *Tmp.* we see the ancient genre deliberately utilized and lifted to new dimensions, turned to a new vision of reality. Gesner argues that Greek romance served as a major fabric of Renaissance narrative and drama and functioned as a source and an influence on Shakespeare.

An older book, in need of revision, is Robert K. Root's *Classical Mythology in Shakespeare* (Holt, 1903). After an Introduction in which Root assesses Shakespeare's use of mythology, principally drawn from Ovid, the major part of the book consists of an alphabetical listing of the mythological characters in Shakespeare. The book includes discussion of these characters, references to them, and likely source of the story or quality being alluded to in a play or poem. Root also lists Shakespeare's works individually, with a brief summary of the mythology involved in each.

Two studies explore in some detail the dramatist's reliance on the Bible. First, Richmond Noble, in *Shakespeare's Biblical Knowledge* (Society for Christian Knowlege, 1935; New York: Macmillan), considers both Shakespeare's general and his specific knowledge of the Bible. Noble also discusses the version of the Bible available to Shakespeare, as well as the Book of Common Prayer. Primarily the book lists allusions and parallels for each play (except *Per.*); but it also includes a useful list of Biblical proper names, identified and cross-referenced to the plays in which they appear. An index of books of the Bible, with all the plays listed by act and scene, that quote or paraphrase that particular book of the Bible, proves helpful also.

Of a different sort, James H. Sims's *Dramatic Uses of Biblical Allusions in Marlowe and Shakespeare*, University of Florida Monographs, Humanities no. 24 (U of Florida P, 1966), explores Shakespeare's dramatic use of the Bible. In the comedies the misuses and misunderstandings of scripture add to the ludicrous element and sometimes provide insight into particular characters. The Biblical echoes make the audience conscious of the moral and spiritual order of the universe. In the histories and tragedies, Shakespeare underscores theme and foreshadows action by Biblical allusion. Sims includes a useful bibliography.

PERIODICALS

Some periodicals especially relevant for Shakespearean studies have been mentioned earlier in this chapter. In the journals cited, students will find many essays on particular Shakespearean topics, as well as other helpful materials. Since 1948, Cambridge University Press has published *Shakespeare Survey,* an annual publication now edited by Stanley Wells. In volume 11, students will find a helpful index to volumes 1-10; similarly, in volume 21, an index to volumes 11-20. In addition to essays on particular plays or poems, each issue includes annual reviews of the year's contribution to Shakespearean study, arranged under three topics: critical studies; life, times, and stage; and textual studies—exceptionally valuable reviews of recent studies. *Shakespeare Quarterly,* founded in 1950 by the Shakespeare Association of America, has since 1972 been published by the Folger Shakespeare Library. Its annual bibliography has already been cited. The forerunner of this journal was the *Shakespeare Association Bulletin,* published from 1924 to 1949, volumes 1-24. The annual publication *Shakespeare Studies,* begun in 1965, edited by J. Leeds Barroll, contains reports on research, critical essays, and book reviews. Louis Marder has since 1951 edited and published the *Shakespeare Newsletter,* which presents news items, abstracts of articles, essays, and dissertation digests, plus other features.

Periodicals not specifically devoted to Shakespeare also contain valuable information. *Studies in Philology* has always contained essays on Shakespeare; from volume 19 (1922) through volume 66 (1969) it included a Renaissance bibliography, with a section on Shakespeare. Begun in 1961 at Rice University, *Studies in English Literature* devotes one of its four issues, usually the spring number, to Elizabethan and Jacobean drama in which essays on Shakespeare frequently appear. Usually a review article may include Shakespeare items. *Research Opportunities in Renaissance Drama,* begun in 1956 and edited by David M. Bergeron, occasionally has articles, check lists, or other materials relevant to Shakespeare, though primarily it focuses on his fellow dramatists.

BIOGRAPHICAL STUDIES

Students who wish to investigate the life of Shakespeare will find few facts available but a plenitude of theories. Despite the relatively small number of facts about his life, we actually know more about Shakespeare than about most of his contemporaries. Parts of his life remain tantalizingly vague even after four centuries. Charles Sisson presents a summary of some of the biographical studies in his essay "Studies in the Life and Environment of Shakespeare since 1900," *Shakespeare Survey* 3 (1950): 1-12. Students will find quite helpful G. E. Bentley's *Shakespeare: A Biographical Handbook* (Yale UP, 1961), a sensible, quite readable basic summary of the dramatist's life. Bentley discusses such topics as the nature of Shakespearean biography in the seventeenth and twentieth centuries; legends; Anti-Stratfordians; Shakespeare in Stratford and London; Shakespeare as actor, playwright, and nondramatic poet; the printers; and Shakespeare's reputation. Bentley includes a bibliography, as well as a list of books and documents from which he quotes.

More extensive research would take one to E. K. Chambers's massive *William Shakespeare: A Study of Facts and Problems,* 2 vols. (Clarendon, 1930). Volume 1 contains chapters on Shakespeare's origin, the stage in 1592, Shakespeare and his company. Volume 2 is primarily a reprinting of all the records that Chambers could find pertaining to Shakespeare's life—nearly 200 pages. Chambers reproduces the records and comments on them; topics covered include the grant of arms, christening, law suits, marriage, epitaphs. Biography is much too narrow a term to describe what these volumes contain, for they provide a collection of materials rather than a straight narrative biography. In a much briefer account, *Sources for a Biography of Shakespeare* (Clarendon, 1946), Chambers discusses the records (court, national, legal, municipal), allusions, and traditions that provide materials for a life of Shakespeare.

One of the early standard biographies is Joseph Quincy Adams, *A Life of William Shakespeare* (Houghton Mifflin, 1923). This is, in fact, the first substantial American biography and the first major biographer to emphasize the place of the theater in Shakespeare's life, that is, to place him in the context of the theater world. As a consequence, many of the chapters discuss matters of the theater. Though frequently reprinted, this biography needs to be checked against more recent ones. A good, reliable biography is F. E. Halliday, *The Life of Shakespeare* (Duckworth, 1961), who breaks down the life into segments of certain years. A more specialized study is Mark Eccles's *Shakespeare in Warwickshire* (U of Wisconsin P, 1961). This intensive study focuses on the life in Warwickshire, Shakespeare's home country. Eccles traces family relationships of the Shakespeares and the Ardens, the neighbors in Stratford, the school in Stratford, Anne Hathaway, gentlemen and players in Stratford (dramatic performances), Shakespeare at New Place, and Shakespeare's friends.

The most controversial biographer has been the historian A. L. Rowse. His first study, *William Shakespeare: A Biography* (Macmillan, 1963), though a substantial biography by a renowned historian, adds no new information to what we already had. What has alienated many literary scholars is Rowse's tone and boastful claims. He believes that only a historian, such as himself, could unravel the mysteries of Shakespeare's life, especially the problems of the Sonnets. He dates the Sonnets 1592-95, names the earl of Southampton as the young man and Marlowe as the rival poet. The only problem that he could not solve then was the identity of the dark lady. But historical method or no, Rowse has not solved the "mysteries" of the Sonnets. Beneath all the drum beating and tub thumping comes a rather hollow sound.

In 1973 Rowse came back to the subject with *Shakespeare the Man* (Macmillan, 1973), which bears many striking resemblances to his earlier book. The major contribution is Rowse's "discovery" of the identity of the dark lady, a problem that had previously been elusive. He claims that she is one Emilia Lanier. With characteristic immodesty Rowse says: "For the first time we can now write a three-dimensional biography of William Shakespeare." Conveniently, this discovery corroborates all his previous theories. Rowse suggests that this new book "puts out of court all the biographies of Shakespeare." Rowse's much-celebrated historicity aside, he can be quite romantic as he analyzes the life; for example, he sees Prospero as Shakespeare bidding farewell to the stage. But the epitome comes on the last page of the book where we learn of Shakespeare's final memories as he lay dying, with the chapel bell tolling in the background; not surprisingly, Shakespeare remembers Emilia in his final earthly vision. Obviously, no historical records substantiate such an analysis.

One of the nagging problems in Shakespearean biography has been that hardy group of denigrators who raised questions about the authorship of his plays, sometimes referred to as the Anti-Stratfordians. No doubt the general public is still teased by the possibility that one William Shakespeare did not write the plays generally ascribed to him. Suffice it to say, there is no evidence to support such a view; but such perversity continues to rear its head. This problem has been adequately dealt with in H. N. Gibson's *The Shakespeare Claimants* (Methuen, 1962). Many claimants have been put forward, but Gibson focuses on the four principal ones: Francis Bacon, the Oxford syndicate, Lord Derby, and Marlowe. He finds no convincing argument and certainly no evidence recommending any of these positions. About half of this book examines the "evidence" common to two or more of the theories. The book includes a brief bibliography. In *The Mysterious William Shakespeare: The Myth and the Reality* (Dodd, Mead, 1984), Charlton Ogburn devotes nearly 800 pages to arguing for the authorship by the earl of Oxford.

Another book that deals with such problems and many more is S. Schoenbaum's *Shakespeare's Lives* (Clarendon, 1970). This book reviews and analyzes the many Shakespeare biographies, including the "Deviations," that is, the Baconians and others. The first seventy pages or so deal with the materials for a life of Shakespeare, reviewing the evidence that we have. The remainder evaluates and describes the biographical ventures, from comments in the seventeenth century through Rowse's 1963 biography. The book is divided more or less along historical lines—for example, the Victorians, the twentieth century, and so on. The book, written with verve and enthusiasm, also demonstrates great learning. Students will find it extremely interesting and easy to use. Another book by Schoenbaum, *William Shakespeare: A Documentary Life* (Clarendon and Scolar, 1975), emphasizes facts. One of the unusual features of the book is the inclusion of the Shakespeare records, manuscripts and print, in facsimile, the facsimiles joined to the text. A certain amount of material is not strictly biographical but is of interest to biographers: sketches of Holy Trinity Church in Stratford, prospects of Stratford, panoramas of London, and so on. In all there are about 220 facsimiles. Students will find this book, produced by an outstanding authority, a delight to look at and to read. Two years later, Schoenbaum and his publisher provided an abridged version, entitled *William Shakespeare: A Compact Documentary Life* (Oxford UP, 1977). Minus many of the illustrations of the larger book, this handy and reliable guide to Shakespeare's life has become the standard one to consult, assaying as it does the myths and facts of the poet's life.

A sequel to the *Documentary Life,* Schoenbaum's *William Shakespeare: Records and Images* (Oxford UP, 1981) contains 165 facsimiles and illustrations of documents and pictures pertaining to Shakespeare's life and career. Here one can see examples of Shakespeare's handwriting, the Shakespeare forgeries, facsimiles of the Stationers' Register records, and, especially interesting, the various portraits of Shakespeare. This beautifully produced book offers a priceless treasure of photographic reproductions.

Upsetting some notions of biography and chronology, E. A. J. Honigmann in *Shakespeare's Impact on His Contemporaries* (Macmillan, 1982) questions assumptions about Shakespeare's life and the dating of his plays. He also assesses Shakespeare's reputation among his contemporaries, especially Ben Jonson. The idea of a sweet and gentle Shakespeare, Honigmann suggests, is, in part, the fabrication of bardolatry; a very different man, sharp and businesslike, appears in some of the principal life records. The most unambiguous evidence of Shakespeare's preeminence during his lifetime derives from the exceptional number of surreptitious publications based on his plays. Honigmann devotes considerable attention to the relationship between Jonson and Shakespeare and their relative artistic standing; and he concludes, contrary to some scholars, that Shakespeare enjoyed the higher reputation. Reassessing the chronology of the early plays, Honigmann pushes them back a few years, some into the late 1580s. He also argues that Jonson was the rival poet in the Sonnets and that *WT* in part responds to Jonson's criticism of Shakespeare's art. Honigmann offers a challenging evaluation of evidence and assumptions about Shakespeare's life and works, much of it passed on unquestioningly by earlier scholars.

Honigmann continues his search in the most recent book to grapple with Shakespeare biography, his *Shakespeare: The 'Lost*

Years' (Manchester UP, 1985). Honigmann tries to pin down the whereabouts of Shakespeare before 1592 and concludes that Shakespeare spent time in the early 1580s in Lancashire, in the employ of the Houghtons and then the Heskeths as a schoolmaster. Because these families were Catholic, Honigmann argues that so was Shakespeare, at least during this period of his life, only to change later. In Lancashire, Honigmann suggests, Shakespeare got his start as an actor, and eventually he came to serve Lord Strange and became associated with his acting company. Admittedly a highly speculative book, it must nevertheless be considered seriously by any future biographer. Honigmann's superb detective work often convinces.

CHAPTER THREE
The Research Paper

Preparing a research paper on a Shakespearean topic may strike fear into the hearts of many students, but it need not. This book has already provided access to many of the tools that can help in doing research on Shakespeare. After all, there is nothing especially mysterious about research procedures; they are not rituals reserved for the holy few who have fathomed them. Our daily lives contain many examples of research as we sift through conflicting newspaper accounts or editorials, as we try to determine which is the better product to buy. The process consists largely of gathering evidence and drawing inferences.

Considering the monumental amount of material published on Shakespeare, and no end is in sight, one feels frustrated just contemplating launching an investigation. But this book cuts through at least part of the material. Students frequently complain that there is nothing new to be discovered or said; probably every generation of students has reached this conclusion, believing, quite wrongly, that all Shakespearean materials have been discovered and that the final critical word has been uttered. And as surely as we look back to the nineteenth century with some smugness at its apparent naïveté about Shakespearean matters, the next century will doubtless come to regard us as a bit quaint, if not altogether wrong. Students preparing undergraduate research papers need not think that their function is to say something original about Shakespeare or to unearth some previously hidden fact about Shakespeare's life.

Briefly, the research paper is an investigative, formal essay with a thesis or argument. Its style should be concise without being cryptic; its form should have adequate documentation without drowning in a sea of pointless notes. The paper and the research process itself constitute in part an exercise in logic and sound thinking. The paper should be persuasive and convincing and also creative and imaginative. Unfortunately, research papers often have a bad name among students, as if they are something that sooner or later one must endure and, like most illnesses, survive. Contrary to common myth, the creative energies needed to produce a successful paper can be as rigorous as writing a poem or a short story. It is not altogether perverse to suggest that a research paper can be fun. Certainly producing such papers may be one of the most valuable learning experiences that students can have during their formal training.

Doing the research involves both a trustworthy method and maximum efficiency. Some students waste incalculable hours in helpless wandering about in a library, not knowing where to head. Again, this book should offer enough guidance so that students can make efficient use of their effort. The process of research can be applied to other endeavors, becoming indeed one of the most useful tools that students can gain. Research consists of more than methodology, though it must contain that; it is also hard work—it must involve sufficient commitment of time and resources. The final product is, of course, greater than the sum of its parts. Students should feel some exhilaration at finishing such an assignment, at having grappled with an intellectual problem, resolved it, and given it some coherent shape. Perhaps more than anywhere else in our academic procedures, having to do a research paper forces one to grow and mature as an analytical thinker.

For additional assistance or information, students can consult textbooks on composition and rhetoric for discussion of the research paper and other matters of style. Some colleges have developed their own style manuals and guides to research. Note and bibliographical form suggested below corresponds to that outlined in the manual published by the Modern Language Association of America, *MLA Handbook for Writers of Research Papers,* second edition (1984). Because scholarly journals devoted to literature and some university presses regularly adhere to the *MLA Handbook,* students will profit by learning and following this guide. If it is unavailable in the college bookstore, one may purchase a copy from the Materials Center, Modern Language Association, 10 Astor Place, New York, N.Y. 10003.

SELECTING A TOPIC

Grandiose, sweeping topics often characterize the beginning researcher as he or she sets out to make the world safe for Shakespeare. But unless one is developing a book-length study, ambitions must be scaled down. Naturally one starts with the larger idea; the twin processes of thinking and research will lead to a narrowing of the subject. The matter of a topic may be decided for you by your instructor, who may assign the project to be worked on; your instructor may suggest general approaches to a research study of Shakespare, or you may be left to your own devices. Where to start becomes then a matter of paramount importance.

To oversimplify, three broad areas exist for research topics in Shakespeare: his life and times, the plays or poems themselves, and textual problems. What do we know about Shakespeare's close links to his hometown of Stratford, the place to which he always returned despite his popularity and success in London? What do we know about Shakespeare's children or his son-in-law, John Hall, the well-known physician in Stratford? Certain parts of Shakespeare's life before he arrived in London remain a mystery. What theories have scholars proposed? What about Shakespeare as a wealthy man of property? Who were Shakespeare's companions or fellow dramatists? The nature of the theater itself affords many topics for investigation.

The plays and poems offer almost limitless possibilities. Generally, such broad topics as Shakespeare's tragic vision or the nature of Shakespearean comedy should be avoided because these require book-length development. But more narrowly focused topics within those broad concepts can work; for example, how *A Midsummer Night's Dream* is a comedy. Different approaches can be followed. Certainly an investigation of how critics have treated a particular play or dramatic character is both manageable and valuable. You might want to examine themes, images, language, or structure. Shakespeare's Sonnets remain a rich area for investigation. Here research into what the critics have theorized about the possibly autobiographical nature of the Sonnets could be fascinating, revealing, perhaps, more about the critics than about Shakespeare.

The textual problems of the early editions of Shakespeare's plays and Sonnets can be especially perplexing and probably should not be approached by beginning students, though advanced Shakespeare students may find some possible topics with which they can deal. Textual matters often necessitate a highly specialized knowledge. But you might, for example, undertake a generalized study of how eighteenth- and nineteenth-century editors approached the Shakespearean text, or do research into who were the most notable early editors. The nature of the Elizabethan printshop, government regulations and censorship, the matter of copyright, the relationship of author to printer—all are worthwhile topics as they shed light on Shakespeare's texts.

In any event, you must select some kind of topic, no matter how vaguely defined it may be at the moment. Whatever the initial choice, it should not be whimsical or altogether arbitrary; it should be grounded in some knowledge, however slight, of the subject. Topics picked out of thin air often yield exactly that. Many of the materials discussed earlier in this book suggest possible topics. At least three criteria should be kept in mind: you must be reasonably sure that there is adequate material available for your subject (usually one faces the opposite problem in working on a Shakespearean problem); the topics must be susceptible to adequate treatment within the limits of the paper, determined either by you or your instructor (a five-page paper on "style in Shakespeare" is preposterous, whereas a similar length paper on the light/dark imagery in *Romeo and Juliet* may work); the proposed investigation must be interesting to you. This last point, while obvious, cannot be overemphasized; for if you are bored with your topic, the chances are quite good that your reader will be also. In choosing a topic, you basically evolve a working hypothesis that you take with you to your investigation in order to give that effort some shape and direction. The clearer the topic, the more efficient the research can be.

DEVELOPING A TOPIC

Assuming that a topic has been chosen, then what? If you have chosen to work on one of the plays or some of the poems, you must thoroughly familiarize yourself with those works of art. This is absolutely crucial. Only with a firm grasp of the basic material can you go forward to develop a topic. No matter what topic has been chosen, reading and studying the pertinent matter in a reliable edition of Shakespeare will help the pursuit greatly.

As some ideas about the topic begin to take shape, jot them down on a work sheet so they won't be lost, even if later they are discarded. Already the original concept may begin to be modified in some way. Occasionally, students find that their final thesis bears little resemblance to the first idea, and this is not necessarily undesirable. Many things happen along the way in the process of thinking about and investigating the subject. After all, you should approach the whole project with an open mind. Often the subject seems to choose the researcher, rather than the other way around.

You might now venture to the library with a specific and limited purpose: namely, to do additional background reading. A good place to start might be with *The Reader's Encyclopedia* and other such collections of information cited earlier in this book. If you are working on a problem in criticism, you might read appropriate parts of Mark Van Doren's *Shakespeare,* a book that never fails to provide insight into the plays or Sonnets, even if you do not finally agree with Van Doren's analysis. But his essays are brief and pithy. This guide offers you access to many other books that may generally or specifically pertain to your topic. The point is to begin to gain sufficient familiarity with the critical terrain so that you may wisely pursue investigation. In a real sense you begin to get some feel for the subject. Then, and only then, are you prepared in an intelligent and informed way to launch your full-scale work.

PREPARING A WORKING BIBLIOGRAPHY

To prepare a bibliography and to take notes will, of necessity, send you to the library. Despite the best efforts of teachers, many students unfortunately remain intimidated by the library. A humbling sense of awe at the knowledge contained within the materials in a library is understandable; but it makes just as much sense to view the library as a potential place of enjoyment, pleasure, and learning. Far too many students complete their undergraduate education without having come to terms with the library, some claiming, in fact, never to have been in it. Some of this regrettable attitude has to do, one supposes, with myths perpetuated among generations of students. After all, scholars are supposed to be gray-headed, slightly stooped old men, with terrible coughs engendered by the dust from the books, who only occasionally emerge into the real world. Such a portrait constitutes a travesty of what a researcher is. Scholars come in all sizes, ages, shapes, genders, and temperaments. The library may be for Shakespeare students what the laboratory is for those in scientific disciplines. Armed with this book, you should have some reason to feel a degree of confidence.

As you begin to work in the library, record on 4 x 6 index cards or something similar all potential sources, *using one entry per card;* this method provides an efficient way of keeping up with the references. Information on the card should include the author's full name (last name first), the exact title of the book or essay, place of publication, publisher, and date of publication. It is useful to record in the upper left-hand corner the library call number. Two examples illustrate the procedure:

| book: | PN 2592 B4 | Bentley, Gerald Eades. *The Jacobean and Caroline Stage.* 7 vols. Oxford: Clarendon Press, 1941-68. |

| article or note: | PR 2885 S63 | Boswell, Jackson C. "Shylock's Turquoise Ring." *Shakespeare Quarterly* 14 (1963): 481-83. |

Cards containing references to sources not actually used in preparing the paper can be discarded; the remaining ones will help prepare the final bibliography or list of Works Cited.

Information for the working bibliography can come from at least four places: (1) obviously, this book would be one place to begin. The books analyzed here on the tragedies, comedies, Romances, histories, Sonnets, and other topics may provide a number of possibilities. But of course, this book makes no attempt to cite thousands of essays published in scholarly journals, and these will prove to be of great value.

(2) You would then need to consult in the library the standard bibliographies on Shakespeare (listed in the section on reference sources in chapter 2), especially the annual bibliographies found in the MLA Bibliography and in *Shakespeare Quarterly*. To use the *SQ* bibliography most efficiently, you should consult the indexes provided in it. Other more generalized bibliographies can help also.

(3) The library's card catalogue will provide titles of books on Shakespeare and confirm whether it has the books you have already begun to list. Most catalogues are arranged alphabetically according to author, title, and subject. The subject classification under Shakespeare, if well done, can be of considerable help. The call number for the book is usually placed in the upper left-hand corner; this indicates where the book is located on the shelves in the library. Most libraries now use the Library of Congress classification system, but some still use the Dewey Decimal system. Without trying to penetrate the mysteries of either system, you need only realize that the number tells you where to find the work. Librarians are often themselves great storehouses of knowledge and should be consulted if you need assistance.

(4) Another place, often overlooked, to find valuable references is in the books and essays that you read. The notes and bibliographies included in these discussions will point the way to other materials. Having canvassed at least these four areas for resources, you are now ready to begin reading and sifting through the materials to determine what you need to help you develop your paper.

TAKING NOTES

The initial temptation of all beginning researchers is to take too many notes, a wholly natural impulse which can be conquered only through experience. But if you must sin, do so in the direction of too much, not too little. As painful as it may seem, it will be easier in the long run to discard a few notes rather than repeat some of the research effort in order to get sufficient information.

One safeguard against excessive note taking comes from reading and rereading the material so that you can better judge what is important, what is truly note-worthy. Thus, you should read the entire essay or portion of the book before taking notes; then on a separate scratch sheet, you should jot down page numbers for those passages that seem important at first glance. Some students choose to photocopy whole essays or portions of books. Without getting into the issues of possible violations of copyright, suffice it to say that photocopying cannot replace careful reading and analyzing of the material to determine if it truly contains something worthwhile. A mound of photocopies does not constitute research; it reflects money spent and possible laziness. It may, of course, on occasion reflect time saved. But postponing the process of sifting through the material carefully may not in the long run save time.

Finding something important, you can do one of at least three things in making a note card: (1) quote the comment directly from the printed page and enclose it in quotation marks, inserting ellipsis marks (three spaced periods) for anything deleted; (2) paraphrase the statement; or (3) summarize the argument very briefly, perhaps simply to note that this critic opposes another critic, whose view is already recorded. Different circumstances will demand different techniques. As a beginning researcher, you may find it more efficient to use direct quotations; if so, quote accurately.

Notes should be written in ink on 4 x 6 cards, one piece of information per card. Recording information in a notebook may ultimately be inefficient because the material cannot be easily filed or shuffled about. On the first line of the card on the left indicate the *author* of the statement (this assumes that a separate bibliography card will be made); then, in the middle, a word or phrase to reveal the *subject* or topic; and on the right, the appropriate *page number*. There is nothing particularly sacred about this system, but it works fairly well; more experienced researchers may devise some other method.

The samples below demonstrate the technique:

> Smidt—   Changes in text of *R2*—   p. 89
>
> "Such confusions and omissions—and there are others—reinforce the impression derived from a study of the larger movements of plot and theme that *Richard II* underwent some major changes of design in the course of its shaping. Stage adaptation and condensation would account for some, but certainly not all, of the irregularities."

Paraphrase:

> Smidt—   Changes in text of *R2*—   p. 89
>
> Confusions and omissions in the text of *R2* indicate that the play underwent major changes of design, only some of which can be accounted for by stage adaptation and condensation.

Summary:

> Smidt—   Changes in text of *R2*—   p. 89
>
> Smidt argues that *R2* underwent many changes of design and that only some of them may be attributed to stage adaptation or condensation.

Taking good notes is as much an art as it is a science. And your whole project will come to naught if your notes are sloppy, inaccurate, or irrelevant.

OUTLINING THE PAPER

History contains many students (and others) who prepare an outline of their papers *after* the writing has been completed—usually to satisfy the teacher or a requirement. Human nature being what it is, this situation will never change completely; but it does reveal a failure to understand the function of an outline. It also, no doubt, grows out of students' scarred past, when they were required to produce outlines and thus grew quickly to detest them. Admittedly, making outlines for hypothetical subjects should be an exercise reserved for the idle. For an outline to have any efficacy or justification as part of the total writing process, it must be tied to a concrete, immediate need.

Constructing an outline requires no mystical insights. An outline is simply a practical tool in the process of organizing a paper— no more, no less. In many ways it becomes the acid test of the whole process of thinking about the subject, investigating, and taking notes. The outline constitutes the skeletal structure for the logical development of the paper. Presumably you have jotted down ideas along the way, but the evidence collected through research provides the major basis for your conclusions and for the structure of the argument of the paper. If you cannot produce an outline that is logical and coherent about the subject, then something has gone wrong—either your thinking has been fuzzy or your evidence is inadequate in some way.

Develop either a sentence outline or a topic outline; in any event, you should simply produce one that best suits your needs. At a minimum, the outline should contain a statement of your thesis (the argument, the main idea) that the paper sets out to develop, and a logical organization usually set up in the following manner:

Thesis statement
Introduction
I.
  A.
  B.
    1.
    2.
II.
  A.
  B.
  C.
III.
  A.
    1.
    2.
  B.
Conclusion

This structure suggests that the paper has three main ideas (represented by Roman numerals I, II, III) with subcategories under them. Logical development of ideas determines why the sequence is as it is—Why, for example, does point III come where it does? Does it naturally follow point II? (Obviously the paper may have a varying number of developed ideas, largely dependent on the subject and the length of the paper.) The outline should be taken seriously, not because it has some special significance in and of itself but because it serves as a means to an end—the logical organization and presentation of the paper.

WRITING THE PAPER

The ultimate test of research comes in the ability to communicate the findings in some persuasive, comprehensible form, usually in writing; research has limited value if no one else ever learns of the results or understands them. To negotiate the various procedures suggested here successfully and then to fail to produce an effective paper means failure. To shuffle the note cards, organize the ideas, but then bore people to death by the paper is unforgivable. All the skills of good writing must prevail in the research paper. One myth that should be discarded is that scholarly writing must be dull if it is to be respectable—not that one need go in for stylistic fireworks either. Imaginative writing embraces clarity and forcefulness.

One problem that often besets the inexperienced researcher and writer is how to achieve the right balance between reliance on sources and one's own ideas. A research paper is not a string of quotations, the proverbial "scissors-and-paste job" in which the writer provides only an occasional transitional phrase or connective. Instead, the paper amalgamates the writer's ideas with selected documentation, used either for corroboration and support or for refutation. The writer is not a reporter; he must demonstrate his synthesis and analysis of the materials on the subject, and he must exhibit his own conclusions in a forceful and effective manner. As in all good writing, one cannot divorce form from content.

Because quotations will be used, several matters of form should be considered. If you are quoting one or two lines of poetry, run them on within the text of the paper and enclose them in quotation marks. Two lines of verse should be separated by a slash, as in "Down, down I come, like glist'ring Phaeton, / Wanting the manage of unruly jades." More than three lines of verse should be indented (usually ten spaces) from the left margin; *no* quotation marks are needed. Quoted prose passages of fewer than four prose lines should be run on in the text. Longer passages should be set off and indented from the left margin; again, no quotation marks. Unless you are instructed otherwise, all quoted material should be double-spaced. After the edition of the play or poem has been established in a note or parenthetical documentation, you can simply locate other quoted material from the play in parentheses by citing act, scene, line numbers or line number for a poem. Examples: As Sebastian says, "This is the air; that is the glorious sun" (IV.iii.1). In Sonnet 60, Shakespeare writes, "Like as the waves make towards the pebbled shore, / So do our minutes hasten to their end" (1-2). The first example presupposes, of course, that the writer has already indicated that he is discussing *Twelfth Night.* Style manuals, such as the *MLA Handbook,* offer additional instruction about matters of form in writing the paper.

Writers and painters of the Renaissance depicted Truth as the daughter of Time, and on a very practical level that seems worth remembering for the research paper. To enable a sensible, intelligent argument grounded in evidence (Truth) to emerge in your paper, you must allow sufficient time to bring this about. Nerve-wracking, desperate last-minute efforts seldom achieve satisfactory results. The key to much of this is pace, determining how long you should spend on the various steps along the way. You should allow enough time so that you can write a rough draft of the paper, put it aside for a few days, and then try again. Sometimes a little detachment can reveal startling things about our own flaws and confusion in a paper. But the paper prepared by dawn's early light on the due day offers no time for reflection; it barely affords time for the ink to dry.

DOCUMENTATION

Whether quoted directly, paraphrased, or summarized, any material that you borrow from others will need some kind of documentation to indicate where you got your information or ideas. Such procedures reveal the nature and extent of your research and obviously give credit to others. By careful documentation you provide your readers with access to additional resources beyond your paper. You also reflect an indebtedness to a community of scholars and critics.

Two basic systems of documentation prevail at the moment. What follows attempts to epitomize what is more extensively dealt with in the *MLA Handbook*. Please consult it for problems not covered here. Your instructor may make special requirements about how to handle documentation. The two systems are: (1) parenthetical documentation and (2) notes. Each system may contain something of the other; in some ways each is the inverse of the other.

Simply put, parenthetical documentation means that you cite within parentheses in the body of your paper whatever reference you need; such references get full bibliographical treatment in a Works Cited list. The other system includes footnotes or endnotes that come at the end of the paper, revealing the specific references that you have made. This system may include a separate Bibliography or List of Works Consulted, if the instructor so requires. The instructor may also express a preference about which system to follow. In any event, you will need to choose one or the other.

Parenthetical Documentation

This system has two parts: parenthetical references within the body of your paper and a separate list of Works Cited, to which your references are keyed. Several variations are possible in your parenthetical references, depending on how you refer to the sources. For example:

1. A direct quotation, naming the source and page in parentheses: [your paper]: "No conventional language of word or gesture seems able to convey the enormity of the family's tragic experience" (Bevington 31). [Bevington refers to the author and his book listed in your Works Cited, and 31 refers to the page number for the direct quotation.]
2. The same quotation but citing the author in your sentence: Bevington says that "no conventional language . . ." (31).
3. A summary of the same quotation: again you can either cite

author and page in parentheses or name the author in your sentence and put the page number in parentheses.

4. To cite a multivolume work, give the volume number, colon, and page reference: (Bentley 2:5-6).

5. Two or more works by the same author:
Bevington in his *Action Is Eloquence* says that . . . (55). Bevington says that . . . (*Action Is Eloquence* 55).
[Here use appropriate short title of the work.]

6. Citing literary works:
[your paper]: Polixenes describes his son to Leontes: "He's all my exercise, my mirth, my matter" (*Winter's Tale* I.ii.166).
[If it is already clear that you are discussing *The Winter's Tale*, simply cite act, scene, line number(s); your Works Cited will indicate what edition of the play you use.]

These examples cover the probable requirements for documentation in critical research papers; again, consult the *MLA Handbook* for additional examples.

Works Cited

Having made documentation within your paper, then you need to construct a Works Cited list, an alphabetical listing of sources referred to in your paper. This double-spaced list comes at the end of your paper on separate sheets. Each entry typically has three main parts: author, title, and publication information, each part set off by a period. The first line of the entry is flush with the left margin; subsequent lines are indented five spaces. The last name of the author comes first.

1. A book by a single author:
Bevington, David. *Action Is Eloquence: Shakespeare's Language of Gesture*. Cambridge: Harvard UP, 1984.
[The full title is given, with the subtitle preceded by a colon. The *MLA Handbook* recommends that the abbreviation "UP" be used for "University Press."]

2. Two or more books by the same author:
Frye, Northrop. *Anatomy of Criticism: Four Essays*. Princeton: Princeton UP, 1957.
- - -. *The Secular Scripture: A Study of the Structure of Romance*. Cambridge: Harvard UP, 1976.

[The three hyphens indicate that this item is by the same author cited immediately before.]

3. A book by two or more persons:
Kay, Carol McGinnis, and Henry E. Jacobs, eds. *Shakespeare's Romances Reconsidered.* Lincoln: U of Nebraska P, 1978.
[Only the first name is reversed; a comma separates the names. If there are more than *three* authors, name only the first and add "et al.".: Edens, Walter, et al., eds. *Teaching Shakespeare.* Princeton: Princeton UP, 1977.]

4. A multivolume work:
Bentley, Gerald Eades. *The Jacobean and Caroline Stage.* 7 vols. Oxford: Clarendon, 1941-68.
[List the total number of volumes, whether you have used all of them or not.]

5. An edition.
Shakespeare, William. *William Shakespeare: The Complete Works.* Gen. ed. Alfred Harbage. Baltimore: Penguin, 1969.

6. An unpublished dissertation:
Smith, Mary Allen. "Shakespeare's View of Tragic Women." Diss. U of Kansas, 1985.

7. An essay within a collection:
Yoch, James J. "Subjecting the Landscape in Pageants and Shakespearean Pastorals." *Pageantry in the Shakespearean Theater.* Ed. David M. Bergeron. Athens: U of Georgia P, 1985. 194-219.

8. A later edition or reprint:
Partridge, Eric. *Shakespeare's Bawdy.* 2nd ed. London: Routledge, 1968.
Bradley, A. C. *Shakespearean Tragedy.* 1904. London: Macmillan, 1968.
[In the second example this is a reprint of the same text, not a revised or altered edition. Indicate original date of publication, then cite the copy that you are using.]

9. Essays in periodicals:
Greenblatt, Stephen. "Invisible Bullets: Renaissance Authority and Its Subversion." *Glyph* 8 (1981): 40-61.
[The name of the journal is followed by the volume number, year of publication, and then inclusive page numbers.]

10. A signed review:
Bergeron, David M. Rev. of *Art and Power: Renaissance Fes-*

tivals 1450-1650, by Roy Strong. *Renaissance Quarterly* 39 (1986): 401-02.

In the parenthetical works cited system of documentation, two reasons exist for also having notes (placed at the end of the paper on separate sheets): (1) for additional bibliographical information; and (2) for further explanation of points that cannot be fully dealt with in your paper.

In the body of your paper, the note number (a superscript Arabic number placed slightly above the line) comes after the final mark of punctuation. Thus: [your paper] Many critics have debated the staging of medieval drama.[1]

On your notes page, you then cite the necessary information:
[1]The following critics have argued for a fixed, single stage on which the plays were performed: . . . .
[First line indented five spaces; subsequent lines flush with left margin.]

Notes System

Simply stated, the Notes system places bibliographical information about works being quoted or used in some way at the end of the paper on separate sheets. Thus, the body of your paper would record the reference thus:

[your paper]: One critic observes: "If similarities in design and execution are an indication of closeness in time *King John* and *Richard II* must be near companions."[1]

Then, on a separate Notes page:
a. A book.
[1]Kristian Smidt, *Unconformities in Shakespeare's History Plays* (London: Macmillan, 1982) 86. [In this system the first name comes first, then the last name, followed by title and publication information, set off in parentheses, followed by the page to which you refer. The first line of the note is indented 5 spaces; subsequent lines are flush with the left margin. Commas replace periods for separating units of information in the Notes.]
b. An article in a periodical.
[2]Jeanne Addison Roberts, "The Merry Wives: Suitably Shallow, but Neither Simple nor Slender," *Shakespeare Studies* 6 (1970): 110.

[Here 6 indicates the volume of the periodical; the year of publication is in parentheses, followed by a colon and the page that you cite.]

c. A multivolume work.

³Gerald Eades Bentley, *The Jacobean and Caroline Stage*, 7 vols. (Oxford: Clarendon, 1941-68) 2:115.

[This includes the total number of volumes. After the publication information, indicate which volume and page(s) are being cited.]

d. An edition.

⁴William Shakespeare, *William Shakespeare: The Complete Works*, gen. ed. Alfred Harbage (Baltimore: Penguin, 1969) II.ii.33.

[Assuming that you are quoting from the text, indicate act, scene, line number(s). You should then add a sentence indicating that all quotations come from this edition; then cite the remaining quotations parenthetically within your paper. Thus in the paper: Richard II says: "Arm, arm my name" (III.ii.86).]

If you have already cited a work in a note, then use shortened references to it thereafter. Thus:

⁵Smidt 75.

If there is more than one work by the same writer, then use a shortened form of the title in the note. Thus:

⁶Smidt, *Unconformities* 78.

Even in the notes system, feel free to use parenthetical documentation when it would be clear to your reader what work you are citing, as in the reference above to a quotation from *Richard II*.

If required, you will want to construct a Selected Bibliography or List of Works Consulted, placed on separate sheets after your Notes and arranged alphabetically. The advantage is that this lets the reader get a fuller picture of your research than may be apparent in your Notes. The form of the references in such a bibliography follows that of the "Works Cited," indicated above.

Your paper should be typed on 8 1/2-by-11-inch paper and be double-spaced throughout. Page numbers go in the upper right-hand corner, 1/2 inch from the top. Generally, leave 1-inch margins on all sides, unless given other instructions. Do not underline or put in quotation marks the title of your essay.

PLAGIARISM

In its simplest definition, plagiarism is stealing. And with regard to papers, plagiarism refers to the use of the ideas or words of another person without giving that person credit.

Plagiarism may spring from carelessness, ignorance, or dishonesty. Of the last, not much can be said, because it involves a willful act of stealing. Students bear the responsibility of being both sufficiently accurate and sufficiently informed so that they will not inadvertently commit plagiarism. Borrowing material from a copyrighted source without giving credit is, of course, illegal.

How can you avoid accidental plagiarism? First, by taking very careful notes. By so doing, you run less risk of confusing the author's words or ideas with your own. In the research paper itself, the problem can be avoided by carefully documenting all borrowed material, unless, of course, the matter is common factual information. Sometimes students mistakenly believe that if they change a word or two or generally tinker with the author's style, then they may claim it for their own—nothing could be farther from the truth because the original idea is still the author's. Obviously no defense exists for using direct quotation and not citing the source. Even ideas gleaned from class lectures and used by you in a paper ought properly to be cited, giving credit to the person who voiced the ideas. Again factual information, such as the date of Shakespeare's birth, for example, need not be documented. Experience will go a long way toward making clear when and how to document; the guidance of instructors and style manuals will also assist.

A MODEL RESEARCH PAPER

What follows is an example of a research paper, illustrating how one can be put together and demonstrating several matters of form. You may be required to include a title page, an outline, or other materials. This example simply begins with the title page, followed by the text, but it does include appropriate documentation.

All the Forest's a Stage

David Paul Fidler
English 332
23 April 1986

When one visits Stratford to pay homage to the great poet and dramatist, there is a twinge of sorrow to see that the forest of Arden no longer exists. Thanks to decades of encroaching civilization, we have to imagine what the forest of Shakespeare's childhood and later life looked like. For us, Arden can only exist in our minds. Our efforts to visualize Arden might be guided by our knowledge of *As You Like It,* which takes place mostly in Arden. The initial picture we form of the Arden of *As You Like It* is a "pastoral" picture. Perhaps our attempts to visualize the Arden of Shakespeare's day can be enlightened by an understanding of how Shakespeare uses pastoral in *As You Like It.* Curiously, nowhere in *As You Like It* does a "traditional" pastoral world appear. Shakespeare uses the literary heritage of the pastoral, but he questions that heritage and attempts to present a new pastoral idea.

A popular theme in Renaissance literature sees the pastoral world as providing a haven and regenerative stimulus for virtue. In works such as Sidney's *Arcadia* and Spenser's *Faerie Queene* (Book VI), the authors create a pastoral world that stands apart as an alternative world to that of the court. One critic describes the Renaissance pastoral world as

> . . . an innocent world where the sun always shines and the shepherd inhabitants pass their time playing their pipes, competing in eclogues, and wooing their mistresses. The pressures of society, the obligations of work, are not there and man and nature are in accord with each other. (Evans 36)

Many pastoral "alterations," however, exist in the works of pastoralists. Spenser's pastoral world of *Faerie Queene* Book VI includes night and day, hard work, and vulnerability to the "civilized" world. Pastoral tinkering, however, does not affect the essence of a pastoral world: a place for the nourishment and growth of human virtue. Hallet Smith writes: "The central meaning of pastoral is the rejection of the aspiring mind. The Shepherd demonstrates that true content is to be found in this renunciation" (10). Although some shepherds, such as Tamburlaine, do not thus belong in a pastoral world, the dominant characteristic of most pastoral worlds derives from their existence as an alternative world to the pressure- and vice-ridden courtly world. The pastoral world exists as a world that can be escaped to or retreated into, even if the escape or retreat is only temporary.

Shakespeare, aware of the tradition of pastoral when he introduces Arden in *As You Like It,* does not begin, however, with a strictly Renaissance pastoral; instead, he goes back to Ovid and the Middle Ages. Charles the wrestler informs Oliver and the audience that the old usurped Duke now lives in the

> . . . Forest of Arden, and a many merry men with him; and there they live like the old Robin Hood of England. They say many young gentlemen flock to him every day, and fleet the time carelessly as they did in the golden world. (I.i.107-11)

Shakespeare chooses to link the notion of an Ovidian golden world with the legend of Robin Hood. In a strictly logical sense, an outlaw and the golden world are incongruous. If Shakespeare had wanted to depict a perfect golden world, he might simply have followed his source—Thomas Lodge's *Rosalynde*—more closely (Lodge 5:16). In rejecting the pastoralism of Lodge, Shakespeare shows his different approach to the pastoral.

Arden, then, initially becomes a Sherwood Forest and the golden world rolled into a kind of virtuously defiant paradise. Charles's vision of Arden is an unusual description in pastoral literature. The Robin Hood allusion is important not only because it links Robin Hood and Duke Senior but also because the mention of Robin Hood with the golden world brings two pastoral heritages together.[1] When Ovid and Robin Hood join, the audience recognizes that the court sees Arden as a pastoral world. But the unusual description leaves us unsure about the nature of that world.

The key to comprehending Shakespeare's approach lies in the relationship between characters and Arden. When we look closely at the play, we notice that Shakespeare creates not one distinct Arden but a series of individual Ardens. These Ardens reflect the various personalities of the characters. Shakespeare, I believe, suggests that psychology and its expression through language constitute the heart of the pastoral tradition.

Hazlitt once wrote that:

Shakespeare has here converted the forest of Arden into another Arcadia, where they "fleet the time carelessly, as they did in the golden world." It is the most ideal of any of this author's plays. (qtd. in Halliday 201)

As we have already seen, Shakespeare has not created another Arcadia. The virtuously defiant paradise that Charles describes can only be interpreted as an individual opinion, an individual creation. Since the corruption and wickedness of Oliver and the new Duke Frederick enhance the magical and mythical vision that Charles has described, our desire to partake of Arden increases as we suffer through the rottenness of vice's persecuting virtue at the court. An alternative to the court world exists. Unlike Lodge's details, Shakespeare makes Charles imply more than he states. The pastoral world is at the mercy of a character distant from and ignorant of the world that he believes exists. Even with this in mind, though, we are eager to see if appearance is reality as we plan with Rosalind and Celia to escape the wickedness of the court and enter Arden.

When we finally see Arden, reality takes on a different shape from appearance. In II.i, we hear Duke Senior talking about Arden. Senior's Arden, however, is not the Arden we expected on the basis of Charles's description. In one respect, the forest world of Senior satisfies our expectations: "Hath not old custom made this life more sweet / Than that of painted pomp? Are not these woods / More free from peril than the envious court?" (II.i.2-4). But then Duke Senior talks of "the icy fang / And churlish chiding of the winter's wind" (II.i.6-7), which does not correspond to the eternal spring of the golden world. Although Arden is an English golden world, Shakespeare introduces the biting breeze of winter to show that the Duke cannot ignore or wish away the harsh elements and the hard life of living in a forest. The Duke's noble and virtuous personality, however, turns these discomforts into benefits: "Sweet are the uses of adversity" (II.i.12). Duke Senior finds "tongues in trees, books in the running brooks, / Sermons in stones, and good in everything" (II.i.16-17). His language emphasizes a spirit of optimistic transformation, and his Arden reflects that spirit. Judy Kronenfeld observes:

> Shakespeare does present the Duke as a model of pastoral
> virtue; at the same time, however, he underscores those
> aspects of the Duke's behavior that suggest a perfor-
> mance, a pastoral masquerade. (337)

As a blast of icy wind and the sting of adversity dispel the golden
world creation, the Renaissance pastoral world that replaces it
must be created by Duke Senior, making the pastoral Arden peculiar to his personality.

The one member of the Duke's party who is not merry is
Jaques, and his Arden reflects a melancholy and almost bitter
man. The sight of a wounded deer triggers Jaques to comment
on his idea of Arden, reported by one of the other lords:

> Yea, and of this our life, swearing that we
> Are mere usurpers, tyrants, and what's worse,
> To fright the animals and kill them up
> In their assigned and native dwelling place. (II.i.60-63)

We can interpret Jaques's melancholy as the depression he suffers
as a result of the loss of his ideal of the golden world. Jaques's
melancholy temperament results from his absolutism: nothing
but perfection will satisfy his spirit. The logical conclusion would
be that Jaques is creating an antipastoral world. Like Duke Senior,
Jaques creates an Arden that links organically to his personality.
Jaques and the Duke live in the same forest yet live in very different forests. Shakespeare gives creative powers to his characters,
bringing the pastoral closer to the subjectivity and idiosyncrasies
of individual psychologies and away from the literary pastoral
tradition.

Examples illustrate my point. Touchstone, who creates an
Arden that is a base, crude wasteland and—to him—far inferior
to the life at the court, could never be happy in the pastoral
world of Sidney, Spenser, or Duke Senior. The nourishment of
virtue emphasized in traditional pastorals remains a useless idea
to a man who cares nothing for virtue but embraces ease and
luxury. The court is Touchstone's pastoral world because in the
court Touchstone finds happiness. His language constantly criticizes and belittles notions of "higher things," whether they be
Arcadian forests or romantic relationships: "Ay, now am I in

Arden, the more fool I. / When I was at home, I was in a better place . . ." (II.iv.14-15). Whereas Sidney, Spenser, Lodge, and other pastoralists create a pastoral wrapped in a virtuous atmosphere, Shakespeare allows his characters to cloak Arden in whatever pastoral garb suits them best, thereby drawing us closer to the characters. Shakespeare in *As You Like It* is something of a radical pastoral writer. He probes the pastoral world further in his use of what critics usually call the "obviously" pastoral characters—Corin, Silvius, Phebe, and Audrey.

Corin, for example, does not view his existence in Arden as "pastoral" in the idealized sense. Arden, to Corin, partly symbolizes his serfdom; and he is all too willing to sell his master's property for gold. As he makes the transaction, we cannot help but sense that the world of Arden is not separate and distinct from the civilized world. If so, why then does an economy and exploitation exist within its verdant boundaries? In the distinct pastoral world of Spenser's *Faerie Queene* Book VI, the idyllic world is ruined by an attack from without, from the Brigants who inhabit a different world. With Corin, we see that Arden is part of the "real" world, as is the court; the minds of the characters create a "regenerative" green world from what seems just a forest, plain and simple.

Phebe, on the other hand, exposes her discontent with her life in Arden by rejecting Silvius's ardent wooing. Phebe is a simple shepherdess who is not very beautiful ("What though you have no beauty . . ." [III.v.37]). I find it revealing that she rejects Silvius but immediately falls in love with the figure of Ganymede (Rosalind) in III.v: "Dead shepherd! now I find thy saw of might, / 'Who ever lov'd, that lov'd not at first sight?' " (III.v.80-81). Phebe, it can be argued, falls in love with Ganymede because Ganymede represents to her something new and exciting, something that will rid her of the shepherd trappings that she wears day after day. Like Silvius, she is dissatisfied with her rustic existence and craves something more from life. Her idealized world becomes union with Ganymede. Here we see the supposedly pastoral characters displaying atypical pastoral behavior: they have "aspiring minds."

What about Orlando and Rosalind, the most virtuous characters in the play? Orlando and Rosalind do create Ardens, and the Ardens that they create are far from traditional. Once again,

Shakespeare concentrates on letting the character create a world for happiness, instead of letting a literary tradition create a happy character. Orlando creates two Ardens to fulfill his needs for happiness: a Hobbesian Arden and a Petrarchan Arden. The Hobbesian Arden comes from Orlando's heroic side. When Orlando and old Adam struggle into the forest in II.vi, almost starved to death, the language that Orlando uses indicates that he sees Arden as a dangerous and very harsh place: "uncouth forest . . . savage . . . bleak air . . . desert." We in the audience, having seen all the other Ardens, view the creation of a Hobbesian Arden with delight because Orlando goes into his dramatically heroic high gear, characteristic of his personality:

> If this uncouth forest yield anything savage, I will either
> be food for it or bring it for food to thee. . . . For my
> sake be comfortable; hold death awhile at the arm's
> end. (II.vi.6-9)

Orlando creates his own heroic melodrama to energize his heroic spirit. Orlando's psychology demands that he at times see life in the forests as "poore, solitary, nasty, brutish, and short" (Hobbes 186). Orlando is a creative hero who enhances his dilemma and energizes his heroic abilities with his attitude and language. Orlando, therefore, as a result of the heroic need in his personality, creates a Hobbesian Arden when challenged.

Orlando's other Arden, the one he creates when not being heroic, seems a Petrarchan forest in which he romantically (and somewhat foolishly) expresses his love for Rosalind. As Ganymede tells Orlando:

> There is a man haunts the forest that abuses our young
> plants with carving 'Rosalind' on their barks, hangs odes
> upon hawthorns, and elegies on brambles. . . . (III.ii.
> 339-42).

Just like his heroic side, Orlando's romantic, loving side never does things half-heartedly or stoically. Orlando's psychology flares dramatically in all that he does. His two Ardens reflect the heroic and the loving aspects of his personality. The synthesis of Orlando's forests occurs when he saves his brother Oliver's life by battling the lioness. Orlando would never survive the tranquillity and simple routine of traditional pastoral life; hence, his "pastoral" world comes alive with energy, extremes, emotion, and dramatics.

Of the inhabitants of Arden, Rosalind seems least concerned with creating a personal forest. Rosalind's personality does not need a traditional pastoral world, for she is content with reality. Rosalind finds happiness by juggling the pressures of "this working-day world" (I.iii.12) into a tempered balance. Her pastoral world is whatever world she finds herself in, because her psychology finds fulfillment in controlling the moment and skillfully preparing for the future. Rosalind's motto is "a woman's thought runs before her actions" (IV.i.127-28); and Rosalind lives up to her motto with tempered, reasonable actions backed by a strong will and a quick wit. Her pastoral becomes the most relative of them all because she finds happiness in whatever world she lives in: happy in the court with Celia, although she suffered the banishment of her father; happy in the forest, testing and loving Orlando. In terms of Shakespeare's pastoral idea of individual happiness, Rosalind's pastoral becomes the ultimate pastoral because it is not a particular pastoral at all. That is, Rosalind can find happiness in any world; so all the world, to Rosalind, is a pastoral.

In *As You Like It,* then, the heart of the pastoral tradition for Shakespeare is the creative search for happiness present in each individual. The profusion of Ardens in the play parallels the many distinct and rich characters we find in the forest. Shakespeare has changed the notion of the pastoral from a concept created by a poet for characters and readers to a concept in which the characters and the readers create their own pastorals in the search for happiness. We must now alter Smith's "central meaning" of the pastoral from the "rejection of the aspiring mind" to the utilization of the creative spirit in the search for happiness.

All the forest, then, in *As You Like It* is a stage where the characters create their worlds and act within them. Jaques seems to find his metaphor to be a pessimistic outlook on life; but in *As You Like It,* when the forest becomes a stage, life comes alive in a "rich tapestry" of human experience. In making the pastoral the pursuit of happiness, Shakespeare frees the creator in all of us. So, when we look out over the farmland of Warwickshire, trying to imagine the Arden of Shakespeare's time, we should keep in mind Shakespeare's conception of the pastoral in *As You Like It;* then we can feel free to create Arden, and any other personal world, as we like it.

Note

¹H. H. Furness believes that Shakespeare was appealing to English pride: "nowhere else on the habitable globe could its scene have been laid but in England, nowhere else but in Sherwood Forest has the Golden Age, in popular belief, revisited the earth, and there alone of all the earth a merry band could, and did, fleet time carelessly" (vii).

Works Cited

Evans, Maurice, ed. *The Countess of Pembroke's Arcadia*. Harmondsworth. Penguin, 1977.

Furness, H. H., ed. *As You Like It*. New Variorum Edition. Philadelphia: Lippincott, 1890.

Halliday, F. E., ed. *Shakespeare and His Critics*. London: Duckworth, 1958.

Hobbes, Thomas. *The Leviathan*. Ed. C. B. Macpherson. Harmondsworth: Penguin, 1968.

Kronefeld, Judy Z. "Social Rank and the Pastoral Ideals of *As You Like It*." *Shakespeare Quarterly* 29 (1978): 333-48.

Lodge, Thomas. *The Complete Works of Thomas Lodge*. 6 vols. Glasgow: Hunterian Club, 1881-90.

Shakespeare, William. *William Shakespeare: The Complete Works*. Gen. ed. Alfred Harbage. Baltimore: Viking, 1969.

Smith, Hallett. *Elizabethan Poetry*. Cambridge: Harvard UP, 1966.

Note Documentation Sample

What follows is a sample page from the model research paper, showing how one might use the note documentation system instead of the parenthetical documentation system. A page demonstrating the proper citation of notes follows the sample page of the paper.

Hallet Smith writes: "The central meaning of pastoral is the rejection of the aspiring mind. The Shepherd demonstrates that true content is to be found in this renunciation."[1] Although some shepherds, such as Tamburlaine, do not thus belong in a pastoral world, the dominant characteristic of most pastoral worlds derives from their existence as an alternative world to the pressure- and vice-ridden courtly world. The pastoral world exists as a world that can be escaped to or retreated into, even if the escape or retreat is only temporary.

Shakespeare, aware of the tradition of pastoral when he introduces Arden in *As You Like It,* does not begin, however, with a strictly Renaissance pastoral; instead, he goes back to Ovid and the Middle Ages. Charles the wrestler informs Oliver and the audience that the old usurped Duke now lives in the

> . . . Forest of Arden, and a many merry men with him;
> and there they live like the old Robin Hood of England.
> They say many young gentlemen flock to him every day,
> and fleet the time carelessly as they did in the golden
> world. (I.i.107-11)[2]

Shakespeare chooses to link the notion of an Ovidian golden world with the legend of Robin Hood. In a strictly logical sense, an outlaw and the golden world are incongruous. If Shakespeare had wanted to depict a perfect golden world, he might simply have followed his source—Thomas Lodge's *Rosalynde*—more closely.[3] In rejecting the pastoralism of Lodge, Shakespeare shows his different approach to the pastoral.

Notes

[1]Hallett Smith, *Elizabethan Poetry* (Cambridge: Harvard UP, 1966) 10.

[2]William Shakespeare, *William Shakespeare: The Complete Works,* gen. ed. Alfred Harbage (Baltimore: Viking, 1969). All quotations from the play will be from this edition.

[3]Thomas Lodge, *The Complete Works of Thomas Lodge,* 6 vols. (Glasgow: Hunterian Club, 1881-90) 5:16.

Index of Authors